A THIRD HUNDRED SERMONS

Other Books By the Same Author

ONE HUNDRED SERMONS

RESTORATION HANDBOOK

THE LETTERS TO THE SEVEN CHURCHES IN ASIA

GOD AMID THE SHADOWS

THE BEAUTIFUL GLEANER

LET US PRAY!

ANOTHER HUNDRED SERMONS

A THIRD HUNDRED SERMONS

A Collection of Bible Subjects Homiletically Treated

By

LESLIE G. THOMAS

GOSPEL ADVOCATE COMPANY
NASHVILLE, TENNESSEE
1963

To James E. Laird, who was the first to encourage me to preach the gospel; to the late J. W. Shepherd, and to B. C. Goodpasture, who encouraged me to assemble a library; to my wife, Metta N. Thomas, who helped me collect my books and has stood by me in my work; and to the hundreds of people, who by their response to my efforts, have made my work a pleasure, and, I trust, to some extent profitable, this volume is gratefully inscribed by

THE AUTHOR

I like my friendships, as I like my fires,
* Open, ruddy to the seasoned core;*
Sweet-fibred, hickory-hearted;
* The sort to warm a life by, when, with storm,*
Winter smites hard on wall and pane and rooftree.

—HILTON ROSS GREER

Search for the truth is the noblest occupation of man; its publication is a duty. — MME. DE STAEL.

The grand character of truth is its capability of enduring the test of universal experience, and coming unchanged out of every possible form of fair discussion. — SIR JOHN FREDERICK HERSCHEL.

The grandest homage we can pay to truth is to use it. — RALPH WALDO EMERSON.

Truth lies in character. Christ did not simply speak the truth; he was Truth—Truth through and through, for truth is a thing not of words but a life and being. — FREDERICK WILLIAM ROBERTSON.

Truth is not only violated by falsehood; it may be equally outraged by silence. — HENRI FREDERIC AMIEL.

If a man does not keep pace with his companions, perhaps it is because he hears a different drummer. Let him step to the music which he hears, however measured or far away. — HENRY DAVID THOREAU.

A man's true greatness lies in the consciousness of an honest purpose in life, founded on a just estimate of himself and everything else, on frequent self-examinations, and a steady obedience to the rule which he knows to be right, without troubling himself about what others may think or say, or whether they do or do not that which he thinks and says and does. — MARCUS AURELIUS.

FOREWORD

As the title of this book indicates, this is the third volume of "one hundred sermons" which the author has prepared for publication. He has also published two other books of sermons— *God Amid the Shadows* (fifty sermons), and *Let Us Pray!* (twenty sermons).

All of the lessons in these five volumes have been homiletically treated. This particular arrangement, of course, was for the study, rather than for the pulpit. This plan has been helpful to the author in clarifying his thinking, and he has assumed that it would be helpful to others, too. This, however, is the last work which the author plans to prepare for publication, following the homiletical arrangement.

These notes, like those in the volumes which have gone before, have been gathered from many sources, covering a period of many years; and the author is deeply grateful to every writer who has in any way contributed to the contents of this book. It is his hope that these sermons will be used by others as they endeavor to extend the borders of the kingdom of Christ here on earth.

The author is deeply grateful for the wonderful reception accorded his previous books, and it is his hope that this one, too, will find a place in the lives and libraries of those who make it possible for books to be published.

LESLIE G. THOMAS

INTRODUCTION

Preachers, teachers and students of God's word are always looking for material that will enrich their minds and improve their usefulness in the Master's vineyard. This book of sermon outlines will serve that purpose. It will find its place with the companion volumes by this Author and with the rich literature of the church.

Alexander Maclaren has said, "The secret of success in everything is trust in God and hard work." Those who study this volume will know that it is the result of hard work by a man who trusts in God. It is the latest and perhaps the last book of sermons that Brother Thomas will publish, and is therefore the fruit of a life rich in the Master's service, mellowed by time and experience. We predict for "A Third Hundred Sermons" the same ready sale that all of his works have enjoyed.

J. Roy Vaughan

TABLE OF CONTENTS

*An additional subject suggestion

xi

*An additional subject suggestion

*An additional subject suggestion

xiv

THE FIRST GOSPEL SERMON
Acts 2: 1-42

Introduction: 1. The history of the scheme of human redemption is the most thrilling story that has ever been told. The story begins with the first part of the Old Testament scriptures, and continues on through the Bible to the closing words of the Book of Revelation. 2. It would be interesting and profitable to consider everything that is said regarding the Lord's plan for saving the lost, but that would not be possible in a single sermon. Our lesson for this time is concerned with the first gospel sermon that was preached under the world-wide commission which Christ gave to his disciples just before he left them to return to his Father's throne in heaven. 3. When this sermon was preached Jesus had made possible the salvation of the human race by his death, burial, and resurrection—he had, therefore, become the Saviour of men, and was beginning his reign at the right hand of God. He was ready to make intercession for all who would draw near to God through him. All down through the ages this plan had been developing and unfolding; but it was not completed until Jesus made the supreme sacrifice and had been made both Lord and Christ. 4. It is a recorded fact that God drafted the plan for saving the race, Jesus executed the plan, and the Holy Spirit made it known. The plan, of course, is perfect, and surely no thoughtful person would want either of the Divine Members of the Godhead to do his work over. Our only concern should be to learn what the plan is and then meet its requirements. But in studying this lesson, let us ask,

I. WHEN WAS THIS FIRST SERMON PREACHED?

1. The text leaves no doubt about this question. See Acts 2: 1-4.

2. If one would understand the purposes of God regarding the scheme of human redemption, he must trace their progressive development through the Patriarchal and Jewish dispensations, and the first four books of the New Testament.

(1) In doing this he will find that all these records point to a time in the future when salvation would be offered to a sin-cursed and dying world.

(2) That time was reached on the first Pentecost after the resurrection of Christ from the dead. On that day we reach the point of rest and see the grand culmination of the plan for saving the race. On that day we witness the setting up of the kingdom, the establishing of the church which the Saviour said that he would build. See Matt. 16: 18,19.

3. Pentecost was one of the three annual feasts of the Jews, that is, the time for keeping one of those feasts came on the day of Pentecost. All able-bodied Jewish males were required to

1

attend these feasts. Cf. Deut. 16: 16,17. And since the condemnation of Jesus had occurred during the preceding feast, the feast of unleavened bread, it was most appropriate that the next feast in order be chosen as the occasion for his vindication and the inauguration of his kingdom.

II. THE CHARACTER OF THE AUDIENCE

1. Acts 2: 5-11. Not only was there a vast crowd present; the Bible declares that they were *devout* people. That means that they were devoted to that which they believed to be right. These people were in the city of Jerusalem for the express purpose of worshipping God.

2. But notwithstanding their devotion to that which they believed to be right, they were guilty of crucifying the Son of God. See Acts 2: 23, 26. Deeply religious people can sometimes be very wrong.

3. So far as Christ and his mission were concerned, the people who heard this first gospel sermon were unbelievers. The audience, therefore, was not very favorable for the gospel of Christ. But if we can see how sinners like those were reconciled to God, then surely we can know how any disobedient person can find mercy.

III. THE PREACHER

1. It is always interesting to know who the preacher is when a great sermon is preached, especially a sermon which is recorded in the Bible. This information is not lacking in the text; for we are told that it was the Apostle Peter. See Acts 2: 14.

2. However, before considering his sermon on this occasion, it will be both interesting and profitable to ask about his authority for preaching and his qualifications for proclaiming the first gospel sermon.

(1) His authority: Matt. 16: 13-19; 28: 18-20; Mark 16: 15, 16; Luke 24: 46, 47.

(2) His qualifications: John 14: 26; 16: 13; Acts 2: 4.

IV. THE SERMON

1. *The introduction—the miracle explained, verses 14-21.* This discourse was skillfully opened. Peter's first effort was to remove prejudice from the hearts of his hearers. Some preachers, alas! *create* more prejudice by their rash statements at the beginning of their sermons than they are able to remove during the remainder of their effort.

2. *Jesus proclaimed as Lord and Christ, verses 22-35.* Peter boldly declared that Jesus was approved of God, although condemned by the very people who were listening to him; and that after they put him to death, God raised him from the dead. (See

verses 22-24.) This, of course, placed the audience in direct opposition to God. The speaker then proceeded to prove the resurrection and exaltation of Jesus:

(1) By their own Scriptures, by passages which, by their own admission, referred to the promised Messiah. (Verses 25-31.)

(2) By the testimonies of eye-witnesses. (Verse 32.)

(3) By the supernatural manifestations of the hour. (Verses 33-35.)

3. *The irresistible conclusion—a conclusion armed with unspeakable terrors for his guilty hearers, verse 36.*

V. The Effects of the Sermon and the Results that Followed

1. They were pricked in their heart which clearly implies that they believed that which Peter had spoken. (Verse 37a.)

2. They asked, "Brethren, what shall we do?" They realized their undone condition and wanted to know how they could be freed from their terrible guilt. (Verse 37b.)

3. Peter gave them a straightforward answer, one which they could not misunderstand and which was within the reach of every one of them, so far as their obedience was concerned. (Verses 38, 39.)

4. He then continued his testimony regarding Jesus, and exhorted them to save themselves "from this crooked generation." (Verse 40.) The only way that they could save themselves was by doing as Peter had instructed them.

5. The result that followed. (Verse 41.)

6. Some pertinent questions:

(1) Did Peter give them the right answer to their question? or, Was he true to the commission which the Lord gave to him and his fellow disciples not many days previous to this?

(2) If his answer was correct then, what is wrong with it now? Has God changed his plan for saving the lost since then?

(3) Does the record indicate that any who really wanted to be saved from their sins argued with Peter regarding the terms of forgiveness? They wanted to be free from their guilt, and asked in all sincerity what to do; and Peter, guided by the Holy Spirit, told them. "They then that received his word were baptized."

(4) Did Peter make a mistake in naming baptism as a condition of pardon? See Mark 16: 16; cf. 1 Pet. 3: 21.

7. Verse 42 shows what is expected of people who are saved from their sins, according to the Lord's plan which is, of course, the only plan.

Why do you wait, dear brother,
Oh, why do you tarry so long?
Your Saviour is waiting to give you
A place in his sanctified throne.
What do you hope, dear brother,
To gain by a further delay?
There's no one to save you but Jesus,
There's no other way but his way.

✦ ✦ ✦

APOSTOLIC CHRISTIANITY*
Acts 2: 42

Introduction: 1. The words of the text set forth the characteristic marks of the Christian life to which the converts of Pentecost were pledged by their acceptance of the gospel message. God himself set the apostles in the church (1 Cor. 12: 28), and they constituted the visible center of unity of the newly established institution. The new disciples were gathered around them, and from them the doctrine and discipline of the infant church proceeded. 2. The early church was one body. The world recognized its unity and felt its power. The very first statement of church history is the inspired declaration, "And they continued stedfastly in the apostles' teaching and fellowship, in the breaking of bread and the prayers." The early church was united in what it was and in what it did, and the text sets forth the four elements which express the unity of the primitive Christian life. They are,

I. THE APOSTLES' TEACHING

1. The teaching of the apostles was the necessary instrumentality for bringing the new converts into full and complete discipleship. Their rudimentary faith needed careful and continuous instruction.

2. The apostles were the ones who were chosen by the Lord to make known his will to men. See John 16: 13, 14; 2 Cor. 4: 7. Their teaching in the first days of Christianity was done orally, but that which they taught by word of mouth was not different from that which was later reduced to writing. We now have "in book form" that which they then had "in earthen vessels."

3. Thus, from the very beginning the church of the Lord possessed and depended upon a "teaching ministry;" and it can be seen from what the Lord and the apostles taught that it is just as necessary for us today to continue stedfastly in their teaching, as it was for the early disciples. Cf. Matt. 28: 19, 20; John 8: 31, 32; 2 Tim. 3: 14-17.

II. FELLOWSHIP

1. This, according to Vincent, is "a relation between individuals which involves a common interest and a mutual, active participation in that interest and in each other." Cf. Phil. 1: 5, where

---

*Or, What the Early Church Did

the same word signifies *cooperation* in the widest sense.

2. There were three aspects in which this principle of fellowship was applied by the early church—viz:

(1) It is evident that they continued to encourage each other in all spiritual matters. Cf. Heb. 10: 24, 25.

(2) They continued to demonstrate their mutual regard for each other's welfare. See Rom. 12: 15; 1 Cor. 12: 25-27.

(3) They continued to see to it that regular, systematic provisions were made for practical help as it was needed. Cf. 1 Cor. 16: 1, 2. As the number of disciples multiplied, it was found necessary to appoint deacons, or special servants, to look after this business, so that the apostles might "continue stedfastly in prayer, and in the ministry of the word." See Acts 6: 1ff.

III. THE BREAKING OF BREAD

1. There is little doubt but that the reference here is to the Lord's supper. Cf. Acts 20: 7.

2. The New Testament nowhere teaches, as some have erroneously thought, that the Lord's supper is the most important part of the worship, but from such passages as Luke 22: 29, 30 and Acts 20: 7 we naturally get the idea that the Lord's day worship is centered around the Lord's table.

3. Something of the purpose of the Lord's supper may be seen from the following considerations:

(1) *It is a commemorative institution, 1 Cor. 11: 24.* We are to remember *Christ,* his birth, life, teaching, obedience, etc., as well as his death. Here is a monument, the elements of which are perishable, but it has stood the test of time; let the skeptic account for it.

(2) *It is declarative, 1 Cor. 11: 26.* Here is a proclamation in which every Christian can and should have part; and the more inconvenient and difficult the circumstances under which it is done, the more eloquent is the preaching. Can the Lord depend on you for this service? Cf. Luke 12: 46; Rev. 21: 8, where the term "unfaithful" or "unbelieving" signifies, according to Thayer, one who cannot be trusted.

(3) *It is a communion, 1 Cor. 10: 16.* The marginal reading for communion is "participation in", and it means that we participate in the benefits of Christ's death. See Rom. 6: 3, where it is taught that the alien is baptized into the benefits of Christ's death. Cf. 1 John 1: 7.

IV. THE PRAYERS

1. These were doubtless their public prayers, although it is possible that they also included their private devotions.

2. Prayer, in its widest sense, is "man's supreme effort to find the right answer to the meaning of life"; and, in its practical application, it may be thought of as "intercourse with an Ideal

Companion." With this view of the question, it is easy to see that prayer is not primarily a matter of our talking, God's listening, and then answering, as is so commonly assumed. When Christians "pray without ceasing" (1 Thess. 5: 17), or continue "stedfastly in prayer" (Rom. 12: 12), they are enjoying continuous intercourse with an Ideal Companion. Cf. 1 John 1: 6, 7.

3. *The value of united prayer.* The story is told of a Negro woman who was once asked by the governor of a state why she and her fellows always prayed *together.* Could they not each pray for himself? The governor happened to be standing at the time before a fire of coals, and the woman answered, "Dear sir, separate these coals from each other, and the fire will go out; but see how brisk the flame when they burn together!" Thus, when in fellowship with others our hearts grow warm, and it is much easier to understand the meaning of the Saviour's language in Matt. 18: 19, 20.

V. THEY CONTINUED STEDFASTLY

1. Sudden conversions are not always lasting. This is especially true if there is not some definite and wholesome teaching done immediately. Not every one who changes his views does so because of enlightened conviction. When a group of people has been deeply stirred by impassioned eloquence, it is difficult for the most self-possessed to retain the mastery of his emotions; and it often happens that when the feelings which ran through the crowd die down, the effect disappears. Like a house without a foundation, the profession which was assumed may be swept away into utter and irretrievable ruin by the first tempest that beats down upon it.

2. The test of sincere loyalty to Christ which is emphasized in the text is stedfast adherence to his doctrine or teaching. This implies a daily life in harmony with his mind and precepts. That is what the first disciples did: They continued stedfastly in the apostles' teaching and fellowship, in the breaking of bread and the prayers.

3. Stedfastness implies both *definiteness* and *diligence.* The faithful Christian must take his *stand* in that which the Lord requires, and exercise *diligence* in maintaining that stand; he must have a definite *aim,* and use *diligence* in achieving it.

◆ ◆ ◆

PETER'S SECOND SERMON
Acts 3: 12-26

Introduction: 1. This sermon followed immediately the healing of the crippled man at the Beautiful Gate of the temple. The record of that miracle is found in the first ten verses of the third chapter of Acts. Peter and John were going into the temple at the hour of prayer, being the ninth hour—three o'clock in the afternoon, our time. The lame man was placed at the door of the temple which was called Beautiful, to ask for alms of those who entered the temple. As Peter and John were about to go in he asked them for something; and it was then that Peter healed him. 2. When the people saw that which was done their admiration was directed toward the two apostles, as if they themselves had effected the cure by their own power. When Peter saw how they felt about the matter, he took advantage of the circumstance and delivered the sermon which we are about to study. 3. The crowd had gathered in a porch or portico of the temple which was called Solomon's, and it was evidently there that the sermon was delivered. The following quotation from J. W. McGarvey, *A New Commentary on Acts of Apostles, Vol. I., p. 52f.,* will give some idea for the setting for the sermon:

> The structure that is here called a "porch" was a colonnade constructed along the inner face of the inclosing wall of the outer court. It consisted, according to Josephus, of rows of stone columns twenty-seven feet high, with a roof of cedar resting on them and on the wall, so as to constitute a covered portico, with its inner side open toward the temple. On the eastern side of the court there were two rows of these columns, making that portico sixty feet deep and as long as the wall, which Josephus estimates at a furlong, though its exact measurement today is fifteen hundred and thirty feet. Across the southern end, which now measures nine hundred and twenty-two feet, there are four rows of columns, making three walks or passages between them, each thirty feet deep, and consequently the depth of this portico was ninety feet. These immense covered porticos, or cloisters, as Josephus calls them, served as a protection from the sun in the summer, and from the rain in the winter. They contained space sufficient for the great multitude of the disciples when assembled in one mass; and also for many separate meetings of large numbers to listen to different preachers speaking at the same time. All the twelve apostles might be preaching in them at the same hour, each to a large audience, and yet be far enough apart to avoid confusion of sound. In which of these porticos the present meeting was held we cannot tell, because we are not informed as to which was distinguished by the name "Solomon's," this being of course an honorary title.

But in studying this lesson, let us begin by considering,

I. The Statement of the Theme of the Discourse

1. Since the people were greatly wondering, their minds, of course, were not settled, and Peter took advantage of that situation and endeavored to turn their thoughts into the right channel. The complimentary address, "Ye men of Israel," was a very tactful beginning.

2. In his first sermon Peter set forth an array of facts con-

cerning Jesus and showed by Old Testament quotations that his death, burial, and resurrection were according to divine prearrangement. In his second sermon the same apostle said about the same things about Jesus, but on the latter occasion he employed the antithetical method of approach.

3. The four points of contrast which he stated gradually led up to a climax, They are,

(1) He whom the God of our fathers glorified, you delivered up to die. You, therefore, were in direct opposition to God.

(2) When the heathen ruler of our people pronounced him innocent and desired to release him, you denied him and cried out against the decision of the governor.

(3) You rejected one who was holy and righteous, and asked that a man whom you knew to be a murderer be granted unto you.

(4) You killed the Author of life, your life and that of all mankind, but God raised him from the dead.

4. It is doubtful if a grander climax, or a happier combination of climax and antithesis, could be found in any literature. Each fact which Peter presented must have fallen like sledge-hammer blows upon the consciences of his hearers; for they were all undeniable, except the resurrection, and Peter declared that he and John were witnesses of that.

5. *The miracle explained.* Having reached his antithetical climax, Peter gave an explanation of the miracle, stated his theme, and at the same time demonstrated the reality of the resurrection and glorification of Jesus.

(1) The fact that it was by faith in the name of Jesus that the miracle of healing was wrought shows that there was no peculiar charm in the mere name of Jesus. Cf. Acts 19: 13-17.

(2) The faith which effected the cure was not the faith of the cripple, but that of the apostles themselves. See Acts 3: 4-7.

II. AN EXHORTATION TO SUBMIT TO THE AUTHORITY OF JESUS, VERSES 17-21

1. The fact that Peter called these wicked men *brethren* shows that he was making a tactful effort to conciliate them as far as possible. His reference to their ignorance was evidently to encourage them, so that they would not feel themselves hopeless. Cf. 1 Tim. 1: 13.

2. The sovereignty of God and the free agency of man brought into juxtaposition. Cf. Acts 2: 23.

3. An exhortation to repent and turn, together with a promise of the blessings to follow.

(1) Repentance is a change of mind, brought about by godly sorrow, and resulting in a reformation of life. Cf. Matt. 21: 28, 29; 2 Cor. 7: 10; Matt. 3: 8. But they were told to repent *and* turn.

(2) "Repent ye therefore, and turn again, that your sins may be blotted out, that so there may come seasons of refreshing from the presence of the Lord; and that he may send the Christ who hath been appointed for you, even Jesus." Cf. Acts 2: 38-47.

(3) The coming of Christ will evidently be at the end of the world. See 2 Thess. 1: 7-10.

III. A Warning of the Consequences of Disobedience, Verses 22-26

1. *The supreme authority of Christ must be respected.* Moses was distinguished from the other prophets of the Old Testament as a deliverer, lawgiver, and mediator; and it was in these respects that Jesus was like him, as it respects the new order.

2. *The testimony of the prophets.* Peter, in all probability, quoted many of these prophets; for it is very likely that Luke gave only an epitome of this sermon. Cf. Acts 2: 40.

3. *An appeal to his hearers based on their veneration for the prophets of their nation.* This was a tender appeal to their national feelings; and it sets the example for similar appeals, even today.

4. Here is an inspired interpretation of the promise to Abraham. It is fulfilled, according to Peter, when men turn away from their iniquities. Those who turn away from their iniquities are the recipients of the promised blessings.

IV. The Results of the Sermon, 4: 1-4

1. The sermon was cut short by the priests, the captain of the temple, and the Sadducees. Before Jesus died his chief opponents were the Pharisees; but now after his resurrection the Sadducees take the lead in opposition to him.

2. Because it was now eventide, the apostles were put in ward until the morrow.

3. Notwithstanding the excitement that must have arisen over their arrest, the sermon was not without effect; for many of them that heard the word believed; and the number of the men came to be about five thousand.

◆ ◆ ◆

THE NAME THAT SAVES
Acts 4: 12

Introduction: 1. When Jesus was put to death the rulers of the Jews must have felt relieved; but that feeling did not last long. When they thought of that which he had said about rising from the dead, they took what they considered the necessary steps to prevent even a rumor of his resurrection. See Matt. 27: 62ff. But Jesus did arise from the dead; and beginning with the day of Pentecost which came a few days later his disciples began to proclaim openly, not only his resurrection, but also his ascension and glorious coronation at God's right hand in heaven. 2. The fact of his resurrection established his claim as the Son of God and the Saviour of the world; and in keeping with his previous command his followers began to proclaim him as such. This, of course, brought his name again into prominence; and it was the result of this that Peter uttered the words of the text. In studying this lesson, then, let us begin by considering,

I. The Power of a Name

1. A name, when properly used, can be made to stand for a person's character or office. This was especially true of names which God gave. Cf. Isa. 9: 6; Matt. 1: 21; Acts 2: 36.

2. The name of Jesus had been a power to reckon with during his public ministry, but after his enemies had been successful in putting him to death they evidently felt that his name thereafter would lose its power.

3. It was not long after his death, however, until mighty works began to astonish the people, the same kind of works as those which were done by Jesus during his lifetime. Among these miracles was the healing of the lame man at the Beautiful Gate of the temple.

4. The agents through which this deed was done were two of the Lord's disciples, Peter and John, and after being arrested and lodged in prison for a night, because it was then eventide, they were arraigned before the rulers of the people and called upon to reveal the source of their power: "By what power, or in what name, have ye done this?"

(1) It is doubtful if a question could have been framed which would have been characterized by more vagueness than this one. The apostles, of course, had done nothing on which the rulers dared to fix attention, or on which they could base a charge of wrong-doing. They evidently framed with cunningness the indefinite question in the hope that the defendants, in their confusion, could furnish a basis for accusation by speaking unguarded words.

(2) That was a dastardly act—the cowardly execution of a malicious design. It is a pity that the practice didn't die with those rulers; but it didn't. There are people today who think that they have a charge of some kind against another, but when it develops that their charge is groundless, they will endeavor to get the supposed victim to say or do something which will yet give them a basis for accusation!

(3) Although cunningly devised, no question could have served Peter's purpose better. It left him free to select the answer he desired to give; and when the answer was given his opponents found that it was one which they neither desired nor anticipated.

(4) Peter's statement needed no proof; for, with the man standing before them, the rulers could not deny it. Therefore,

with their answer vindicated and those who asked the question confounded, Peter was free, for the moment, to continue his exaltation of the glorious name of Jesus.

II. THE MEANING OF SALVATION

1. In its widest sense, salvation includes the cleansing of our consciences from all past guilt, and the delivery of our souls from all those inclinations to evil which now so strongly predominate within us. Cf. Rom. 7: 24. The overall idea of salvation is the total restoration of man from his fallen state.

2. It seems that to some people salvation means no more than deliverance from hell and admittance into heaven. We would be nearer the truth if we thought of these two things as *results* of salvation. We have been redeemed from hell because we are saved, and when we enter heaven it will be because we were saved beforehand. Our eternal salvation will be the result of our having been saved in this life.

3. To use a well-known Bible figure, salvation begins with us as wandering sheep; it puts us upon the shoulders of the Good Shepherd and carries us into the fold, where we are disciplined and cared for through life; and then finally, if we are faithful to the end, we are brought into the green pastures of heaven and beside the still waters of eternal joy.

III. MAN'S NEED OF SALVATION

1. The testimony of the Scriptures: Rom. 3: 10, 23. Being lost in sin, man is wholly unable to save himself. If he is saved at all, it must be by some one other than himself. Cf. Matt. 1: 21; Rom. 7: 24, 25.

2. There are three deadly facts about sin which must be considered — viz., its guilt, its stains, and its power. Psa. 103: 3, 4. Let us study them here in this order.

(1) *The guilt of sin.* A person is guilty when he is justly chargeable for his sin—when the responsibility for his conduct is his. God has a direct claim upon the soul of every man; and when any one sets aside God's law for him, he sins. Our first responsibility is to God. Cf. Psalm 51: 4; Acts 17: 26, 27; Isa. 59: 1, 2.

(2) *The stain of sin.* The soul of every sinner has been defiled by sin. Even the most "respectable" sins leave their mark Cf. a drop of ink in a glass of pure water. Sometimes the stain becomes so foul that we are shocked by the uncleanness of the sinner's speech and taste and actions; and like the spot of blood on Lady Macbeth's hand, the stain of sin is something that *we* cannot wash away. Cf. Isa. 1: 18; Acts 22: 16.

(3) *The destructive power of sin.* The sinner will not go very far before he finds that he is in bondage to sin. See John 8: 34. Sin has an enslaving power. The tyranny of evil may begin with a single sinful act; but it is a universally attested fact that one

sin makes another sin easier. Each sin weaves another thread in the rope which binds us, till at last our liberty is lost and the tyranny of sin is complete. It is just as true with sin that an act often repeated hardens into a habit, and a habit long continued petrifies into character.

IV. The Saving Name

1. A clearer statement of fact regarding the relation of Christ to our salvation, or a more emphatic one, could not have been made. Peter left no doubt about that when he uttered the words of the text. Cf. John 14: 6.

2. To trust in the name of Jesus is to have access into the family of God here and now; and after a life of faithful service in his kingdom here below, the one who depends upon this name is assured a home of eternal bliss in that world which is to come. Cf. Matt. 10: 32, 33; Rev. 3: 5; 2 Pet. 1: 10, 11.

3. It should be remembered, however, that to trust in his name is equivalent to obeying him; for the word is used in no other sense in the New Testament. Cf. John 3: 36; 12: 48-50. Song, *Only in Thee.*

◆ ◆ ◆

"THAT IT SPREAD NO FURTHER"
Acts 4: 17

Introduction: 1. The first part of the third chapter of Acts contains the account of the healing of a cripple man at the Beautiful Gate of the temple. In addition to the blessing it brought to the man himself, the miracle had the effect of bringing together a large congregation of interested people; and Peter, taking advantage of the situation, preached unto them the Lord Jesus. 2. His sermon, however, was cut short; for "as they spake unto the people, the priests and the captain of the temple and the Sadducees came upon them, being sore troubled because they taught the people, and proclaimed in Jesus the resurrection from the dead." The apostles were arrested; and because it was eventide their case was continued "unto the morrow." Howbeit, many who heard the word believed; "and the number of the men came to be about five thousand." 3. On the next day the apostles were arraigned in court; but, not having anything definite to bring against them, the rulers simply asked, "By what power, or in what name, have ye done this?" It is doubtful if a more indefinite question could have been framed. However, Peter, being filled with the Holy Spirit, took advantage of the occasion, and again exalted Christ and practically routed their opponents. 4. This brings us to the immediate context, and to the consideration of the attitude which the leaders of the people assumed in the face

of undeniable facts.   Therefore, in studying this lesson, let us
begin by considering,

I. The Motive Which Actuated the Leaders

1. Their immediate objective was to maintain their *status quo*.
They were not primarily concerned with learning any new truth
which they may not have then known.   Cf. John 8: 32; Eph. 1:
13; 1 Pet. 1: 22.

2. To "prevent spreading" is often a worthy undertaking.   For
example,

(1) Infectious diseases, such as tuberculosis, cancer, blood-
poisoning, etc.

(2) Falsehoods, unwholesome gossip, statements which alienate friends and damage character.

(3) *But their object was to hinder a good thing.*   A cripple
man had been healed; and the name of the Benefactor was being
exalted among men.

II. The Reason Behind Their Action

1. They had rejected Jesus as the Messiah, and had put him
to death.   Cf. Acts 3: 13-15.

2. They had denied his resurrection, the very thing that was
being preached by his followers.   See Mat. 27: 62-66; 28: 11-15;
Acts 4: 2.

3. Being confronted with such preaching, they either had to
continue their rejection of the claims of Christ, or admit their
error and change religiously.

(1) A large number of their brethren had done the latter
on the preceding Pentecost.   See Acts 2: 1-41.

(2) But the men of the text had renewed their attack, and
had refused to back down.

III. Their Course of Procedure

1. Their question, "What shall we do to these men?"

(1) Their private conviction: "For that indeed a notable
miracle hath been wrought through them, is manifest to all that
dwell in Jerusalem; and we cannot deny it."

(2) Their proposed course of action: "But that it spread
no further among the people, let us threaten them, that they speak
henceforth to no man in this name."   See also verse 18.

2. The apostles' reply: verses 19, 20.

3. The final result: verses 21, 22.

IV. A Modern Counterpart

1. One of the chief things in which denominational leaders of
our day are united is their persistent effort to see that the teaching
of Jesus regarding baptism as a condition of salvation "spread no
further among the people."

2. They have both misunderstood and rejected his teaching on this subject, a thing which they could easily see, if they would only read that which the New Testament says about it. Cf. Acts 13: 27; Matt. 22: 29.

3. The testimony of the Scriptures regarding the conditions of salvation. See Mark 16: 15, 16; Acts 4: 12; 18: 8.

(1) It is sad to observe that there is hardly a denominational preacher anywhere now, but that does his utmost to make sure that people reject this teaching. They themselves have been taught to reject it; and, being confronted with preaching which emphasizes the Lord's teaching on this subject, they must either continue their denial of it, or admit their mistake and change religiously.

(2) Privately, they admit that which the Bible actually says; but publicly, they reject both precept and example, as set forth in the Scriptures.*

4. The unalterable reply of the Scriptures: Gal. 1: 6-10; 1 Cor. 4: 6; 2 John 9.

An incident occurred in the Pilot Point church during Rev. J. B. Cole's pastorate, which involved a point of doctrine that subjected Pastor Cole to criticism, and gave the incident much publicity and notoriety. Pastor Cole went fishing one day with a business man who was not a Christian, and he availed himself of the opportunity to talk to the lost man about his unsaved condition, and led him to an acceptance of Christ. Jo Ives, the man converted, said to Pasor Cole, "here is water, what doth hinder me from being baptized?" Obviously Brother Cole thought of the story of Philip and the eunuch, and, taking that incident as an example, he led Mr. Ives out into the water and baptized him. Rev. Cole had been a Baptist but a short time and was not up on their conception of baptism, and hcw and when it should be administered. The news of the incident soon spread among the members, and then the show began. The following Sunday Mr. Ives presented himself to the church, asking membership, and his application was rejected and he was hurt at the action of the church and turned to another church, which readily accepted his baptism. The criticism of the pastor caused him to ask a committee of eminent brethren to sit in judgment upon his conduct —Drs. A. J. Holt, J. B. Link and R. C. Buckner. After reviewing the details of the incident they wrote the church advising it to drop the matter, and Pastor Cole to go his way, but not to repeat the act. (J. N. Rayzor, *History of Denton County Baptist Association and the Sixty Churches within Its Jurisdiction*, page 82f.)

---

*We are accounted righteous before God only for the merit of our Lord and Saviour Jesus Christ, by faith, and not for our own works or deservings. Wherefore, that we are justified by faith only is a most wholesome doctrine, and very full of comfort.—*Methodist Discipline, Ninth* Article of Religion. Cf. James 2: 14-26.

"BUT WHEN THEY BELIEVED"
Acts 8: 12

Introduction: 1. The record of the conversion of the Samaritans is set forth in the eighth chapter of Acts, verses 4 through 17. The great persecution against the church in Jerusalem, which started with the death of Stephen, had driven the disciples, except the apostles, from the city and had scattered them abroad through the regions of Judaea and Samaria. However, instead of being discouraged because of this ill-treatment, they that were scattered abroad went about preaching the word. This was in keeping with the Lord's prediction in Acts 1: 8. 2. Among those who left Jerusalem because of the persecution was Philip, one of the seven. See Acts 6: 1-6. He had developed into an effective preacher of the gospel, and when he reached the city of Samaria, he proclaimed unto them the Christ; and because he had the power to confirm his message by the signs which he wrought, the multitudes gave heed with one accord to the things which he spoke. "And there was much joy in that city." But in studying this lesson, let us consider,

I. THE EFFECT OF PERSECUTION ON A RIGHTEOUS CAUSE

1. It should be observed, in the first place, that there is a wide difference between persecution and punishment. In its true sense, *punishment* is penalty for wrong-doing, and is meted out by properly constituted authority; while *persecution* is ill-treatment, inflicted by uninformed or depraved enemies of the ones so treated.

2. The purpose of persecutors is to hinder or destroy the cause represented by their victims, and they usually think that their action is pleasing to God. Cf. John 16: 2.

3. It is a noticeable fact, however, that persecution always falls far short of its objective. This is because weakness, unfairness, and unreasonableness inhere in it. Thus, instead of destroying the cause against which the persecution is directed, it usually accelerates it. In the case of the early church, the blood of the martyrs indeed became the seed of the kingdom. *The overruling providence of God made the persecution contribute to the success of the cause it sought to destroy.*

II. DEALING WITH A DIFFICULTY

1. Simon the Sorcerer had, for a long time, amazed the Samaritans with his chicanery; and because of that he had exercised a great influence over them.

2. That which Simon did may also be described by such terms as "tricks of magic" or "sleight-of-hand performances"; and while they are inexplicable to the uninitiated, yet all intelligent people know that their sole purpose is to excite mere idle curiosity and entertain. Such deeds are in no sense to be classed with

the genuine miracles which were performed by the Lord and those to whom he gave such power.

3. Philip, however, supplanted Simon's chicanery by preaching and confirming the gospel; and in that way he was able to show the infinite superiority of the real over the false, and the divine over the human.

4. There are many difficulties in the way of those who proclaim the gospel of Christ, but many of them will melt away if they will give the gospel message a chance to do its work. Cf. Isa. 55: 10, 11; Acts 2: 12ff.

III. "BUT WHEN THEY BELIEVED"

1. When Philip reached Samaria he "proclaimed unto them the Christ." See Acts 8: 5. However, in verse 12 it is recorded, "But when they believed Philip preaching good tidings concerning the kingdom of God and the name of Jesus Christ, they were baptized, both men and women."

2. To preach Christ, therefore, is to tell about the kingdom of God and the name of Jesus Christ. No one can preach Christ fully (and nothing else will please God) who does not tell the facts concerning him and the work he came to do, together with his method of accomplishing it.

3. The story of the conversion of the Samaritans is as simple and direct as the Great Commission under which Philip preached. See Mark 16: 15, 16. *When sincere people are taught the truth about Jesus, they will gladly do that which he commands.* Cf. *Acts 2: 41.*

IV. THE FORMAL ACCEPTANCE OF THE SAMARITANS

1. The gift of the Holy Spirit, or the Holy Spirit as a gift, had been promised to all who become the Lord's people by obeying the gospel. See Acts 2: 38, 39; cf. John 7: 7: 37-39; Acts 5: 32. However, any informed Bible student knows that during the age of miracles the Lord could withhold that gift temporarily, if conditions justified a miracle, without being inconsistent with his will.

(1) Except in the case of miracles, all of God's gifts to his people, including the gift of the Holy Spirit, are conferred according to the terms of his law governing them. His only provision for imparting the Holy Spirit to his people is found in Acts 2: 38, 39. No one under Christ, so far as the record goes, ever received the Holy Spirit, except in cases where miracles were needed, but those who met the conditions set forth in Acts 2: 38, 39. Four notable exceptions to this rule were the apostles on Pentecost, Acts 2; the Samaritans, Acts 8; Cornelius and his household, Acts 10; and the twelve men at Ephesus, Acts 19.

(2) A miracle is an act of God without regard to law. A law and a miracle, therefore, cannot operate with reference to the

same thing at the same time. If the law is being adhered to, then there is no miracle; but if there is a miracle, then there is either no law covering that particular thing, or the law was suspended for the time being.

(3) In the case of the Samaritans, the case now under consideration, the record plainly states that the Holy Spirit was not given to them at the time of their baptism. They had met the conditions set forth in Acts 2: 38, 39, but they had not received the Holy Spirit. The law in their case was temporarily suspended; for there was need for a miracle.

(4) Some people have tried to explain this record by saying that the Samaritans received "the gift of the Holy Spirit," but that the Holy Spirit with his *miraculous power* had fallen on none of them. Such a distinction is nowhere found in the New Testament. The Holy Spirit is a person, a member of the Godhead, and as such he has miraculous power wherever he is. If it is his will to manifest miraculous power, he does so; but if it is not his will he does not do so. See 1 Cor. 12: 11.

2. These new converts (the Samaritans), on account of their semi-heathen origin, were considered by the Jews almost as idolaters. It was necessary, therefore, that they be formally accepted by the duly accredited apostles of the Lord, that is, apostolic approval was given to the reception of the Samaritans into the church. Cf. Matt. 16: 19. This was the first step toward bringing the great outside world of Gentiles into the body of Christ.

3. The miracle did not consist in giving the Holy Spirit to them, but in the *manner* in which he was given. Instead of giving the Spirit according to the provision set forth in Acts 2: 38, 39, the provision was temporarily suspended and the Spirit was given through the laying on of the apostles' hands. It is easy for most people to see that a miracle was needed in the case of Cornelius and his household, in order to convince the Jewish Christians that the Gentiles were entitled to gospel privileges, including church membership; but it is not always so easy for some to see that something out of the ordinary had to be done, in order to convince the Jewish brethren that the Samaritans should also be accepted: "for Jews have no dealings with Samaritans." (John 4: 9.)

❖ ❖ ❖

THE HUMAN AND DIVINE IN CONVERSION*
Acts 8: 26-40

Introduction 1. The Book of Acts is a book of conversions. It contains that which the Lord wants people to know about the subject. Just before Jesus left his disciples to return to his Father he gave what is called the Great Commission, and every

*Or, The Work of Four

case of conversion recorded in the Book of Acts was worked out according to the terms of that commission. 2. There is no better way of making plain any proposition than by effective illustration. Not only does the writer of the Book of Acts give examples of conversion—examples which took place under the preaching of inspired men—he gives a variety of examples which illustrate how the conversion of men and women was accomplished under various and sundry conditions. The attending circumstances often differed widely, but it is a fact capable of demonstration that in every case those who were converted to the Lord did exactly that which he set forth in the Great Commission—no more, no less. 3. In the case of the conversion of the Ethiopian, the one now under consideration, we have one of the clearest illustrations in all the Book of Acts of the parts which the human and Divine accomplish in conversion. It is our purpose in this study to consider carefully that which each did, and thereby distinguish between the human and the Divine. Let us begin, then, by considering,

I. THE WORK OF THE ANGEL

1. "An angel of the Lord" literally means a *messenger* of the Lord. The artist's conception of an angel is usually that of a white being with golden hair and long wings. But in the Bible sense of the term, an angel is simply a messenger, one who is sent. An angel, therefore, could take the form of a human being. Cf. Heb. 13: 2.

2. The angel in the case now before us represented the Divine side in the conversion of the eunuch, and his work was to bring the preacher and the man to be converted together. The angel did not say a single word to the eunuch; and, so far as the eunuch knew, the angel had no part in his conversion.

3. The angel's instruction to Philip was to "arise, and go toward the south unto the way that goeth down from Jerusalem unto Gaza: the same is desert."

(1) Philip, apparently, was in Samaria when the angel spoke to him, and if so he was about thirty-six miles north of Jerusalem. His instruction was to travel "toward the south unto the way that goeth down from Jerusalem unto Gaza." Gaza was on the seacoast, southwest of Jerusalem.

(2) Philip promptly obeyed the voice of the angel; and when he reached the road running from Jerusalem unto Gaza, he saw a man of Ethiopia who had been to Jerusalem to worship, but who was now returning home and was reading the prophet Isaiah as he rode along in his chariot.

(3) But when Philip reached that road he had done all that he was told to do by the angel, and this brings us to the second agent in the eunuch's conversion.

II. The Work of the Holy Spirit

1. The part which the Holy Spirit did in this conversion is briefly stated in one short sentence: "And the Spirit said unto Philip, Go near, and join thyself to this chariot." Again Philip promptly obeyed.

2. The Spirit did not tell Philip anything else to do, so far as the record is concerned; for he knew that when once a man with the evangelistic zeal of Philip came face to face with an opportunity like this, he would preach Jesus unto him. That was what he had been doing in Samaria. See Acts 8: 5.

3. The Holy Spirit did not say a word to the man to be converted. Like that of the angel, his part was to get him and the preacher together. There is not, in fact, an example in all the New Testament in which the Holy Spirit, or any one representing the Divine side of the question, ever dealt directly with the sinner in an effort to convert him. This brings us to the end of the work that was done by the agents of the Divine side in the conversion of the eunuch. We shall next consider,

III. The Work of the Evangelist

1. It is well to keep in mind that Philip was not an apostle in the sense that the twelve were. He is specifically called an *evangelist*. See Acts 21: 8. An evangelist is a herald of the gospel message, the message which was first made known by the inspired apostles of Christ.

2. As already suggested, Philip promptly obeyed the voices of the angel and the Spirit. His zeal for God and the salvation of men is indicated by his running to the chariot. When he reached the chariot he heard the man of Ethiopia reading the prophet Isaiah; and upon asking if he understood that which he was reading, he received the polite reply, "How can I, except some one shall guide me?" *It is never difficult for the preacher and the man who needs to be converted to get together, when they manifest the sincerity that these two men did.*

3. The eunuch was reading from the Book of Isaiah (Isa. 53: 7f), and Philip, "beginning from this scripture, preached unto him Jesus." How much is condensed in this statement! How much is implied in these words of the inspired text! *He preached unto him Jesus!* He could begin at this scripture and preach unto him Jesus; for it was Jesus about whom Isaiah was speaking. What would a man preach to another man, if he preached unto him Jesus?

(1) He would tell of his coming into the world and of the principal events in his life, climaxing them with the significance of his death, burial, and resurrection. Cf. 1 Cor. 15: 1-4. These are the fundamental facts of the gospel, and no one can preach Jesus who does not emphasize them.

(2) He would likewise tell of the provisions the Lord made

so that men might enjoy this salvation. See Mark 16: 15, 16; Luke 24: 46, 47; cf. Acts 2: 36-39.

(3) He would also tell of the promises which Jesus made to all who obey the gospel. These promises include,

a. The remission of sins.

b. The gift of the Holy Spirit.

c. Eternal life to all who are faithful to him until death. Cf. 2 Pet. 1: 4.

IV. What Did the Eunuch Do?

1. He gave evidence of his desire to know the truth, and listened earnestly with an open heart. Cf. John 7: 17; Acts 17: 11.

2. He believed that which Philip preached unto him, as his subsequent actions show. Cf. Rom. 10: 17.

3. He translated his faith into action—he did that which Jesus commanded people to do, if they would enjoy his salvation. Cf. Matt. 28: 19; Acts 2: 38, 41.

4. Let us suppose that the eunuch, as he went on his way rejoicing, met some one who observed that he was very happy and ventured to ask him the reason for his happiness. What would the eunuch have told him? He could not have told him about the instruction which the angel and the Spirit gave Philip; for he did not know of that. He could only have told him of that which happened at the time and subsequent to the time Philip approached him as he rode along the road reading the prophet Isaiah. He had learned of the Lord, obeyed his commandments, and was then enjoying his promises. These are the requirements and blessings of conversion.

❖ ❖ ❖

THE BRINGING IN OF THE GENTILES
Acts 10: 34-48

Introduction: 1. With the Bible as our guide, along with our knowledge of human nature, we know that the best and most effective way of getting the facts of the plan of salvation before others is to state the plan and then illustrate it by showing how the plan was carried out in the case of individual instances of conversion. The most satisfactory illustrations of conversions, of course, are those which have been recorded in the New Testament. 2. The case of conversion now before us is remarkable, first, because it was the initial case of conversion from among the Gentiles, but also, and chiefly, because it plainly implies that, regardless of the righteousness of any one's character, all men need a Saviour. 3. The one converted on this occasion was not a bitter enemy of Jesus, as was Saul of Tarsus; he was not a cruel and rapacious man, like the Philippian jailer; neither was he guilty of crucifying the Son of God, as were the people of Acts 2; instead, he was a man of benevolence, devotion, and uprightness of life. The story of his conversion, therefore, will be of unusual interest to us. Let us begin the lesson, then, by considering,

I. The Character of Cornelius

1. It is interesting to observe than when we meet with a representative of the Roman military system, he is always a man who wins our esteem and admiration. For example,

(1) The centurion at Capernaum, who built a synagogue for the Jews, whose servant Christ healed, and whose faith he singled out for the highest praise. See Luke 7: 1-10.

(2) The centurion, Julius, who was in command of the soldiers and prisoners on the ship which carried Paul to Rome. See Acts 27: 1ff.

(3) The centurion who was in commond at the crucifixion of the Lord, and who, when Jesus died, exclaimed, "Truly this was the Son of God." See Matt. 27: 54.

(4) Last, but not least, Cornelius, the Roman centurion at Caesarea.

2. To express the matter in our language, Cornelius was in command of a crack company of soldiers, part of a Roman legion, known as the Italian band.

3. The age in which Cornelius lived was one of unspeakable corruption and licentiousness (cf. Rom. 1: 28-32), with Roman soldiers exercising great power. But with all this, Cornelius was an unusually good man. See Acts 10: 1, 2, 22.

(1) Much is being said in these times about the relative importance of heredity and environment. They are both important and any one is vitally affected by them; but, in the final analysis, it is the individual himself who is responsible for channeling these influences.

(2) Even the casual observer knows that in many instances men with the best of environments have failed: while others have come to nobility of character and greatness of achievement in spite of unfavorable environments. Compare,

a. Adam and Eve in the garden of Eden.

b. Joseph in Potiphar's house.

c. Daniel in the house of Nebuchadnezzar.

d. The saints in Caesar's household, Phil. 4: 22. In spite of his position and the temptations which went with it, Cornelius was a remarkably good man.

II. How the Preacher and the Congregation Were Brought Together

1. The statement of the text, Acts 10: 3-8.

(1) Will God hear the prayer of an alien? See Acts 10: 31;

9: 11; cf. John 9: 31. This last passage contemplated people who were in covenant relationship with Jehovah.

(2) God will not hear the prayer of any person, child or alien, who turns away his ear from hearing his law. Cf. Prov. 28: 9.

2. While the messengers were on their way from Caesarea to Joppa, the Lord was preparing Peter for his task. See verses 9-20. Peter had referred to the bringing in of the Gentiles some eight or ten years before, but he did not comprehend that which he said about it. See Acts 2: 38, 39.

3. The men sent from Cornelius contacted Peter and he returned with them to Caesarea where he was welcomed by Cornelius, who had an audience waiting for Peter. See Acts 10: 21-33.

III. THE SERMON THAT CONVERTED CORNELIUS

1. Peter began his sermon with a declaration which has often been sadly misinterpreted, verses 34, 35. Some have thought that Peter taught that a good moral life is all that is necessary.

(1) If that had been what Peter meant, then Cornelius was already pleasing to the Lord; for he was a good moral man. Cf. Acts 11: 14.

(2) To fear God is to reverence him, while to work righteousness is to do that which he commands—that which will result in one's becoming righteous in God's sight. Cf. Rom. 10: 1-3.

(3) Peter made it plain that the gospel of Christ is for all who will accept it.

2. What did Peter preach to Cornelius? He did not eulogize him for his exalted character; instead, he proclaimed unto him the Christ as the Saviour of men. See verses 36-43. According to Peter, Christ commissioned his disciples to proclaim three great facts concerning him:

(1) That all the prophets bore witness to him. Christ was not merely an accident in the great drama of life. He came in the fulness of time and in the fulness of God's great purpose and plan to redeem the world.

(2) God ordained Christ to be the Judge of the living and the dead. All men, therefore, must stand before his judgment-seat, regardless of their moral character. Cf. 2 Cor. 5: 9, 10; John 12: 48-50.

(3) That *through his name* every one that believeth on him shall receive remission of sins. The Scriptures themselves are the best commentary on this proposition. See Luke 24: 46, 47; Acts 2: 37, 38; 10: 47, 48.

3. While Peter was speaking a miracle occurred which showed the Jews who were present that the Gentiles were entitled to gospel privileges, including church-membership. Cf. Acts 11: 1-18.

IV. ALL MEN NEED A SAVIOUR

1. The conversion of Cornelius, more than any other conversion recorded in the New Testament, proclaims the truth that all men, regardless of their moral character, need a Saviour. Cf. Rom. 3: 10, 23; 1 Tim. 2: 5; John 14: 6.

2. It is important to remember that the first man who was converted to Christ from among the Gentiles was not a thief or a drunkard or a malefactor of any kind; instead, he was a high-minded man, the very pick of the Gentile world.

3. Although the miraculous has passed away, and no one need expect an angel to appear to him, as was true in the case of Cornelius; but there are reasons for believing that the providence of God is often responsible for one's being placed in the position, and under favorable circumstances, for being taught the truth regarding himself and his salvation in Christ.

◆ ◆ ◆

PAUL'S FIRST RECORDED SERMON
Acts 13: 16-41

Introduction: 1. The thirteenth and fourteenth chapters of Acts contain the record of the first missionary journey which was made by Paul and Barnabas. They started from the church in Antioch in Syria, with John Mark as their attendant, and their first preaching was done in the synagogue of the Jews in Salamis, on the island of Cyprus, about 130 miles from Antioch. After spending some time on that island they sailed toward the mainland and came to Perga in Pamphylia. 2. The missionaries probably intended to preach the gospel in Pamphylia, a small province lying next to Cilicia where Paul had evidently already preached in Tarsus, its chief city. Cf. Acts 9: 30; 11: 25. But just what happened in Perga is still shrouded, to a great extent, in mystery. However, we do know that it was there that John Mark left the missionaries and returned to his home in Jerusalem, and that Paul and Barnabas went up from the low-lying coastland of Pamphylia to the highlands of South Galatia. From Acts 15: 36ff. we learn that Paul was not pleased with John Mark's action in leaving them, and from a statement which Paul made in his letter to the Galatians, written at a later date (see Gal. 4: 13, 14), it is thought by some that Paul contracted malaria in the low, sweltering caldron of Pamphylia. If Paul was thus stricken it is easy to understand why they sought the mountainous regions; for the best possible antidote for a malarial attack would be the mountain air. The pestilential climate of Pamphylia may also explain John Mark's sudden decision to return to Jerusalem. 3. Their first stop in the highlands of Galatia was an Antioch, known as Antioch of Pisidia, about 100 miles almost due north of Perga. The

elevation of Antioch was nearly 4,000 feet above sea level, and
like other centers of Paul's activities, it was a favored place.
Augustus, the emperor, had made it a Roman colony, and that
meant that its citizens enjoyed certain special rights, such as personal freedom and immunity from certain taxes. From its elevated location, the city over-looked the far-reaching plain to the
southeast, where the great Roman highway, which crossed the
highlands of Asia Minor, swung to the north to get around the
large lakes on its way to the Greek cities on the Aegean Sea.
Antioch was only a few miles from these mountain lakes, high in
the Taurus range, and it was one of the thriving, busy cities of
the uplands of South Galatia. 4. The sabbath found the missionaries in the Jewish synagogue, and they must have made a favorable impression; for they were invited to speak to the congregation. "And after the reading of the law and the prophets the
rulers of the synagogue sent unto them, saying, Brethren, if ye
have any word of exhortation for the people, say on. And Paul
stood up, and beckoning with the hand" he began his first recorded
sermon. In studying this lesson, then, let us begin by considering.

I. The Introduction to the Sermon, Verses 16-22

1. One of the first things that we notice about Paul as a
preacher is the fact that he stood up and beckoned with the hand.
This was according to the manner of the Greek orator, and was
in contrast with the sitting position of the Jewish teacher.

2. The audience that day was made up of both Jews and devout proselytes, and Paul addressed both classes.

3. He began his sermon with a review of Israel's early national history, for he knew that that would gratify the patriotic
sentiments of his Jewish hearers; but he was careful not to overlook the devout proselytes who were in the congregation. Cf.
verse 26.

(1) Not only would such an introduction please his Jewish
hearers, it was also calculated to direct their minds toward the
main theme of his discourse.

(2) The Jews had a glorious history, of which they were
justly proud; and any happily expressed reference to the more
outstanding events in it would awaken their most lively emotions.

(3) These incidents furnished the inspiration for their songs,
the themes of their orators, and afforded them comfort in their
persecutions. Any one, therefore, who showed the highest appreciation of these great events had the readiest access to their sympathy. Paul knew this, and he readily passed through this door
into the hearts of his hearers.

II. Jesus Proclaimed As a Saviour, Verses 23-29

1. The proposition stated, 23, 24.

(1) When Paul reached the name of David in his introductory

review of their history he touched a responsive chord; and from there he passed immediately to the main theme of his sermon—the appearance and work of David's promised Son.

(2) In a brief, but skillfully worded, sentence Paul introduced Jesus as the promised Son of David who was to deliver Israel, and also stated the time of his public appearance, viz., during the closing days of John's ministry. In this way he fixed attention, not upon the time of the birth of Jesus, but upon the time that God brought him forth unto Israel as a Saviour.

(3) The "baptism of repentance" was the baptism of penitents; for none but that class could be baptized according to divine authority.

2. The testimony of John, 25.

3. Prophecies fulfilled in the death of Jesus, 26-29.

(1) After asserting that the messiahship of Jesus was authenticated by the testimony of John, it became necessary for Paul to explain the singular fact that the Jews in Jerusalem had put him to death as an impostor.

(2) The speaker did this by showing that it was the result of their ignorance; and he took that which would have been regarded by any Jew as *prima facie* evidence that Jesus was not the Messiah and turned it into an unanswerable argument in his favor.

4. The resurrection of Jesus set forth, 30-37.

(1) In this section Paul presents the crowning fact of gospel evidence of the messiahship of Jesus, and as he does so he quotes from their beloved prophets in support of his contention. This, of course, would make his Jewish hearers more willing to listen to him.

(2) The average reader would understand the expression "Thou art my Son, this day have I begotten thee" (Psalm 2:7), as referring to the birth of the person under consideration; but Paul, as is done elsewhere in the Scriptures, makes it refer to the resurrection of the Messiah. This shows that Bible students should be careful to let God say what he means by any expression he uses.

(3) Paul next proceeds to show that these blessings predicted by Old Testament prophets (Isa. 55:3; Psalm 16:10) could not have been intended for David himself, but for the promised Messiah, the Son of David.

5. Remission of sins proclaimed through Jesus, 38, 39.

III. A Warning, Verses 40, 41

1. Although Paul had plainly showed that remission of sins can be had only in Jesus, it is a signal fact that, so far as the record is concerned, he did not tell his hearers how to obtain this blessing. Cf. Acts 2:36-38. This was evidently due to the fact that he saw from their attitude toward that which he had said that they were not prepared for such information.

2. Thus, instead of telling them how to obtain remission of sins, he uttered a fearful warning. See Hab. 1: 5.

3. It is not always necessary that a sermon have a pleasing ending. Jesus closed his sermon on the mount with a profound warning. The attitude of the audience usually determines the type of closing for any worthwhile sermon. It is a dangerous thing to listen to a sermon, if one does not intend to put into practice that which he learns.

◆ ◢ ◀

GOD NEVER GETS IN A BLIND ALLEY
Acts 13: 42-52

Introduction: 1. The events recorded in the text must be considered in the light of the preceding sermon preached by Paul, if we are to comprehend their full significance. The people who had heard Paul's discourse were deeply impressed by it; and as they left their places in the synagogue they requested "that these words might be spoken to them the next sabbath." 2. The audience which heard Paul preach was made up of both Jews and devout proselytes; and as we shall see in the course of this study, they manifested two distinct attitudes toward the word which was spoken. Cf. 2 Cor. 2: 15, 16. 3. This trait of human nature is common to all ages, and if we will keep this fact in mind it will help us immeasurably in our efforts to reach the hearts of men with the gospel. But in studying this lesson, let us begin by considering the statement,

I. WHEN THE SYNAGOGUE BROKE UP

1. This is a significant remark, and in order to appreciate its force we should try to visualize that which usually happens when one of our meetings is over. Ordinarily we begin to talk about other things, usually of a worldly nature, perhaps compliment the sermon or maybe criticize it to others, and then hurry away to a big dinner.

2. How different it was on the occasion which we are now considering! Many of the worshippers followed Paul and Barnabas in their eager desire for more light on the great questions which had been discussed.

(1) This attitude on the part of the people was remarkable in view of the fact that the sermon which Paul had just delivered was full of condemnation of the action of the Jews, full of controversial arguments which collided with their habitual way of thinking, and full of warning.

(2) To use a modern-day expression, they had received a crack on the head, but instead of manifesting a feeling of anger and resentment, many of them eagerly followed Paul and Barnabas and sought after more information. Cf. Acts 24: 25; Gal. 4: 14,

15. (Some of these very people were likely among those to whom Paul later wrote the letter to the Galatians.)

(3) And to use another present-day expression, many of our people today just can't take that which those people took. Instead, irate hearers whose pet prejudices have been jostled cry out, "This man is dangerous. He ought to be silenced."

3. What should happen after a gospel sermon has been preached? This should be a direct challenge to both preacher and hearer. A few questions may help us here.

(1) Every gospel preacher should ask himself whether or not he has a right to expect any response to his sermon. Did he present definite truth? or was he just talking in generalities? Cf. 2 Tim. 4: 1-4.

(2) Does the hearer have an open mind and is he sincerely and eagerly seeking after the truth? Cf. Acts 17: 11, 12. It frequently happens that some hearers face the preacher and in their self-confidence practically challenge him to interest them. Such an attitude frustrates even the grace of God.

II. GOD IS NOT MOCKED

1. The general attitude of the people toward the word of God, as presented by Paul and Barnabas, may be learned from verses 44 and 45. It is implied in these verses that Paul preached another sermon on the second sabbath.

2. If the obvious and traditional instruments of God's purposes reach the point where they no longer function according to his plans, he always has others which he can use. He never gets in a blind alley, nor is he mocked. Cf. Gal. 6: 7a; Isa. 55: 10, 11.

3. This is one of the most important and sobering lessons in history; and it ought to be an eternal warning to every individual, group, or institution which considers itself an agent or instrument of God's will.

(1) The orthodox Jew of the New Testament times could not even remotely imagine the possibility of God's carrying on his work without his chosen people, the Jews. But God showed that when any individual or institution fails to accomplish his will, such will be rejected and the work will go on through other means. No man nor institution is indispensable to God's work. Cf. Matt. 21: 43; Acts 10: 34, 35.

(2) Paul's momentous announcement, "Lo, we turn to the Gentiles," is a classic illustration of this truth. Cf. Rev. 2: 5.

III. SELF-CONDEMNATION

1. Some people seem to think that they have a point when they assert that God is too good to condemn his people eternally. What they need to learn is that God does not condemn any one

until he makes himself unworthy of that home which God has for them who love and serve him.

2. God did not turn away from the unbelieving Jews until they themselves thrust the word of God from them, and judged themselves unworthy of eternal life.

3. The Bible plainly teaches that God has good things in mind for all people. See 1 Tim. 2: 3, 4; 2 Pet. 3: 9. But it is also true that he allows men the freedom to exercise their own will power. Cf. John 5: 40.

IV. ORDAINED TO ETERNAL LIFE

1. The exact meaning of the expression "ordained to eternal life" has long been a matter of question among Bible students.

(1) When the question is considered in the light of the context and the general teaching of the Scriptures, the correct translation of the passage would probably be, "As many as were disposed to eternal life, or as many as were determined to secure eternal life, believed."

(2) The context implies that they were brought to this determination before they believed. Some experience or condition, either before or after they heard Paul preach, produced this mental state in them; and upon hearing him tell how eternal life can be secured, they readily believed.

2. The general attitude of those who were "ordained to eternal life" and of those who rejected Paul's preaching stand in sharp contrast with each other.

(1) Three things are affirmed of those who rejected the gospel:

a. They were filled with jealousy.

b. They contradicted the things which were spoken by Paul, and blasphemed.

c. They judged themselves unworthy of eternal life.

(2) In contrast with the attitute of the unbelieving Jews, three things are said of those who believed:

a. They were glad when they heard the things which Paul said.

b. They glorified the word of God.

c. They were ordained to, that is, disposed to or determined to secure, eternal life.

3. Thus it can plainly be seen that the word for ordained (*tetagmenoi*) stands in contrast with the mental state of the Jews who judged themselves unworthy of eternal life.

(1) The one group had an open mind on the question and a desire to gain the goal of which he spoke, while the other group, although professing to want eternal life, closed their mind to that which God said about securing it. Cf., again, Acts 17: 11, 12.

(2) Two men may sit side by side under the sound of the same gospel sermon. One is awake to the importance of the life

which is to come, while the other is absorbed in the life that now is. The latter will turn a deaf ear to the preaching and thereby judge himself unworthy of eternal life, while the former will gladly consider the message; and if he finds it to be true, he will gladly believe it and cheerfully do that which it enjoins. Cf. Mark 16: 15, 16; Acts 18: 8.

V. THE FINAL RESULTS IN ANTIOCH

1. The word of the Lord was spread abroad, not only in Antioch itself, but in all the region in which the city was located.

2. When those of the character of the unbelieving Jews are unable to meet the arguments of another, they usually turn to their most formidable weapon—that of stirring up prejudice and persecution. That is what happened in Antioch of Pisidia.

3. While Paul and Barnabas were ignominiously expelled from the city, they did not leave without forecasting the righteous judgment of God upon those who rejected his word. Cf. Mark 6: 11; Luke 10: 16.

4. Although born into the family of God in the midst of persecution, and no doubt compelled to endure much suffering without the companionship and encouragement of their spiritual fathers, the newly made disciples were, nevertheless, "filled with joy and with the Holy Spirit." Cf. Rom. 5: 1-5.

◆ ◆ ◆

WHEN PLANS MUST BE CHANGED
Acts 16: 6-10

Introduction: 1. Life is full of efforts and failures. Practically every person starts out toward some desired goal, and for a while things seem to be going well; but with most of us there comes a time in our experience when we reach a point beyond which we cannot go. There we stand and look upon our frustrated plans which must be abandoned. Such an experience can lead one to despondency and bitterness, but if he is sincerely trying to follow the Lord he will simply realize that his plans must be changed. 2. One of the chief things which God requires in all his people is the development of a pure and spotless character, and this often requires divine discipline; but if one is willing to be directed by the Lord in all that he does, he will soon come to realize that he can serve best in the field where the Lord leads him. Whatever our experiences in life may be, we are taught that to them that love God all things work together for good, even to them that are called according to his purpose. This is the divine answer to all the baffling experiences which come to us. 3. The lesson before us today sets forth one of the most impressive examples of the necessity for a change in plans, together with the glorious results which followed, to be found in all liter-

ature. Paul and his companions had passed through the region
of Phrygia and Galatia, having been forbidden of the Holy Spirit
to speak the word in Asia; and when they were come over against
Mysia, they assayed to go into Bithynia; and the Spirit of Jesus
suffered them not; and passing by Mysia, they came down to
Troas. , It was at Troas that Paul had his vision of the man
of Macedonia calling for help, which resulted in their conclusion
that God was calling them to preach the gospel to the people of
that country. But in studying this lesson, let us begin by considering,

I. OUR GOALS VERSUS CHARACTER BUILDING

1. One of the first things that any Christian should learn is
that God does not see as man sees. Cf. 1 Sam. 16: 7; Isa. 55: 8,
9.

2. God is omniscient, and, as such, he sees the end from
the beginning. He knows, therefore, what is best for each of us,
both from the standpoint of the work which he wants us to do
and the development of our own characters.

3. Every child of God, of course, should sincerely endeavor
to do that which he believes the Lord wants him to do; but if and
when it becomes clear to him that he will not be able to accomplish that on which he had his heart set, he should not hesitate
to change his plans and enter whole-heartedly into the new situation.

II. THE EXAMPLE OF PAUL

1. The narrative which we are considering today records an
experience in the life of Paul which is so simple and commonplace that the average reader little suspects that the writer was
dealing with one of the most significant events in human history—
namely, the passing of Christianity from Asia into Europe.

2. But great as the result was, Paul had not planned to go to
Europe at that time. He and those with him had "assayed (attempted or endeavored—Thayer) to go into Bithynia; and the
Spirit of Jesus suffered them not (that is, would not allow or
permit them to go.)"

3. Although wanting Bithynia but getting Troas, Paul was
able to make this change in his plans one of the greatest opportunities of his life. This was because he had the spirit, attitude, and
technique which were necessary in order to deal with an unes-
capable problem.

III. WHAT, THEN, ENABLED PAUL TO TURN DEFEAT INTO VICTORY?

1. *His deep religious conviction entered into the new plan.*
Whatever his disappointments may have been regarding Bithynia,
he had no complaint to offer when he reached Troas. Instead,

he remained stedfast in his conviction that God had a purpose for his life; and since he had been led to Troas, there must be something there worth discovering; for God plans and purposes include Troas as well as Bithynia. He never leads any man to a place where all the doors of opportunity are shut. Cf. 2 Cor. 2: 14; Rom. 8: 28.

(1) It is just such situations as this that one can tell how much real religion he has.

a. A man, for example, might proclaim his faith in certain divine propositions, but no matter how serious he may seem about them, no one can tell from his proclamation alone just how real they are to him.

b. One might sing,

> He leadeth me! O blessed thought!
> O words with heav'nly comfort fraught!
> Whate'er I do, where'er I be,
> Still 'tis God's hand that leadeth me,

but however much in earnest he may seem, no one can tell from that alone how much it means to him.

c. But when one sees a man who wants Bithynia but gets Troas, and still feels certain that there is a divine purpose for his life, and enters enthusiastically into that which he finds in the new situation, that man's religion is the kind that honors God and benefits his fellow men.

(2) The story of Joseph also, in a very effective manner, illustrates this theme. Give the highlights of his experience from the time his brothers sold him until he was made known to them as the governor of Egypt. Can any one suppose that he, during all that period of humiliation and disgrace, could see that God was taking care of him? See Gen. 41: 51, 52; 45: 5, 8; 50: 20; Cf. Matt. 10: 29, 30.

2. His interest in people. This was the fruit of his religion. Instead of feeling sorry for himself, he immediately began to think of other people. It may be that he remembered that which was said of him when he saw the Lord on the Damascus road. See Acts 26: 15-19. Thus, filled with a desire to advance his Master's cause, together with an ever-present sense of his responsibilities, he doubtless felt that he would have in Troas an opportunity to help some one see the light. Cf. Acts 16: 9, 10.

(1) As has already been suggested in this study, practically all of us are in Troas; and if we will only try to adjust ourselves to our new situation and open our eyes, we will, in all probability, get a clear vision of great opportunities which lie out before us.

(2) Some one has said that "nothing makes a man strong like a cry for help." Cf. a mother who, completely fatigued, finds her child ill and in need of her. She, seemingly, takes on new strength and can go for days without stopping. Just think what

this spirit would do in the followers of Christ when they see the lot of the helpless, some of them so helpless that they do not even know that they need deliverance!

3. *The example of Jesus.*   This, perhaps, was that which helped Paul most.   Jesus wanted the people to accept him as the promised Messiah—his Bithynia, but they rejected him and he was finally brought to Golgotha—his Troas.   However, it was on the cross that he made his greatest sacrifice for mankind, so much so that Jesus took a hard thing and made a triumph out of it.   Cf. Matt. 23: 37-39; 26: 36-46.

> All the light of sacred story
> Gathers round its head sublime

◆ ◆ ◆

A HEART THE LORD OPENED
Acts 16: 11-15

Introduction: 1.   The first part of the sixteenth chapter of Acts contains the story of the "Macedonian call" and the effect it had on Paul and his company.   Feeling certain that God had called them to preach the gospel in Macedonia, they made their plans to go there at once.   After a very few days they were in Philippi, "a city of Macedonia, the first of the district, a Roman colony;" and while waiting for an opportunity to begin their work, they tarried there "certain days."   2.   Still carrying out the policy of preaching the gospel first to the Jews, they evidently waited for the sabbath day, which would give them such an opportunity; and with the coming of the sabbath they went out by a river side, where they found a place of prayer.   The group which had gathered there was made up of women; and Paul and his company, taking their seats, spoke unto them.   Among the women who had gathered there was Lydia; and since it was her heart the Lord opened, let us begin this study by considering,

I. SOME FACTS CONCERNING LYDIA

1. She was a merchant-woman and had come from Thyatira, a city of Asia in which was located one of the seven churches of Revelation, 2 and 3.

2. Her business in Philippi was that of a dealer in purple; and since purple dye was very costly, it was only used on expensive fabrics.   That, together with the fact that she was a dealer in that material and the added fact that she was the head of a household, with a house large enough to entertain Paul and his three companions, indicates that, while not above the necessity of working, she was, nevertheless, in comparatively easy circumstances.

3. Something of her character may be learned from the statement of the text, "one that worshipped God," and from the

further consideration that in this heathen city, where the sabbath of the Jewish Scriptures was unknown to its inhabitants, she was faithful in observing it.

(1) Thus, while other dealers in purple goods were, in all probability, busy on that day, she closed her shop, regardless of the demands of competition; and while there was no synagogue in which she might worship, and no male Jews to conduct the accustomed service, she and those associated with her habitually left the noisy city, and spent the holy day in prayer on the bank of the river.

(2) Such fidelity to God, under circumstances so unfavorable, is not often seen in our own more favored times. There are many professed Christians today who will let business, pleasure, company, and almost anything else, keep them from observing the Lord's day as the New Testament directs. Cf. Luke 8: 14; Rev. 1: 10.

(3) The practice of the early Christians, Acts 2: 42; 20: 7; Heb. 10: 25ff.

II. Why Did Her Heart Need Opening?

1. The fact that the Lord opened it implies that in some way it was closed; and the question as to why it was in that condition naturally suggests itself.

(1) It was certainly not due to inherited depravity, nor yet to the hardness of a sinful life. Her character at the time we meet her is wholly against that idea.

(2) It was closed in the same sense in which the hearts of other pious and earnest Jews and Jewish proselytes were closed, that is, by their misconception, and consequent attitude, regarding Christ. Because they thought that he was coming to establish an earthly kingdom, their hearts were stedfastly closed against him as the crucified Redeemer. Cf. 1 Cor. 1: 23.

2. This condition of Lydia's heart would have to be corrected or she would, like the masses of her Jewish brethren, reject the gospel of Christ.

3. The correction was made by removing this mistaken conception regarding Christ from her mind; and the effect of the opening of her heart was precisely that which was aimed at—viz., it led her "to give heed unto the things which were spoken by Paul."

III. What Is the Heart That Is Involved in the Acceptance or Rejection of Christ?

1. It is certainly not the lobe of flesh that is located in the left side of our bodies—that organ which pumps the blood through our bodies; for its function in man is no different from that in any beast of the field. What thoughtful person would contend that that is what the Lord opened in the case of Lydia?

2. The Scriptures teach that we have both an inward and an outward man; and that each has a heart. See 2 Cor. 4: 16; 2 Sam. 15: 1-6; Matt. 6: 19-21; Col. 3: 1, 2; Luke 24: 45 (cf. 24: 13ff.)

3. Functions of the heart:

(1) It thinks, Matt. 9: 4; it reasons, Mark 2: 8; it understands, Matt. 13: 15; it believes, Rom. 10: 9, 10. These are purely intellectual processes.

(2) It desires, Rom. 10: 1; it loves, Matt. 22: 37; it trusts. Prov. 3: 5. These are emotional processes.

(3) It purposes, Acts 11: 23; it determines, 1 Cor. 7: 37. These are processes of the will.

(4) It may be pricked, Acts 2: 37; it condemns or approves, 1 John 3: 19-21, depending on what we do about that which we think to be right or wrong. Cf. Rom. 6: 16-18. These processes have to do with the conscience.

IV. How Did the Lord Open Lydia's Heart?

1. The statement of the text:

(1) She "heard us," that is, she listened to that which was spoken to her.

(2) "Whose heart the Lord opened." This followed the hearing.

(3) "To give heed unto the things which were spoken by Paul." That was the reason why the Lord opened her heart, so that she might do the things which were appointed for her to do.

2. That which Lydia did in response to Paul's teaching was in complete harmony with that which the Lord commanded when he sent his disciples out to try to convert the world to him. See Acts 16: 15; Mark 16: 15, 16.

V. Reaching the Heart of the Honest Soul

1. The context plainly shows that the Lord followed a deliberate plan in bringing Lydia and Paul together. See Acts 16: 1-10.

2. Barring any miraculous element that may have been in the case now before us, it is altogether probable that the Lord, in his providential oversight, is doing the same for people today, especially those whose lives and attitudes are like Lydia's. Cf. John 7: 17; Heb. 1: 14.

◆ ◆ ◆

WHAT MUST I DO TO BE SAVED?
Acts 16: 16-34

Introduction: 1. It sometimes happens that a prisoner confers a great blessing upon his jailer. This was certainly true of Paul and the Philippian jailer. The apostle to the Gentiles, along with his companion Silas, had been falsely accused and shamefully beaten, and then, without being shown any mercy, "they cast them into prison, charging the jailer to keep them safely: who, having received such a charge, cast them into the inner prison, and made their feet fast in the stocks." 2. If the magistrates had only taken the time to investigate, they would not have been guilty of mal-treating innocent men; but with the human race depraved as it is, it often happens that the would-be benefactor must bear a cross before his blessings reach the needy. 3. The condition of these prisoners was distressing in the extreme, but there was no resentment in their hearts. There was no room for such a feeling, as long as their hearts were filled with prayer and praise unto God. It would be useless to speculate on which songs they probably sang, but we do know that their prayers and songs reached the hearts of their fellow prisoners.

> Down in the human heart, crushed by the tempter,
> Feelings lie buried that grace can restore:
> Touched by a loving heart, wakened by kindness,
> Chords that were broken will vibrate once more.

If the Lord's people, instead of so much complaining and criticizing, would spend more of their time praying and singing praises unto God, it is likely that they would often meet with this request:

> Sing them over again to me, wonderful words of life;
> Let me more of their beauty see, wonderful words of life.
> Words of life and beauty, teach me faith and duty:
> Beautiful words, wonderful words, wonderful words of life.

I. The Occasion for the Question of the Jailer

1. As Paul and Silas were praying and singing hymns unto God, while the prisoners were listening to them, a great earthquake suddenly shook the prison-house to its foundations, throwing open the doors, and loosing the bands of all the prisoners.

2. Upon being roused from his sleep and seeing the prison doors open, the jailer "drew his sword and was about to kill himself, supposing that the prisoners had escaped."

3. But before the jailer had time to act, "Paul cried with a loud voice, saying, Do thyself no harm: for we are all here. And he called for lights and sprang in, and, trembling for fear, fell down before Paul and Silas, and brought them out and said, Sirs, what must I do to be saved?"

II. What Salvation Was He Seeking?

1. It was not salvation from the earthquake; for its terrors were passed and he was free from them.

2. He was not seeking salvation from the wrath of the Roman Government for letting prisoners escape; for they were all still in the prison.

3. The context plainly shows that he was seeking the salvation which involved his relation to God—salvation from his sins; for that is what Paul and Silas told him about.

4. Although his resolution to seek salvation was made in the midst of events which were both sudden and dramatic, it is interesting to observe that his conversion was carefully directed by the word of the Lord. See Acts 16: 32. Sudden and terrifying events often start men in the direction of better things. Cf. Saul of Tarsus, Acts 22: 1-16; Martin Luther.*

III. THE WAY OF SALVATION

1. The question of the jailer and the answer of Paul give a splendid view of the way of salvation. But, let us ask, who is responsible for the ideas of "save" and "lost", and who inspired the answer which Paul gave? See Luke 19: 10; Acts 16: 32; cf. Acts 10: 43.

2. Just what it means to believe on the Lord, and how faith saves a man, Paul, we are sure, made clear in his sermon to the alarmed jailer. He did not stop with merely telling him to "believe on the Lord Jesus, and thou shalt be saved"; for he spoke unto him the word of the Lord. No one can believe on the Lord who does not know who Jesus is, what he did to bring about the salvation of the lost, and that which he said regarding the method of obtaining it. Cf. 1 Cor. 15: 1-4; Mark 16: 15, 16.

3. Inasmuch as the jailer is presented to us by the inspired historian as an example of a man who was saved by faith, it is in order to ask,

(1) How strong must faith be before it will save? Cf. James 2: 14-26; Heb. 11: 7.

(2) How did the jailer prove that he had faith? See Acts 16: 33, 34.

◆ ◆ ◆

ARE ALL RELIGIOUS PEOPLE CHRISTIANS?
Acts 17: 22, 23

Introduction: 1. There are serious difficulties involved in discussing a question of this nature, because of the attitude most people already have toward it; for with many even the raising of

---

*The sudden death of a friend, which was followed shortly afterward by a narrow escape from death by lightning in a forest between Erfurt and Eisleben, caused Luther to resolve to obey what he then regarded as the commands of a higher law. Terrified by the violence of the storm that was raging around him, and especially by the bolts of lightning that were crashing through the trees, he addressed one of the patron saints of his childhood in these words: "Help me, dear Saint Anna, I will be a monk." Those who know something of the life of Luther understand that it was this terrifying experience that caused him to resolve upon the course which led to his great influence in the Protestant Reformation.

◆ ◆ ◆

a question like this one is to them a reflection on their honesty and integrity with reference to their religion. 2. But let it be emphasized at the very outset that it is not the purpose of this investigation to call in question any one's honesty or sincerity. Our aim, instead, is to determine in the light of God's word whether or not there is a difference between being religious and being a Christian; and whether or not one can be honestly mistaken in religious matters. 3. It is a well known fact that a person must be religious in order to be a Christian; but the question now under consideration is, Can one be religious and not be a Christian? If he cannot, then all religious people, regardless of the character of their religion, are Christians; but if one can be religious and not be a Christian, then some people are certainly mistaken in thinking that they are Christians, just because they are religious. But in studying this lesson, let us consider,

I. The Need for a Careful Examination

1. The fact that one can be religious and not be a Christian ought to cause each one present to make the closest personal examination possible. Each one of us needs to know just what the Lord has said about this matter, and just what our religious status is.

2. The testimony of the Scriptures: 2 Cor. 13: 5; 1 Thess. 5: 21; 1 Peter 3: 15.

3. Unless we are willing to do as these scriptures suggest, that is evidence enough to show that our hearts are not right before God. Cf. Prov. 23: 7.

4. To take a thing for granted, without making the proper investigation, has often resulted in the bitter experience of being deceived; and it is certain that nothing could be worse, if it concerns the soul. Cf. Matt. 16: 26.

II. The Definition of the Terms

1. It is very necessary that we know the meaning of the words "religion" and "Christianity," if we are to have a clear understanding of the subject now before us.

2. *Religion* is a system of faith and worship which may or may not be of divine origin. Cf. James 1: 26, 27.

3. *Christianity* is the system and life taught by Jesus Christ and his apostles. Cf. Heb. 1: 1, 2; 12: 2; Matt. 28: 20a.

4. Christianity, indeed, is a religion; but it differs from all other religions in that Christ is its author. There are many systems of religion, but only one that can rightfully be called Christianity. Cf. Rom. 10: 1-4.

(1) Were these Jews religious? Indeed they were.

(2) Were they Christians. No thoughtful person would affirm that they were.

III. SOME OTHER RELIGIOUS PEOPLE WHO WERE NOT CHRISTIANS

1. The people of Athens, Acts 17: 16, 22, 23.
2. Saul of Tarsus, Gal. 1: 13, 14; Acts 26: 1-11. Cf. Acts 23: 1; 24: 16.
3. Cornelius, Acts 10: 1, 2; 11: 13, 14.
4. Lydia, Acts 16: 11-15.

(1) Surely no one can fail to see from these examples that it is possible for a man to be religious and not be a Christian. And if that was true in Bible times, it is true now; and therein lies the necessity of making sure that we are right before going forward. Cf. 2 John 9.

(2) One may search the entire New Testament through but he will not find a single case of conversion, except in the case of those who discovered that they were wrong religiously, and who turned from their error and sought salvation by obeying the gospel of Christ. Cf. Mark 16: 15, 16; Rom. 1: 16, 17; John 1: 11, 12.

IV. A PICTURE OF THE RELIGIOUS WORLD

1. There are many different religions in the world, but they may all be listed under five heads—viz:

(1) Paganism or idol worshippers. There are many different systems under this heading, and practically all professed Christians will readily admit that here is a difference between religion and Christianity; for they are making efforts, through their missionaries and other methods, to convert them to their conception of Christianity. Cf. the idea that it doesn't make any difference what one believes, just so he is honest!

(2) The Jewish and Mohammedan religions which are neither pagan nor Christian; for they do not accept Christ, but claim God as their author.

(3) Catholicism which is a mixture of paganism, Judaism, and Christianity. The adherents of this religion are classed as Christians; but the classification is made without any regard for the New Testament idea of that term.

(4) Protestantism or denominationalism. While there are many branches under this heading, there is in reality only one system; and taken as a whole it is a mixture of paganism, Judaism, Catholicism, and Christianity. Notwithstanding their claim to be Christian, it is a well known fact that many of them will not fellowship others of this classification; and not one group among them claims to teach all that Christ commanded, hence the popular slogan, "Go to the church of your choice."

(5) Christianity, the unadulterated system of faith and worship which was taught and authorized by Christ and his inspired apostles.

2. The New Testament authorizes Christianity and Christianity alone; and if one will believe and obey that which is taught in this inspired volume, he will become a Christian and nothing else. One will have to obey something outside the inspired record, if he becomes anything other than a simple New Testament follower of Christ—a Christian.

3. If the Bible cannot be relied upon as an infallible guide, then there is safety in nothing else; but if the Bible is the inspired word of God, it must be obeyed implicitly. Cf. Matt. 7: 21-23; 2 Tim. 3: 16, 17; Gal. 1: 6-10.

◆ ◆ ◆

LET YOUR PREACHER PREACH
Acts 20: 17-27

Introduction: 1. The ministry of preaching has been a custom among the followers of Christ since the beginning of his kingdom, nearly two thousand years ago. That kind of work was responsible, perhaps more than any other, for the rapid growth and development of the early church; and yet every faithful preacher of the gospel knows that his ministry cannot be effective —cannot have the full release of its power, and thereby fulfill its mission in the most effective manner—unless the people understand something of the way in which he is able to serve them. Cf. a physician. His work is limited, unless the people know how he is fitted to serve them. 2. Every one who has any conception of what it means to be loyal to Christ, readily understands that all preaching which meets with Divine approval must be in harmony with the principles of the New Testament. But there is one thing that is not generally understood, or else is ignored— viz., that the preacher is not the only one who has responsibility in the matter of preaching. More will be said about this as the lesson proceeds. But in considering this subject, let us begin with the proposition,

I. Let Your Preacher Preach

1. Perhaps some one is ready to say, Why make such a request as that? no one is going to hinder him from preaching. In fact, if he does not appear before the congregation to preach at every appointed hour, the leaders will take immediate steps to replace him.

2. All that is true, and is well understood; but there is something that is not so well understood, or else is ignored—viz., Each individual member of the church has a responsibility in preaching which is not fulfilled by a contribution that helps to pay the preacher, so that he can stay with the congregation and preach at the appointed times.

3. It is this individual responsibility that we are concerned

with today. Therefore, it is in order to say, *Let your preacher preach to you.* This would require two things on the part of each individual: (1) Be present, Heb. 10: 25; (2) Be in the proper frame of mind to receive instruction, Acts 17: 11, 12.

II. THE PURPOSE OF PREACHING

1. Preaching is not something that we may or may not have, just to suit our own conveniences and fancies. It was ordained by God himself, and commanded by the Lord Jesus Christ and his apostles. Cf. 1 Cor. 1: 21; Mark 16: 15; Acts 10: 42; 2 Tim. 4: 1, 2.

2. Gospel preaching proceeds from the basic conviction that life, if acceptable to God, must be lived on his terms, and that his will regarding man is revealed in Christ Jesus. See Matt. 7: 21; 1 Cor. 2: 1, 2; cf. Rom. 15: 4.

3. Every normal individual has what is known as a "frame of reference" to which he consciously or subconsciously refers his questions as to what he shall or shall not do, or what he shall or shall not believe. This "frame of reference," however, is not always dependable, worthy, or intelligent. If it were, then the Bible would not be needed. The purpose of preaching is to call people's attention to the fact that God's word is the standard to which they must conform, if they would enjoy the blessings he has prepared for them. Cf. Isa. 55: 8, 9.

III. VOICES FROM THE OPPOSITION

1. While the preacher is trying to get your attention to help you realize that God's word must be respected, there are other influences which are at work in an effort to make you forget that it is by obedience to God's word that one will enter into life.

2. What are some of the influences which would like to have you forget that you are a child of God? Only two shall be mentioned here, but they should be sufficient to illustrate the lesson.

(1) The voice that says that you are capable of deciding what you should or should not do. Such an attitude totally unfits one for receiving the word of God. Cf. Luke 8: 5, 12.

(2) The things of this world. See Luke 8: 14; James 1: 13-16. One's "own lust" often draws him away from God.

3. It should be obvious to any one that if people are to be benefited by gospel preaching, they will have to attend the meetings of the church with regularity, when at all possible. How many professed Christians seem not to realize this! Habit should be made to serve every Christian in the matter of church attendance. Cf. Luke 4: 16. People are not usually disturbed every Monday morning about whether or not they are going to work; why should they be disturbed on Sundays about whether or not they will attend the meetings of the church? Or, are they past the disturbing point?

SOME WORDS TO REMEMBER
Acts 20: 35

Introduction: 1. The words of the text form the closing part
of Paul's address to the Ephesian elders. He was finishing his
third missionary journey, and was hurrying to Jerusalem for the
day of Pentecost. Inasmuch as Ephesus was off of his route, he
asked the elders of the church there to meet him in Miletus; and
it was at the latter place that he delivered his address to them.
Every Christian, and especially every elder in the church, should
read and carefully study this speech. 2. When the words of
the text are read as a basis for a sermon, many people expect a
discourse on giving; but when their real significance is understood,
it will be seen that they were spoken for another purpose. Perhaps no violence would be done to the Scriptures, if the text were
used as a basis for preaching on giving; but when the facts in
the case are carefully considered it will be very obvious that Paul
had something else in mind when he spoke these words. But in
studying this lesson, let us begin by considering.

I. Some Interesting Facts

1. These words of Jesus were rescued from oblivion; and have
been preserved for the use of the Lord's people in every succeeding age. Cf. John 20: 30, 31; 21: 25.

2. In all the writings of the apostles to the church, Paul is
the only one who ever made a direct quotation from Jesus; and
he only made two. See Acts 20: 35; 1 Cor. 11: 23-25.

3. While not quoting directly from the Saviour, his chosen
ambassadors did make known his will, and set forth precisely
that which he wants men to believe and do today. Cf. John
16: 13, 14; 13: 20; Gal. 1: 6-12.

II. Paul's Use of the Lord's Words

1. As already indicated, these words were the closing part
of Paul's address to the Ephesian elders; and he used them to
inspire the elders to follow his example of serving. See Acts 20:
34, 35.

2. Such service had always been Paul's rule as a Christian;
and in following that rule, he was but imitating the example and
teaching of Jesus. Cf. 2 Cor. 12: 14, 15; 1 Thess. 2: 7-9; Matt.
20: 28.

3. But Paul points out that Jesus said that it is *more* blessed
to give than to receive.

(1) *There is a blessing, then, in receiving.* What would be
the condition of one if he should refuse the gifts of nature, human
love, and divine grace?

(2) *But there is a greater blessing in giving.* Cf. Matt. 10:

8b. What gifts and opportunities do we have for helping others as a result of our receiving?

> He who is loved has gained the highest tribute of earth;
> but he who loves has entered into the spirit of heaven.

4. This was the higher example of Jesus. Cf. 2 Cor. 8: 9; Phil. 2: 1-8.

III. SOME BLESSINGS WHICH CAME TO PAUL

1. *The blessing of a confident faith.* Cf. 2 Tim. 1: 12; Rom. 8: 28; 2 Cor. 5: 1.

(1) Such faith can be reached by the normal individual only by the way of service. Cf. Jer. 22: 16.

(2) Faith is something to use; for faith is made perfect by works. See James 2: 22.

2. *The gift of happiness.* It is doubtful if any follower of Christ suffered more and did more for others than Paul; and yet no one can find an accent of melancholy or sadness in all his writings. Cf. 2 Cor. 7: 4; 12: 7-10; Acts 16: 25; Phil. 2: 17, 18; 2 Tim. 4: 6-8.

3. *A holy character.* Cf. 1 Pet. 1: 15, 16; Matt. 5: 48; Phil. 1: 27a; Gal. 2: 20.

Conclusion: Thus, instead of the text emphasizing the question of an offering, it sets forth the introduction to a fuller life. If its teaching is followed, all selfishness will be destroyed, and a deeper love for the brethren will be promoted. Cf. Matt. 16: 24; 1 John 3: 14-16; 4: 20, 21.

◆ ◆ ◆

WHAT SHALL I DO, LORD?
Acts 22: 10

Introduction: 1. It is always interesting to examine the turning point in any great life, and consider the forces which were responsible for the course that was taken. Regardless of whose life it may have been, we may be sure that it was motivated by the principles of true greatness. One fine example of the way in which these principles work is found in Psalm 119: 59, 60. There the psalmist graphically describes the forces which led to the turning point in his life, and the results that followed. 2. Although one of the most relentless persecutors of the followers of Christ, Saul of Tarsus, the man who asked the question of the text, was honest at heart, and his greatest desire was to please God. Cf. Acts 23: 1; 24: 16; 1 Tim. 1: 13. It was because he was actuated by these principles of greatness that he was ready to say, when he discovered that he was wrong, "What shall I do, Lord?" 3. It is doubtful if there was ever a man who felt less the need of asking such a question. His path, as it always had been, was plain, he was sure of his purpose and of his goal in life, and he was determined, at all costs, to accomplish his purpose and to reach his goal. But in studying this lesson, let us ask,

I. How Did Saul Come to Ask This Question?

1. First of all, as already indicated, he was zealously doing that which he believed to be right. Cf. Gal. 1: 13, 14. God is always pleased with a man who maintains a clear conscience. That means that he is living up to the best he knows, and will readily accept any new light, if and when it comes to him. Cf. John 7: 17.

2. In endeavoring to do that which he believed to be right, Saul obtained letters of authority from the high priest, and set out for Damascus to arrest any whom he might find there who were of the Way, whether men or women, that he might bring them bound to Jerusalem to be punished.

3. As he approached the city, about noon, he saw a light from heaven, above the brightness of the sun. Being struck with its sudden glare, he fell to the ground and heard a voice saying unto him, "Saul, Saul, why persecutest thou me?" Immediately he asked, "Who art thou Lord?" and upon learning that it was Jesus, whom he thought to be an impostor, he promptly asked, "What shall I do, Lord?"

II. Saul's Response to the Lord's Answer

1. It is doubtful if there ever was a man who so completely emptied himself and stood ready to listen to what the Lord had to say, as did Saul of Tarsus. His attitude is a splendid commentary on Matt. 16: 24. Everything was at that time diametrically opposed to that which he believed was right, but that did not deter him; his life-long desire and determination to please the Lord were as pronounced as ever.

2. Having committed the work of making known the way of salvation to men (cf. 2 Cor. 4: 7; 5: 18-20), the Lord did not personally tell him what to do, but simply said, "Arise, and go into Damascus; and there it shall be told thee of all things which are appointed for thee to do."

3. Although still blinded by the light from heaven, Saul was led into the city; and the evidence that he was at that time a penitent believer was seen in the fact that he refused to eat or drink until he learned what the Lord wanted him to do, although he had to wait three days.

4. While Saul was waiting and praying, the Lord sent one of the very men whom he had intended to arrest to tell him what to do. But that did not matter to Saul; for all that he was concerned about was to learn and do that which the Lord required of him. So, when Ananias said, "And now why tarriest thou? arise, and be baptized, and wash away thy sins, calling on his name," Saul did not hesitate: "he arose and was baptized."

5. *When was Saul saved?* If he was saved the "moment that

he believed," then he was saved before his sins were washed away; for it was three days after he believed before he was told to "arise, and be baptized, and wash away thy sins, calling on his name." Saul was saved by faith (Rom. 5: 1), but only when his faith became strong enough to lead him to do that which he was told to do. His faith was made perfect by works. Read James 2: 14-26.

III. "A CHOSEN VESSEL UNTO ME"

1. It is a noticeable fact that of all the cases of conversion recorded in the Book of Acts, that of Saul of Tarsus alone is characterized by the personal appearance of the Son of God himself; yet with all that, as already indicated, Jesus did not tell him what to do in order to be saved: he only directed him to the place where he could find out.

2. The personal appearance of Jesus was not to save Saul; its purpose was to qualify him as a minister—as an apostle, both to the Gentiles and to the children of Israel. See Acts 26: 16-18; 9: 15.

3. "For I will show him how many things he must suffer for my name's sake." The fact that Saul was determined, at all costs, to please the Lord made him a fit instrument for the Lord's use; and since suffering must often be endured before the truth is seen and accepted by some, the Lord knew that in Saul he had a man who was willing to "endure all things for the elect's sake, that they also may obtain the salvation which is in Christ Jesus with eternal glory." (2 Tim. 2: 10.)

❖ ❖ ❖

THE UNFINISHED SERMON
Acts 24: 24-27

Introduction: 1. It is not always easy to comprehend that which is implied in the universality of the gospel and God's desire and effort to get it into the hearts of all men. With an audience like the Ethiopian eunuch (Acts 8) or Lydia (Acts 16) the task is relatively easy, but when it comes to reaching people like Felix the method of procedure is entirely different. 2. It frequently requires sufferings and hardships on the part of God's faithful messengers in order to reach some people; but we may be sure that God will always give them the necessary grace to enable them to bear such hardships and sufferings. 3. Although the sermon which we are to study today was never finished, the general outline of it and the circumstances surrounding its delivery were of sufficient importance to warrant a place in the sacred record. In studying this lesson, then, let us begin by considering,

I. THE CHARACTER OF THE AUDIENCE

1. This audience was not a large one. So far as the record goes, there were only two people who heard Paul on this occasion —Felix and Drusilla.

(1) Felix was one of those rulers, all too common in that day and this, who exercised great power without conscience. He had formerly been a slave to Agrippina, the mother of Nero, but he had in some way gained his freedom. He was made governor of the province of Judaea, and, according to Tacitus, being guilty of "every kind of cruelty and lust, he exercised the authority of a king with the temper of a slave." This same authority, in his *Annals* (11: 54) represents Felix as considering himself licensed to commit any crime, relying on the influence which he possessed at court to escape punishment.

(2) Felix was married three times, each time to a woman of royal birth. Two of his wives were named Drusilla. One was a Roman, the niece or granddaughter of Antony and Cleopatra, mentioned by Tacitus. The other, his last wife, was a beautiful young Jewess, the daughter of Herod Agrippa I (Acts 12), and sister of Herod Agrippa II and Bernice (Acts 25.) Drusilla was first married to Azizus, king of Amesa, who had been circumcised in order that he might receive her.

(3) Sometime after her marriage to Azizus, Felix saw Drusilla, fell in love with her, and through the influence of one of his friends, a Jew and pretended magician by the name of Simon, he unscrupulously persuaded her to forsake her husband and defy Jewish law by marrying him, although he had not become a Jew. See Josephus, Antiquities 20: 7, 1f.

(4) The cruelty of which Felix was guilty, the manner in which he and Drusilla were brought together, and his lust for gain, give us some idea of the character of the audience which sat before Paul.

2. God desires the salvation of every one (2 Pet. 3: 9), being no respecter of persons (Acts 10: 34, 35); but since people like Felix and Drusilla seldom attend preaching services, how are they to be reached? The manner in which they and Paul were brought together is graphically told in Acts, chapters 21-24.

3. It certainly required courage to preach under these circumstances. It is not easy to go into the homes of the ungodly and tell them plainly of their sins. Felix had the power to release Paul, but Paul had no words of flattery for him.

4. Paul's attitude here appears to be a good commentary on his statement in 1 Cor. 9: 22b. He could always adjust himself to any occasion. Cf. his words to the Philippian jailer, as recorded in Acts 16.

II. THE SERMON THAT PAUL PREACHED

1. The inspired record says that Felix "sent for Paul, and heard him concerning the faith in Christ Jesus."

(1) Inasmuch as "faith" is the leading and characteristic feature of the religion of Christ, it is often used to denote the whole of Christianity.

(2) It is very likely that Felix and Drusilla expected Paul to speak on what is usually thought of as the doctrinal side of Christianity, but instead of that he spoke on the practical side—setting forth the kind of life that must be lived by those who are acceptable to God. This was entirely appropriate for the occasion.

2. *"And as he reasoned."* The word "reason" literally means to discourse or discuss. Thus, in speaking before Felix and Drusilla, Paul discoursed on or discussed some of the great principles which belong to Christian living. The text sets forth three of these principles:

(1) *Righteousness.* This word suggests purity of life, uprightness, correctness in thinking, feeling, and acting; or, which is the same thing, the conformity of personal conduct to the demands of the moral and religious laws of God.

a. In its practical application the term means about the same as our word *justice*—justice to God and justice to man.

b. The cruelty and crime which characterized his administration as governor of Judaea, together with his taking the wife of another man, plainly showed that Felix was not a righteous man; and it was Paul's business, as a messenger of Christ, to make a direct application of his gospel to those who sat before him.

(2) *Self-control.* This means to hold oneself within due limits, as it respects pleasures, duties, and everything else. Cf. Prov. 16: 32.

a. Three of the well-defined stages in the development of this virtue are self-knowledge, self-respect, and self-control.

b. The licentious life which Felix and Drusilla were living was sufficient evidence to show that they were not exercising self-mastery.

(3) *The judgment to come.* Paul followed his denunciation of sin with a warning of the impending judgment. Cf. Acts 17: 30; 2 Cor. 5: 10.

a. The principles which will determine the character of this judgment are plainly set forth in the New Testament. Cf. Acts 17: 31; Matt. 7: 21-23.

b. Every person present should be truly thankful that the coming judgment is a matter of revelation. Cf. Heb. 10: 30, 31.

III. THE EFFECTS OF THE SERMON

1. *"Felix was terrified."* It is to his credit that he was not angry. An awakened conscience was proof that he was not en-

tirely lost. It is always a blessing to one when he can feel the lash of the law. Such feelings, however, must be translated into the resolutions and actions which God requires, if they are to benefit the sinner.

(2) *The sermon cut short.* Felix interrupted Paul just as he was reaching the climax of his sermon. If he had waited another moment Paul would have told him of a Christ who was able to make him right at the very center of his being, one who could free him from all of his sins and make him unspeakably happy. The coming judgment would have had no terror for him then; but the sermon was never finished. Felix himself cut it short.

(3) *He declined to heed Paul's warning.* Although Paul remained in his custody two years longer and Felix frequently sent for him and communed with him, yet there is no evidence that he ever trembled again or showed any inclination to reverse his decision.

IV. WHY WAS FELIX NOT CONVERTED?

1. Because he allowed his lust and ambition to smother the fires of conscience, which Paul's sermon had set burning.

2. Because he deferred his decision to a more convenient season, which never did and never would come. It is never convenient for one to give up his cherished sins.

3. His excuse was only an effort to hide the real reason for his refusal to accept Christ—viz: a reluctance to give up sin.

4. It is dangerous to tamper with God's word and one's own conscience. The Lord has given *you* a chance. Will you follow the example of Felix or Paul? Cf. Acts 26: 19.

◆ ◆ ◀

WHY RIVERS ARE CROOKED
Acts 24: 25

Introduction: 1. Nature has been spoken of as *God's Other Book.* It is, of course, older than the Bible. Nature proclaims the fact that there is a Supreme Being, but it remains for the Bible to tell who the Supreme Being is. Nature declares his nature and power, while the Bible reveals his goodness, mercy, and love. 2. Since God is the Author of both books, the child of God may be sure that his Father is pleased to have him learn the lessons which they have to offer. The student, however, should keep in mind the purpose God has in nature and revelation; and he should endeavor to get from each only those lessons which their Author intended to teach. Therefore, in studying this lesson, let us begin by considering,

I. SOME LESSONS WHICH NATURE TEACHES

   1. The testimony of the Scriptures:
   (1) Psalm 19: 1, 2; Rom. 1: 19, 20.
   (2) Matt. 24: 32, 33; 13: 31, 32; Mark 4: 26-29; Psalm 92: 12.

   2. There are many things in the natural world which remind us of the spiritual, e. g., *sun,* Mal. 4: 2; *star,* Rev. 22: 16; *rock,* Psalm 89: 26; *tree,* Rev. 22: 2; *grass,* 1 Pet. 1: 24; etc., etc.

II. A LESSON FROM RIVERS

   1. The rivers of the earth form a prominent part of God's creation, and all men are more or less familiar with them.

   2. One of the noticeable features of rivers is their serpentine course. No one has ever seen a river which is entirely straight from its beginning to its end.

   3. Why are rivers crooked? *"A river becomes crooked by following* the line of least resistance. So does man."

   4. A careful study of this characteristic of a river will enable man to learn some valuable lessons about himself, if he will make the application to himself.

III. SOME THINGS THE LORD EXPECTS OF HIS PEOPLE

   1. To walk in straight paths. See Heb. 12: 13; and cf. Matt. 7: 13, 14. There are many things in the way of such a course, and we shall consider some of them here under two headings— viz:
   (1) External. Cf. Acts 14: 22; 1 Thess. 3: 3; 1 Tim. 6: 9, 10.
   (2) Internal. See James 1: 13, 14.

   2. To resist evil. See James 4: 7; Rom. 12: 21. Cf. song, "Yield not to Temptation."

IV. SOME OUTSTANDING EXAMPLES

   1. Of those who made crooked paths:
   (1) Cain, Gen. 4: 1-8; Heb. 11: 4; John 3: 11, 12; Jude 11.
   (2) Balaam, Num. 22: 1ff; Jude 11: 2 Pet. 2: 15.
   (3) Korah, Num. 16: 1ff; Jude 11.
   (4) Felix, Josephus, *Ant.* 20: 7; Acts 24: 24f.
   (5) Demas, Phile. 24; Col. 4: 14; 2 Tim. 4: 10.
   2. Of those who made straight paths:
   (1) Joseph, Gen. 39: 1ff.
   (2) Daniel, Dan. 1: 1ff.
   (3) The three Hebrew children, Dan. 3: 1ff.
   (4) Paul, 1 Cor. 9: 27; 2 Cor. 12: 7-10.

V. SOME PRACTICAL APPLICATIONS

   1. It is not beyond the power of people to walk in the way

which the Lord has ordained for them.   Cf. 1 Cor. 10: 13; James
1: 2-8.

2. Christians should remember the word of the Lord when
they are tempted to follow the line of least resistance.

(1) By walking in the ways of the world.   See John 2: 15-17;
James 4: 4.

(2) By absenting themselves from the assembly of the saints.
Cf. Heb. 10: 25, 26.

(3) By seeking to recompense evil for evil.   See Rom. 12: 19-
21.

3. If they will use the strength which God supplies, no obstacle can turn them from the way of righteousness.   See Phil.
4: 13; cf. Psalm 119: 11; Matt. 4: 4.

◆ ◆ ◆

THE HEAVENLY VISION
Acts 26: 19

Introduction: There was one day in the life of Paul that was
unique in all of his experience.   That was the day he met the
Lord on the Damascus road.   From the day his name appears in
history, he was zealous for the faith of his fathers; but a per-
secutor of the church of the Lord.   Although the persecution
which he waged was bitter, his motive was pure; for he verily
thought with himself that he ought to do many things contrary
to the name of Jesus; and that he did with all the power of his
soul.   But because he was always conscientious in what he did, it
was never hard for him to change his course, if he learned that
he was going in the wrong direction.   He was a man for whom a
heavenly vision would never be wasted.   But in studying this
lesson, let us consider,

I. The Setting of the Text

1. When Paul spoke the words of the text he had spent many
years preaching the faith which he once sought to destroy.

2. His conversion to Christ had been genuine; and it is doubtful if any follower of the Nazarene has suffered more for his cause
than did he.

3. When he stood before Agrippa he had already finished
three great missionary journeys, and had been in the prison in
Caesarea two years; but having the opportunity to speak before
Agrippa and the other royal guests, he largely forgot himself in
his effort to win the king for Christ.

4. The speech in which the text is found is one of the truly
great speeches of all literature; but we are concerned today with
that part in which Paul mentions the "heavenly vision."

II. SOME THINGS THAT PAUL SAW THAT DAY

1. *He saw that he was ignorant.* Although trained in the best schools of the land, and regarded as a finished scholar of his day, Paul readily saw that he was really ignorant of the most important things of life. Cf. 1 Tim. 1: 13; Acts 13: 27; 3: 17; Isa. 55: 8, 9. Jesus gave the secret for learning the will of God. See Matt. 11: 25ff; John 7: 17. Cf. Acts 22: 10.

2. *He saw that he was a sinner.* One of the meanings of the term *sin* is "to miss the mark"; and it makes no difference, therefore, how sincere and zealous one may be in his efforts to please the Lord, he sins if he does not do as God has directed. See Rom. 10: 1-3; Phil. 3: 5, 6; Acts 24: 16; 1 Tim. 1: 15.

3. *He saw that his teacher was wrong.* He was brought up at the feet of Gamaliel, one of the greatest teachers of his day, and was "instructed according to the strict manner of the law of our fathers." But with all his learning, he had not before seen the simple truth that the old law had been fulfilled in Christ (Matt. 5: 17), and that God is speaking through him now. Cf. Matt. 17: 5; Heb. 1: 1, 2; Acts 3: 22, 23.

4. *He saw that he must break away from the law and traditions of his fathers.* That is never an easy thing to do, especially for one who is sincere and devoted; and if one will observe it in the lives of Paul and others, he will be able to get some idea of the tremendous price that often must be paid. Cf. Matt. 10: 34-37; Phil. 3: 7ff.

III. THE DISPOSITION MADE OF THE VISION

1. It matters not how important a vision may be, or how vital it may be to one's welfare, the thing that counts most for him is the treatment he gives it.

2. While no one today can have the kind of vision that Paul had, that is, a miraculous one, we are not to understand that he cannot have a vision at all. New light may come to him in many ways, enabling him to see things hitherto unknown to him, and thus increasing his responsibility. *What are we doing with the new light that comes to us?*

3. Some possible ways of dealing with one's visions.

(1) *Allow them to fade from memory.* This may be done swiftly or gradually. Cf. Luke 8: 9-14.

a. The hindrance may be that hardness or slowness of one's nature to receive impressions, which prevents the seed from taking root.

b. It may be an instability of character which causes first enthusiasm, and then draws back before difficulty or persecution.

c. The hindrance may lie in the effects of worldliness, increasing with the passing of time and strangling the plant which had taken root and had begun to grow. *But whether gradual or swift, the result in the end is the same.*

(2) *The experience or new light may be kept for oneself.* This has been the attitude of those who have sought the monastery. In many cases such people have impaired their own spiritual life, have become one-sided in their thoughts of God, and have deprived others of their share in the vision—a share which they so greatly need. Cf. Gal. 6: 1ff.

(3) *The greatest possibility is to follow Paul's example, as expressed in the text.* Although he went to Arabia, he did not remain there. He came back to the busy, noisy, confused, and eager world of Greek, Roman, and Jewish life. He came back to face the hostility and scorn of the Jews, the suspicion and slowness of apprehension of many Christians who were still too much bound by traditions to accept his great message of Christian liberty. He came back to face unparalleled trials and hardships on his missionary journeys, and to take up a daily burden much heavier than any hardship or persecution which he bore—"anxiety for all the churches." All this and much more is included in his simple claim that he had not been disobedient to the heavenly vision.

4. For us, too, obedience to a vision means a return to the ordinary ways of life; perhaps not to such trials and sufferings as awaited Paul, but certainly to faithfulness in all things, great and small. We are responsible to God and our fellows for the use we make of the truth and beauty which we have been enabled to see. Matt. 17: 1-8; 14ff.

IV. PAUL'S MESSAGE AND SOURCE OF STRENGTH

1. It is doubtful if any man ever showed more zeal and sacrifice in carrying out the Lord's commission than did Paul. Cf. 1 Cor. 15: 10.

2. Paul's commission to preach was the same as that given by the Lord to the other disciples before he left them. Cf. Mark 16: 15, 16; Gal. 1: 6-10; Col. 1: 23.

3. Although Paul preached only what the prophets and Moses said should come, his Jewish hearers, for the most part, those who should have known the Old Testament better, refused to hear him and assayed to kill him. The Lord, however, had helped him and he had been able to the day he spoke to continue his good work. Cf. 2 Cor. 12: 9, 10; Acts 18: 9-11; Matt. 28: 18-20.

❖ ❖ ❖

PAUL BEFORE AGRIPPA
Acts 26: 28, 29

Introduction: 1. Paul's defence before King Agrippa, as set forth in Acts 26, is a classic example of the art of convincing and persuasive oratory. The apostle was a prisoner for the sake of the gospel; but, whether in prison or out, he was always ready to take hold of every opportunity which came to him for speaking a word in behalf of the cause for which he was giving his life. Even a casual reading of the record will show that he was much more interested in getting the truth of the gospel before his hearers than he was in merely defending himself. He knew that the faithful messenger of the cross must often suffer if he is to reach the hearts of some men; but he was glad that he was counted worthy of that great honor. Cf. Acts 5: 41. 2. It is not often that a humble gospel preacher has the privilege of preaching the gospel to kings, governors, and the people who are usually associated with them; but it does sometimes happen. God is no respecter of persons; and since all men belong to his creation, he does not want any of them to perish. 3. We are, of course, deeply interested in everything that was said and done on this memorable occasion, but we are particularly concerned with Agrippa's remark, as set forth in the text, and Paul's response to it. But in order to have a clear understanding of those statements, we must be familiar with the contents of the twenty-fifth and the twenty-sixth chapters of Acts. As a beginning point in this study, then, let us consider,

I. THE NEW GOVERNOR AND PAUL'S APPEAL TO CAESAR, 25: 1-12

1. When Festus succeeded Felix as governor of Judaea, he found that the latter had left Paul as a prisoner. See Acts 24: 27.

2. Soon after taking office Festus made a trip to Jerusalem, and while he was there the principal men among the Jews informed him against Paul. Their purpose was to get Paul away from the prison-house so that they might kill him. Cf. Acts 23: 12ff.

3. At first Festus refused to be swayed from Roman law and custom; but when his desire for popularity gained the ascendancy, he yielded to their request and asked Paul if he was willing to go up to Jerusalem, and there be tried before him. This resulted in Paul's appeal to Caesar.

II. THE STATE VISIT OF AGRIPPA AND BERNICE, 25: 13-22

1. This Agrippa was known as Herod Agrippa II. He was the great-grandson of Herod the Great who slaughtered the children of Bethlehem; great-nephew of Herod Antipas who beheaded John the Baptist; and son of Herod Agrippa I who killed James with the sword and imprisoned Peter.

2. Bernice was the eldest of the three daughters of Herod Agrippa I. The youngest of these sisters was Drusilla, the wife of Felix. Both of these sisters were renowned for their rare beauty and personal charms. Bernice was the wife of Herod, king of

Chalcis, "who was both her husband and her uncle." He died and left her a widow when she was but twenty years of age. Following the death of her husband her character was held much in question on the score of chastity. She had retired to the home of her brother, King Agrippa II; and when the report went out that she had criminal relations with him, she persuaded Polemo, king of Cilicia, to marry her, supposing that by this means she should prove those calumnies upon her to be false. But this union did not last long; for Bernice left Palemo, as was said, with impure intentions, and also forsook the Jewish religion. See Josephus, Antiquities 20: 7, 3.

3. These state visits, of course, required a great deal of entertaining on the part of the governor. Sometime after the arrival of Agrippa and Bernice Festus laid Paul's case before Agrippa with the expressed purpose of seeking help in dealing with it; and when Agrippa expressed a desire to hear Paul himself, that not only provided another day of entertainment for the king, but also opened the way for Agrippa to equip himself for advising Festus regarding Paul's case.

III. THE SETTING OF THE STAGE 25: 23-27.

1. It is doubtful if Paul ever faced so brilliant an audience for the purposing of defending himself as a messenger of the cross. But, as already suggested, it is easy to see that the apostle was more interested in getting the truth of the gospel before his hearers, than he was in merely defending himself. *His primary interest was in truth, justice, and honor.*

2. The introduction by Festus.

3. What must have been Paul's feelings as he stood before this gorgeous assembly!

IV. PAUL'S DEFENCE BEFORE AGRIPPA, 26: 1-23

1. When Agrippa said to Paul, "Thou art permitted to speak for thyself," that opened the way for him to say anything he desired to say.

2. Paul's first effort was to bridge the gulf which separated him from his chief auditor; and then he immediately launched into a discussion of the facts which led up to his present status.

3. A simple reading of his address, together with a few well-chosen comments, will be sufficient to impress the lesson which Paul sought to get over to his hearers on this great occasion.

V. HIS APPEAL TO THE KING, 26: 24-29

1. The interruption by Festus and Paul's courteous reply.

2. It is impossible to say just how much longer Paul would have continued his line of thought, if Festus had not interrupted him; but with that break in his address, he did not return to it but instead made a direct, personal appeal to Agrippa himself.

3. It was this appeal that brought forth from Agrippa the expression of the text: "With but little persuasion thou wouldest fain make me a Christian."

4. To this statement Paul replied: "I would to God, that whether with little or with much, not thou only, but also all that hear me this day, might become such as I am, except these bonds."

Conclusion: 1. What must have been the feelings of Paul as his audience marched away from him!

2. Here is another man who was not moved in the direction of God by the gospel. The gospel indeed, is God's power unto salvation, but only to those who believe. The incident now before us plainly shows that the term "believe" does not refer merely to intellectual assent. It involves not only an acceptance of the facts presented, but also a willingness to do that which the Lord commands. Cf. John 3: 36.

3. Agrippa, like Felix, had his opportunity, but he was not equal to the occasion. How different it would have been with him, as he left this world for eternity, had he responded favorably to Paul's appeal! But as it was he could only say,

> Of all sad words of tongue or pen,
> The saddest are these: It might have been.

◆ ◆ ◆

PITCH YOUR TENT AND BUILD AN ALTAR
Gen. 13: 1-4

Introduction: 1. The human race, as history reveals it, has been characterized by three distinct stages—the savage, the nomadic, and the civilized. The savage devoured his food where he found it; the nomad moved about from place to place seeking provisions for his family, his flocks, and his herds; while the civilized man built cities, and brought the rewards of his labors back to his home. 2. Although classified as civilized today, there is, nevertheless, a very real sense in which our lives belong in part to the nomadic type. We have no abiding city, and life is frequently pictured in the New Testament as a journey, or a pilgrimage. Cf. Phil. 3: 20; 1 Pet. 2: 11, 12. It matters not, therefore, under what conditions we may live, life for us in this world is only a temporary stay; and the exhortation, Pitch your tent and build an altar, in its practical sense, is entirely applicable to us. 3. When Abraham and his household returned from the land of Egypt, the whole land of Canaan lay before them; but it was "unto the place of the altar, which he had made there at the first" that he took his family. This ancient story has a message for us today—viz, we, too, need an altar to which we may, and must, come back again and again: and the story itself suggests some reasons why this is so. Let us consider some of them.

I. WE NEED AN ALTAR TO TURN TO AMID THE BUSINESS OF LIFE

1. Few of us are able to stand the pace of modern life; and unless we have an altar to which we may turn, we are likely to find that the poise and strength of soul which should be ours has been worn away by the bustle of life.

2. All of us, therefore, stand in continual need of being refreshed and stabilized in body, mind, and soul; and happy are we if, like Abraham, we know where to turn. Cf. Matt. 6: 33. Faith in God has been called "the best preventative against the maladies of the soul, and the most powerful means of curing them."

3. How often has one turned to the altar of worship, fretting with dark and vexing suggestions, feeling sore in body, mind, and spirit; but who came away calm, refreshed, all his cares gone, and rejoicing in the God of his salvation.

> O the pure delight of a single hour
> That before thy throne I spend,
> When I kneel in prayer, and with Thee, my God,
> I commune as friend with friend.

II. WE NEED AN ALTAR TO TURN TO IN OUR TIMES OF PROSPERITY

1. When Abraham came out of the land of Egypt he was rich in cattle, in silver, and in gold, but he turned instinctively to the altar at which he had worshipped in the days before such prosperity was his. He probably knew something of the perils which lurk in prosperity: how wealth may destroy the finer feelings of the soul, alienate man from God, and estrange him from his brethren.

2. It is not necessarily wrong for one to be wealthy, but any one who is acquainted with life among average people and the teaching of the New Testament knows that there are many things which are more vital than the material things of this life and their pursuit. Cf. Luke 12: 15; Matt. 16: 26; Luke 16: 9-13; 1 Tim. 6: 17-19.

3. The story is told of a man who was led, by its owner, rebuilder, and renovator, through the rooms and gardens of a lovely house which, with infinite thought and discretion, had been reclaimed from decay and made fair and beautiful. At every step, indoors and out, was something charming or adequate, whether furniture or porcelain, whether flower or shrub. Within were long, cool passages, where through the diamond panes sunlight splashed on the white walls, and bedrooms of the gayest daintiness; without were lawns, vistas, and arrangements of the loveliest colors.

When the tour was completed, the hostess asked her guest, "Well, what do you think of it all?" The visitor thought many things, but only expressed that which was uppermost in his mind, which was this, "You are making it very hard to die."

The visitor might have added, "and harder still to live"; for whatever may be the regrets with which one says "Good-bye" to the luxuries of life when the time comes to leave this world, it is not to be compared with the embarrassment of finding oneself faced with the duty of living aright in rich surroundings.

III. WE NEED AN ALTAR TO TURN TO WHEN WE HAVE SINNED

1. Abraham had sinned grievously while in Egypt. Outwardly he seemed none the worse for it; for it was to that sin that he owed much of his great prosperity. But, for all his possessions, he was not at peace. It was not merely that he had incurred the disapproval of Pharaoh, and still smarted from his rebuke; it was the sting of his own conscience which troubled him, along with the knowledge that he had sinned in God's sight. And he knew that there could be no rest for his spirit until, at the altar, he had made a humble confession of his sin, and received God's forgiveness.

2. There are those, of course, who have no sense of sin, and to them Abraham's experience means nothing; but to those of us who know what it means to live with an accusing conscience, because of our sins against ourselves, our fellow men, and our God, the lesson is timely and forceful. We realize that until we have confessed our sins and received God's forgiveness there can be no peace within. Cf. Matt. 5: 23-26.

IV. WE NEED AN ALTAR TO TURN TO FOR A FINER AND NOBLER CONCEPTION OF GOD

1. What man in human history had a grander conception of God than did Abraham? This patriarch lived so close to God and was so devoted to him that his Maker called him "my friend." See Isa. 41: 8; James 2: 23; cf. John 15: 15; 2 Tim. 1: 12; 4: 6-8.

2. Our religion fails to satisfy many; because the dust we stir up at the altar obscures the light and glow of the fire which should warm the hearts of others.

(1) What makes people pray when they are afraid, but indifferent when danger has passed? This attitude comes from a lack of sound teaching—from having glimpsed the altar only at a distance, from having seen it through a haze of error.

(2) Religion is not an opiate. It does not determine what will happen to us, but it does determine what we shall do with that which does happen to us. Cf. Rom. 8: 28; 2 Cor. 12: 9, 10.

3. We who follow Christ are not immune to disaster, cf. 2 Tim. 3: 12; 2 Cor. 11: 22ff; but our religion enables us to turn disaster into triumph. Cf. 1 Cor. 10: 13; James 1: 2-8.

THEY HEARD THE ANGELS SING
Luke 2: 13, 14

Introduction: The song of the angels as recorded in the text now before us is one of the most beautiful, as well as one of the most interesting, songs in all literature. It was their message to the shepherds as they watched their flocks by night—the night in which the Saviour was born. Jesus was both human and divine; and in keeping with that idea, the chief thought of this hymn of praise concerns both God and man. The circumstances surrounding the song are given in the context; and a consideration of it will add greatly to one's interest in the song. But in studying this lesson, let us begin with the expression,

I. Glory to God in the Highest

1. This is the first doxology of the gospel; and it seems to be both an ascription and a proclamaiton; for ascriptions of praise are also proclamations of fact. Thus, in ascribing glory to God, his glory is also proclaimed.

2. How did the coming of Christ bring glory to God? It displayed his attributes to advantage. "The general arranges his forces to display his wisdom; the orator arranges his arguments to display his power; the philantropist arranges his gifts and so displays his mercy. In the coming of Christ we see wisdom and power and mercy displayed in their fullest and sublimest manner. The whole character of God stands out resplendent in faithfulness and love. How many promises were fulfilled, how many obligations were discharged by the coming of Jesus! By setting forth God in his highest glory it brings glory to him." Cf. Eph. 3: 8-11.

3. The word "glory" has been defined as good opinion resulting in praise and honor. This definition carries with it the idea of an outward expression of one's inner thoughts.

4. But who is to give glory to God, and in what? See Phil. 2: 9-11; 1 Cor. 10: 31.

5. How may one give glory to God?

(1) By endeavoring to promote his glory among men, Matt. 5: 14-16.

(2) By declaring one's gratitude for benefits received, Luke 17: 11-18.

(3) By not distrusting God's promises, Rom. 4: 20; 2 Cor. 1: 20.

(4) By celebrating his praises, Rev. 19: 7.

(5) By rendering due honor to God's majesty, Acts 12: 20-23; Rom. 1: 20-23.

(6) By acknowledging that God knows all things, and by showing that one believes it, Josh. 7: 19.

II. On Earth Peace among Men

1. This peace is possible as a result of the coming of Christ and it is, according to Thayer, "the tranquil state of a soul assured of its salvation through Christ, and so fearing nothing from God and content with its earthly lot, of whatever sort that is." Cf. Col. 3: 15; John 14: 27; 16: 33.

2. The peace which Christ gives includes every kind of peace which man can enjoy, such as peace of conscience, peace with his fellow men, the ease of mind regarding worldly matters, as may be seen by considering the elements of this peace. What, then, are the elements of the peace which comes with Christ?

(1) *The peace of an illuminated life.* No one can canvass the literature of the world, listen to his fellows, or interrogate his own heart, without realizing how chafed and bewildered men are apart from Christ. Cf. Rom. 1: 28-32; Matt. 11: 25-30.

(2) *The peace of a purified life.* See 1 John 1: 6, 7; Eph. 2: 13-18.

(3) *The peace of a harmonized life.* Cf. the conflict of Rom. 7. It is not God's will that such a condition exist, and a Deliverer has been provided. See Rom. 7: 24-8: 1ff.

(4) *The peace of a solaced life.* Christians are not allowed to live their lives apart from temptations and troubles; but it is not God's will that such things should overcome them. Cf. 1 Cor. 10: 13; Rom. 8: 28.

III. Who Are the Recipients of This Peace?

1. "Men in whom he is well pleased."

2. This involves an amnesty proclamation and not a mere armistice proposal. Cf. Heb. 8: 12; Mark 16: 15, 16; Acts 2: 37, 38.

3. Such peace was never promised to the wicked. See Isa. 48: 22; Matt. 10: 34-36; 1 Thess. 5: 3.

IV. In Whom is God Well Pleased?

1. Cf. Matt. 3: 13-17 for a similar expression.
2. Those not in the flesh, Rom. 8: 8.
3. Those having faith, Heb. 11: 5, 6.
4. Those not entangled in the affairs of this life, 2 Tim. 2: 4.
5. Those not seeking to please men, Gal. 1: 10; 1 Thess. 2: 4.

V. What Were the Results of the Angels' Song?

1. The immediate results as seen in the case of the shepherds who heard them:

(1) They resolved to investigate that which had been made known to them, v. 15.

(2) They began their efforts immediately and with enthusiasm, v. 16.

(3) Their efforts were rewarded and they made known to others that which had been spoken to them, v. 17.

(4) They gave glory to God for that which they had seen and heard, v. 20.

2. What are the results today as we re-echo this heavenly message?

(1) Do those who hear us as we repeat this message seek Christ?

(2) Do those who learn about him yield themselves to him in obedience to his word?

(3) In a word, Does our testimony concerning the Christ cause men to want to do exactly that which he commanded?

Conclusion: The aim and purpose of the coming of Christ was the glory of God; the effect of his coming was peace on earth among men in whom he is well pleased; the motive of his coming was to induce men to become obedient to the will of God as revealed in his word.

◆ ◆ ◆

THE ANTIDOTE TO ANXIETY
Phil 4: 6, 7

Introduction: 1. The words of the text were written by Paul while he was a prisoner in Rome. The time of his trial was approaching and he, of course, did not know what the outcome of it might be. But he was not worrying about that. On the contrary, he cheerfully bade his beloved brethren at Philippi to be anxious in nothing. Cf. Phil. 1: 21-24. 2. Our individual experience, when considered in the light of world affairs and the providence of God, may be likened to that of a man dwelling between two tall buildings, with only a narrow strip of sky visible to him; and if, perchance, a small bit of cloud covers that strip of sky, he may conclude that the whole horizon is covered. But if we constantly keep in mind our relation to God and his care for us, there will always be sufficient reasons for our doing that which is enjoined upon us in the passage now before us. 3. The text contains a double precept or exhortation—the one forbids our indulgence in a habit which is evil and pernicious, while the other requires that we do that which is not only good within itself, but which also is the effectual cure of the former evil practice. But in studying this lesson, let us consider,

I. THE PROHIBITION—"IN NOTHING BE ANXIOUS"

1. This is a universal and unconditional command. However, it does not prohibit industrious, economical, and prudent forethought.

(2) *The prevalence of anxiety.* There has, perhaps, never been a time when the world was so rich in material things and pos-

sessed so many mechanical appliances for lightening human tasks and toils; yet its people are more nervous and everywhere filled with worry. It is worry, rather than work, which wears out so many before their time.

3. *The folly of anxiety.*

(1) *It accomplishes nothing.* There might be some justificacation for anxiety, if it accomplished anything at all. For example, it does not cause a train to come any sooner, or enable one to cross a bridge before he comes to it.

(2) *It weakens and wears one out, both mentally and physically.* Worry is a waste of energy, and it is utterly useless. It indicates a divided mind. Cf. James 1: 5-8. Not only does anxiety sap vitality and reduce efficiency; it also results in a preoccupation which makes it more difficult to do the things which should be done.

a. Well did Charles Kingsley say, "Do today's duty, fight today's temptation, and do not weaken and distract yourself by looking forward to things you cannot see, and could not understand if you saw them."

b. The mischief done by anxiety is forcefully illustrated by the innocent old farmer who wound up his alarm clock and set it to go off at six in the morning. He then sat up all night to make sure that he would hear it; and when morning came he was so exhausted by his tedious vigil that he could not take his journey.

c. Every one can do his work much better if he does not allow his energy to go to waste in anxiety. Cf. the perfect trust which Christ placed in his Father. See John 14: 27.

4. *The cause of anxiety.* The real cause for this condition is a lack of faith in God. He has promised to do much for us; but on condition that we do our part.

(1) Heb. 7: 25; Rom. 8: 28.

(2) Matt. 18: 3; 6: 25ff. It may be that the father and mother do not know where the next day's food for the family will come from, but their little children do not fail to trust them for their needs.

II. THE PRECEPT—"LET YOUR REQUESTS BE MADE KNOWN UNTO GOD"

1. Relief from anxiety can never be obtained by the efforts of our own will, or by arguing its uselessness and hurtfulness. The text names the only sure way to get rid of this unhappy condition. Cf. 1 Pet. 5: 7.

2. *The means by which God would have us lay bare our hearts before him.*

(1) Prayer, in general. Cf. 1 Thess. 5: 17.

(2) Supplication, that is, put your particular anxieties into

speech. Any Christian should be ashamed to have an anxiety about which he is ashamed to speak to his heavenly Father.

(3) Thanksgiving, never be moody or doubtful on the one hand, nor fail to be thankful for past blessing, and for the opportunity of coming to God with our problem, on the other. "Half our worries," says one, "would immediately melt away if we began to sing a psalm of praise."

3. *The scope of our intercourse with God.* "In everything."

III. The Result—"And the Peace of God, Which Passeth All Understanding, Shall Guard Your Hearts and Your Thoughts in Christ Jesus"

1. God's peace as a sentinel mounts guard over our lives. Cf. Isa. 26: 3.

2. Heb. 13: 5, 6.

> I know not where his islands lift
> Their fronded palms in air;
> I only know I cannot drift
> Beyond his love and care.
> O brothers! if my faith is vain,
> If hopes like these betray,
> Pray for me that my feet may gain
> The sure and safer way.
> And Thou, O Lord! by whom are seen
> Thy creatures as they be,
> Forgive me if too close I lean
> My human heart on thee!
>
> —John Greenleaf Whittier

❖ ❖ ❖

BAPTISM FOR REMISSION OF SINS IS JUSTIFICATION BY FAITH
Rom. 5: 1; 1 Pet. 3: 21

Introduction: 1. The New Testament reveals the Lord's plan for saving the human race; and if one would thoroughly understand the truth regarding this question, he must consider all that is taught on the subject. It will not be enough for him to consider a few passages and then attempt to formulate a plan in keeping with a partial statement of the divine revelation: he must consider *all* that is said on the subject, if he would know the will of God. Cf. Matt. 7: 21-23. 2. Because some have not taken into consideration all that is taught on the subject of salvation from sin, they have erroneously thought that "baptism for remission of sins" is diametrically opposed to "justification by faith." But since we are primarily interested in that which the Lord says, let us turn our attention to that which is found in his word.

I. Salvation Is Promised Only to Believers

1. The testimony of the Scriptures: Acts 10: 43; 13: 38, 39.

2. Thus, the plain teaching of the New Testament is that God has promised to save men on the condition that they *believe*. However, an important question arises just here—viz: What does it mean to believe?

3. There are many people who take these passages to mean that the process of believing is wholly mental or inward, and that those who thus believe are saved without any outward action or physical obedience, whatsoever. Cf. the following statement:

We are accounted righteous before God only for the merit of our Lord and Saviour Jesus Christ, by faith, and not for our own works or deservings. Wherefore, that we are justified by faith only is a most wholesome doctrine, and very full of comfort.—Articles of Religion: IX. *Of the Justification of Man.* Discipline of the Methodist Church, 1948, p. 27.)

4. Such passages as those listed above are quoted to prove that a man is saved before and without obeying the gospel. But if that is true, how, then, are we to understand those passages which plainly state that one must "obey the gospel" in order to be saved? Cf. Heb. 5: 8, 9; 1 Pet. 4: 17; 1: 22; 2 Thess. 1: 7-9; Rom. 6: 17, 18.

This leads us to ask,

II. DOES THE NEW TESTAMENT TEACH BAPTISM IS FOR REMISSION OF SINS?

1. The testimony of the Scriptures: John 3: 5; Mark 16: 16; Acts 2: 38; 22: 16; Rom. 6: 34; Eph. 5, 25; Tit. 3: 5; 1 Pet. 3: 21.

2. These passages, just as they read in the commonly received English versions of the New Testament, teach "baptism for the remission of sins" just about as clearly as anything else is taught in the Sacred Volume; and if they do not put the matter beyond question, it is because it is impossible for language to do so.

3. Moreover, this view is abundantly sustained by scholarly criticism and the history of the church in all ages.

III. A PERTINENT QUESTION

1. In the light of these indisputable facts, why is this doctrine which is expressly taught in the New Testament, and sustained by the fairest inferences from the Scriptures and the strongest analogies, so earnestly opposed by so many professed followers of Christ?

2. The doctrine of "justification by faith" has been so conspicuously and so generally taught by denominationalists since the Lutheran Reformation that many have come to believe that any teaching which involves "works," or "acts of obedience," is untrue.

3. "Baptism for the remission of sins," in their estimation, conflicts with this idea of "justification by faith"; and for that reason the former teaching is condemned as being wholly unscriptural.

Their most potent argument against the doctrine of "baptism for the remission of sins" is substantially as follows:

Any teaching which conflicts with "justification by faith" is unscriptural;

But the doctrine of "baptism for the remission of sins" does so conflict;

Therefore the doctrine of "baptism for the remission of sins" is unscriptural.

4. However, it may be correctly said that no thoughtful and well-informed person has ever discussed the doctrine of "baptism for the remission of sins" in a negative manner, without experiencing much difficulty in disposing of the scriptures presented in its support, even to his own satisfaction; and in view of that which is said in the New Testament regarding both "baptism for the remission of sins" and "justification by faith," is it not possible that both are true, since they are both a part of the revelation which was given by inspiration? If so, then there is certainly no conflict between them.

IV. Some Conceivable Methods of Justifying a Sinner

1. *Justification by law is entirely out of the question.* No sinner has ever been justified by mere law; for it is the nature of law to approve the obedient and condemn the disobedient. And if it were possible for one to keep the law perfectly, he would, of course, be just, but not a justified sinner. He would be approved before the law, because he never violated it.

2. However, that is not the kind of justification the New Testament sets forth. The problem dealt with in God's Word is the justification of a sinner—one who is condemned by law.

3. There are two conceivable methods by which a sinner may be justified—viz:

(1) *Justification by works.* Works of this kind are known as "meritorious" or "compensative" works; and they carry with them the idea that the worker will be compensated as a result of his having done them. Such a view rejects Christ and gives all the value to works. This method is specifically condemned in the New Testament. Cf. Tit. 3: 5; Eph. 2: 8, 9; Gal. 5: 4; Rom. 3: 21-28.

(2) *Justification by grace, mercy, pardon.* This plan justifies the sinner who is condemned by law, and allows nothing which he can do, or offer, as a compensation. It is, therefore, diametrically opposed to the "method of works."

> Just as I am, without one plea,
>   But that thy blood was shed for me,
> And that thou bidd'st me come to thee,
>   O Lamb of God, I come, I come!
> Just as I am, and waiting not
>   To rid my soul of one dark blot,

> To thee whose blood can cleanse each spot,
> O Lamb of God. I come, I come!
> Just as I am, thou wilt receive,
>   Wilt welcome, pardon, cleanse, relieve;
> Because thy promise I believe,
> O Lamb of God, I come, I come!

V. WHAT DOES IT MEAN TO BE SAVED BY GRACE?

1. This method is said to be of faith because faith is the means by which the sinner takes hold of Christ and appropriates the salvation which he made possible for him by his sacrificial death upon the cross. Cf. Rom. 4: 16. But in order for faith to be effective it must be made perfect by works (James 2: 22). The "works of faith," therefore, are as certainly *included* in the plan of salvation, as the "works of a meritorious character" are *excluded*. Cf. Rom. 1: 5; 16: 26; Acts 6: 7.

2. Sin deserved to be punished; but when Christ died for the sinner he satisfied the demands of the law; and the death of Christ was, in the estimation of God, a sufficient cause for withdrawing the sentence of death against the *believer*.

3. As already pointed out in this study, salvation is promised only to the believer; but the question is, How or upon what condition is he to receive it?

(1) It is both reasonable and scriptural that salvation be conditional; for if it were not so, it would be possessed by those who do not want it and who are wholly unfitted for it.

(2) Then, too, it should be remembered that salvation from sin is not mere forgiveness of sin. It would do no good whatsoever for God to forgive the sins of the impenitent. Mere forgiveness does not liberate the sinner from the bondage of sin; he must likewise be saved from the love and practice of sin.

4. How, then, or upon what condition is the sinner to be saved from sin? See Rom. 1: 16, 17; Mark 16: 15, 16; Luke 24: 46, 47; Acts 2: 1-41. Thus, his faith leads him to accept Christ as his Saviour and to do that which he commands in order to have his sins washed away. Cf. Acts 22: 10, 16. Therefore, "baptism for the remission of sins" is "justification by faith"; for baptism is faith acting and appropriating justification which is promised the believer!

◆ ◆ ◆

YOU CAN SMASH THE BAROMETER BUT YOU CAN'T STOP THE STORM!
2 Pet. 3: 8-13

Introduction: 1. A few years ago Gayle Oler published an interesting article on this subject in his paper, *Just A Moment.* He began the article by relating the story of a business man on Long Island, who received an expensive barometer through the mail. The instrument did not look just right to him, for the pointer was away over to one side. He shook it, but still it wouldn't act as he thought it should. 2. In disgust he called in his secretary, dictated a "hot" letter to the manufacturer, and sent the barometer back. That afternoon at four o'clock the wind blew and the rain came; and all that part of Long Island was destroyed. Then the man remembered that he had had plenty of warning, but he had not had the foresight to heed it. This narrative should suggest to us some profitable lessons; and to begin with, let us consider,

I. An Unprofitable and Dangerous Practice

1. There is no profit in becoming angry with the preacher, or the religious paper, when you receive the warning of spiritual danger.

(1) When the alarm clock wakes you up at six in the morning, you can silence the clock or throw it out the window; but it will still be six o'clock.

(2) If you ignore the warning, you have not injured the preacher, the paper, or the alarm clock. Only you are the loser.

2. You may ignore your responsibility to God, and refuse to hear his word; but he is not mocked. You may spurn all thought of the judgment, but that will not delay the day one minute. It simply means that you are going to the judgment unprepared.

3. You may do like the ostrich and bury your head in the whirl of the world and the sands of sin; you may try to forget that you have a soul, and that God has a Son who died for you; you may ignore Christ and the church; but that does not mean that you have escaped the necessity of dealing with these important issues of life. You cannot arrest a cancer by refusing to think about it. Prompt, watchful, and thorough action is necessary, if any benefit is to result.

4. An argument with a barometer, Bible, or bulletin does not change the message of either; and a wise man will not try such a thing. Cf. Matt. 7: 24-27. He will thoughtfully and gratefully endeavor to gather whatever information there is available, and will profit by it. Whosoever does otherwise only injures himself.

II. Some Plain Statements of the Bible

1. The authority of Christ must be recognized and accepted, if we are to escape destruction. See Acts 3: 22, 23. This inspired statement remains true, whether we like it or not.

2. "The wages of sin is death" (Rom. 6: 23) is a fact, regardless of how pleasant or enticing sin may seem. One may talk about how strict and narrow the demands of Christianity are upon him, but that does not lessen the demands of God's word in the least. Cf. 1 Tim. 5: 6; Luke 8: 14; John 15: 1, 2a.

3. Jesus said, "He that believeth and is baptized shall be saved;

but he that disbelieveth shall be condemned." See Mark 16: 16; cf. Rom. 1: 16, 17; John 6: 44, 45.

.(1) The most expert argument cannot remove the fact that the unbeliever and the disobedient will be eternally condemned at the bar of divine judgment. See John 3: 36; 2 Thess. 1: 6-9.

(2) It is also true that those who receive salvation will be baptized believers. See Acts 2: 41. A man spurns this declaration of the New Testament to his own destruction.

III. STEP ACROSS WHERE THE STREAM IS SMALL

1. If one should be walking through the woods near Lake Itasca, and step across a tiny stream not far from where it gushes out of a lovely spring and starts on its southward journey, he might not realize the significance of what he was doing; but if he should go down beside the stream for many miles, looking for a better and more convenient place to cross, he would find that the farther he traveled, the more difficult it would be to cross the stream; for he would be walking beside the mighty Mississippi River.

2. The writer of the Book of Ecclesiastes suggests that it is much easier to obey Jehovah in the days of one's youth, "before the evil days come." See Eccl. 12: 1ff.

3. The writer of the Book of Hebrews speaks of the possibility of people's becoming "hardened by the deceitfulness of sin," and urges that we exhort one another daily, while it is called today, less such a hardening take place. See Heb. 3: 13.

4. The older one gets the more accustomed he becomes to his situation, and the more set he is in his ways. It has been said that only one man out of every thousand becomes a Christian after he reaches the age of thirty. This does not mean that a person *cannot* become a Christian after he is thirty years old; but it does mean that the chances are nine hundred and ninety-nine to one that he *will not*. The older one grows the more difficult it becomes for him to change; hence the folly of delay. Cf. Heb. 4: 7.*

---

*The story is told of a man who once dreamed that he was standing in the midst of a great crowd of evil spirits, with Satan, their lord, sitting over them upon his throne. The archenemy of mankind was seeking some new way in which he might beguile, entrap, and lead to eternal ruin the souls of men.

"Who," the king of the evil spirits cried from his throne, "will go to earth and persuade men to accomplish the ruin of their souls?" One of the dark spirits volunteered to go, and upon being asked how he would accomplish his work, replied, "I will persuade them that there is no God." But Satan answered, "That will never do; for you can never persuade the majority of men that there is no God. They may make the denial, but down deep in their hearts they will not believe it. God created man and he will therefore always believe that there is a God; for the voice of God speaks in his very nature."

Then a second dark spirit came forward and said, "I will go." When the prince of demons asked him about his plan, he said, "I will persuade

A BREAKFAST BY THE SEA
John 21: 1-19

Introduction: 1. There is nothing pertaining to the life of Christ that is not both interesting and instructive. John tells us (20: 30, 31) why he wrote the things which are contained in the book which bears his name; and when we consider that which he said in the closing verse of that book (21: 25) we are impressed, not only with the enormous volume of the Lord's words and deeds, but also, and chiefly, with the great importance of the things which were recorded by John. 2. The story of the breakfast by the sea and the things which happened in connection with it are among those highly important incidents which were chosen and recorded by the apostle whom Jesus loved. So graphic is his narrative of the things under consideration at this time that we almost feel as we read it that we are there with the Lord and the seven disciples as they experienced these things there by the sea. But in studying this lesson, let us begin by reviewing

I. THE NARRATIVE AS RECORDED BY JOHN

1. The third appearance of Christ to his disciples, verses 1, 14.
2. The seven disciples who went fishing and the results, 2-6.
3. The Lord recognized and his invitation to them to breakfast, 7-13.
4. His interview with Peter, 15-17.
5. His announcement regarding Peter's future, 18, 19.

While everything about this narrative is both interesting and profitable, as already indicated, our study today has to do primarily with the Lord's interview with Peter, and our first consideration has to do with the fact that

II. LOVE CLAIMS ITS OWN

1. It matters not how sorry our actions may have been toward

---

men that there is no heaven." "No," replied Satan, "that will not do either; for men expect a future life. The very instincts of their hearts lead them to long for the happy land from whence we have forever fallen."

A third demon came forward with this plan, "I will persuade them that there is no hell." "No," said the devil; your plan will not work. You cannot persuade men that there is no hell. There is too much suffering in the world, and too many pangs of conscience among men, for them to believe that. We must have some other plan, something that will appeal to all men, of all the ages, in all conditions, and of all beliefs."

It was then that a fourth dark spirit came forward and whispered to Satan, "I will go, and I will tell them that there is no hurry; tomorrow will be time enough!" "Go," cried the evil one, "and my presence be with you!"

> "Too late, too late, poor trembling soul,
> O will this be your fate?
> Too late, too late, to be made whole,
> Too late, too late, too late."

the Lord, he never ceases to love his people. Cf. Jer. 31: 3; Rom. 5: 6-8.

2. Just before his betrayal Jesus warned Peter that he and his fellow disciples were in grave danger, and he assured him that he had prayed for him that his faith would not fail. See Luke 22: 31-34. It seems that Peter did not take the Lord's message to him very seriously and evidently did not especially feel the need of his prayer for him.

3. It should be recalled just here that the Lord made a prediction regarding Peter when he was first introduced to him. See John 1: 35-42. "You are Simon: . . . you shall be Peter." Mercurial, temperamental, and impulsive at first, he would in time become as stable as the rock.

III. The Process at Work

1. When they had finished breakfast, Jesus said to Simon Peter, "Simon, son of John, lovest thou me more than these?"

(1) That was exactly what Simon claimed to do before he denied the Lord. Cf. John 13: 37; Matt. 26: 33.

(2) It should be observed here that Jesus addressed him as Simon, not as Peter, or even as Simon Peter.

2. When Peter answered the Lord, all of his boastfulness was gone. He replied, simply, "Yea, Lord; thou knowest that I love thee." (As noted in the margin of the American Standard Version, *love* in these places represents two different Greek words.)

(1) The word for *love* which Christ used in his first two questions is *agapao,* the meaning of which is, Have a preference for, appreciate, a feeling which would lead one to give himself up for the good of another, whether friend or enemy. This is the stronger New Testament word for *love,* and it results, not from mere sentiment, but from moral choice; and it is loftier and less impulsive than the other New Testament word for *love.*

(2) Peter, in all of his replies, and Jesus, in his third question, used the other word for love—*phileo.* This term expresses natural affection, such as a parent feels for a child, or one close friend feels for another. It represents a feeling or inclination prompted, not by moral choice, but by sense and emotion. *Agapao* expresses a love which would give itself up *for* another, while *phileo* indicates a love which gives itself up *to* another.

3. In his second question Jesus omits any idea of comparing Peter's love with that of others. He simply asked him, "Simon, son of John, lovest thou me?" But, as already indicated, Jesus again used the stronger word for love. His question this time seems to ask, "Simon, do *you* really love me?" Peter replied as he did the first time, using the same words, including the weaker term for love.

4. When Jesus asked the third time regarding his love for him he changed terms and used the weaker word for love, the

term which Peter used in all three of his answers. It was the Lord's change in words the third time that grieved Peter; and his answer was, "Lord, thou knowest all things; thou knowest that I love thee." Yes, the Lord did know all things, including Peter's boastfulness and his three denials of him; but he also knew Peter's heart and no doubt remembered his prediction regarding him made in John 1: 42.

IV. LOVE AND SERVICE

1. It is noticeable that each time Peter confessed his love for Jesus the Lord told him to do something: "Feed my lambs"; "Tend my sheep"; "Feed my sheep."

2. No one can read the New Testament without being impressed with the fact that love is always the inspiration for service. Cf. John 14: 15, 21; 1 John 5: 3.

3. No man, therefore, can love the Lord without serving him; and that includes service to one's fellow men. Cf. John 13: 34, 35; 1 John 4: 20, 21; 3: 14-18; Rom. 13: 10.

4. When people begin to question that which the Lord commands, either in the matter of becoming a Christian or in living the Christian life, that is a sure sign that their love for him is not what it should be.

◆ ◆ ◆

THE CHILD IN THE MIDST
Matt. 18: 1-6

Introduction: 1. The subject now before us is one of the most important topics that can engage the attention of men, and especially Christians. It involves the possibilities of childhood, and, to a great extent, the ultimate outcome of manhood, as well as our responsibilities connected with both. 2. No Christian home or congregation of disciples of Christ can give too much of the right kind of attention to it; for if the child is permitted to start its growth and development in the wrong direction, it may end fatally. But if it does not end fatally, it will, in all probability, involve an endless struggle to bring the child to and keep it in the right way. But as a beginning point in this study, let us consider,

I. SOME POINTS TO BE EMPHASIZED

1. *The acid test for every endeavor is the commodity it produces.* This is true regardless of whether the reference is to worldly affairs or to the work of the church. Cf. farm products, manufactured articles, church members and leaders.

2. *The hope of the future lies in childhood.* ("The child is father of the man," Wordsworth.) It is the duty of church leaders to see to the training of future leaders, preachers, teachers, and faithful Christians in general.

3. However, if the leaders are to be successful in this under-

taking, they must have the cooperation of the parents.   Cf. Hannah and Samuel; Lois, Eunice, and Timothy.

4. Unless parents assume their responsibility, there is relatively little that the leaders of the church can do, insofar as the children are concerned.   If one will trace his relation to the church from early childhood, he will easily see the correctness and force of this statement.

5. The idea that children should not be required to attend religious meetings, including classes, for fear that they will form a distaste for them, is inconsistent with other relations of life; for example, public school, work, etc.   There are some teachers who advocate the viewpoint just mentioned, but they want the attendance officer to see to it that the children attend their classes!

II. A LOOK AT THE FIELD

1. The place and importance of the heart.   Cf. 1 Sam. 16: 7b; Prov. 23: 7; 4: 23; Luke 6: 45.   The heart includes the intellect, the emotions, the will, and the conscience.

2. *The meaning of education.*   "Education is concerned, not with the intellect alone, but with everything which makes up the life of the pupil,—his thoughts, feelings, will, choices, attitudes, purposes, ideals, and habits."

3. *Some leading educators hold that a child is born with a large group of capacities and a number of inherited tendencies, none of which is fully developed.*   Many influences are brought to bear upon him, to which he reacts and responds, and thus his education begins immediately.   In a broad sense, these changes which take place in the individual from his birth to maturity constitute his education.

4. "The question to be asked at the end of an educational step is not, What has the child learned? but, What has the child become?"

5. *It should be kept in mind, however, that learning does not result from instruction alone, but through living, that is, experience, as well.*   It is the duty of parents and church leaders, therefore, to furnish such *instruction and guidance* as will enable the child to grow constantly in the ability to share efficiently and happily the life in the home, church, school, community, nation, and world.

III. TRAINING IS NECESSARY, IF GOOD IS TO FOLLOW

1. The training here contemplated is that which results in the development of character; and it should be kept in mind that the church has not reached its educational goal, until its pupils possess both the disposition and ability to meet all the situations of life in the Christian spirit and manner.

2. Failure to train, or if wrongly done, may be disastrous. Cf. Prov. 22: 6.*

3. As has already been seen, education is not accomplished by teaching alone; but also by properly guiding the pupil through the experiences of life.

4. Psychology teaches that the man is largely made during the first twelve years of his life. Comparatively few new habits are formed after the age of twenty-five, and relatively few old ones are given up.

5. It has been said, based on reliable statistics, that only one out of every thousand obeys the gospel after he passes the age of thirty.**

IV. SOME TRAINING AGENCIES—SENSE IMPRESSIONS

1. *The home:* conduct, manner of housekeeping, pictures, flowers, playmates, Bible teaching, etc. Would it be embarrassing if parents had to register the amount of Bible teaching their children receive in the home? They do not hesitate to require their children to study their school assignments, or practice their music lessons, for fear that they will later develop a dislike for them.

2. *The school—literary and church:* the kind of lesson material used, teachers, equipment, etc.

3. *The church:* faithfulness of the members, pride in the buildings and grounds, preparation for worship and service, enthusiasm and devotion of the leaders, etc.

4. *Secular and religious literature:* what kind of literature do your children read, or fail to read?

V. MORE CONCERN DEMANDED

1. Parents and church leaders should be more concerned with children and their training: not only their own children, but those about them—that is, all whom they can reach.

THE SOUL OF A CHILD
The Soul of the Child is the loveliest flower
That grows in the garden of God.
Its climb from weakness to knowledge and power,
To the sky from the clay and the clod.
To beauty and sweetness it grows under care,
Neglected, 'tis ragged and wild.

*The story is told of a woman who called upon a friend to try to persuade her ninth son not to be a sailor, as his eight brothers had done. The mother could not understand why all her boys wanted to be sailors. The friend pointed out to her that a large picture of a ship at sea, which she had put on the wall, was the silent teacher. Indeed, "the child *is* father of the man!"

**The best time for establishing Christian foundations and nurturing Christian behaviour is the plastic years of childhood and youth before habits of conduct have been established." (Antoinette Lamoreaux: *The Pupils in the Church,* p. 28. The Judson Press, Philadelphia.)

'Tis a plant that is tender, but wondrously rare
The sweet, wistful soul of a child!
Be tender, O gardener, and give it its share
Of moisture, of warmth, and of light,
And let it not lack for thy painstaking care
To protect it from frost and from blight.
A glad day will come when its bloom shall unfold;
It will seem that an angel has smiled,
Reflecting from its beauty and sweetness untold
In the sensitive soul of a child.

                                        —*Selected*

2. It has been estimated that less than five per cent of children choose Bible characters for their ideal.

3. How many children who are old enough to think choose their parents as their ideal?

4. Some parents are known to have said, "It is nobody's business if I do not take my children to the Bible classes." Would it be anybody's business if these children should sell whiskey or engage in other sinful practices. Every child who is denied proper training is a potential criminal.

Conclusion: Who can estimate the possibilities of childhood? Reliable figures indicate that eighty per cent of the additions to the church come through the Bible school. Does that fact have any significance? Will not each parent, church leader, and Christian share his part of the responsibility of child-training? Cf. *The Church and the Children,* edited by Sewell and Speck. Firm Foundation Publishing House, Austin, Texas.

◆ ◆ ◆

HOW TO BECOME A CHRISTIAN
2 Cor. 5: 17-19

Introduction: 1. *How may I become a Christian?* is one of the greatest questions which any person away from the Lord can ask. Indeed, for one to understand the full import of that question is to know the difference between life and death. When Paul wrote to the Romans, he told them that all men are under sin; and that, according to the Scriptures, there is none righteous, no, not one. See Rom. 3: 9, 10. 2. Only those who are free from sin can live with the Lord; and since all are sinners in the sight of God, all are in need of salvation. This is true of every person when he reaches the age of responsibility, and no one, therefore, has any advantage over another in this respect. But in studying this lesson, let us begin by considering the fact that

I. JESUS IS THE SAVIOUR

1. If men are to be saved from their sins, there must be a Saviour; and that is the express purpose for which Jesus said that he came to the earth. See Luke 19: 10.

2. But the Bible just as plainly says that there is no remission "apart from shedding of blood." Heb. 9: 22.

3. Blood had been shed for ages past, before the coming of Jesus, but that blood, the blood of animals, could never take away sins. Heb. 10: 4.

4. It remained, therefore, for Christ to shed his own blood, and thereby make possible the salvation of every man. See Heb. 2: 9; 1 Pet. 1: 18, 19.

5. But not only is Jesus the Saviour of men; he is their only Saviour. Acts 4: 12.

II. ONLY THE OBEDIENT WILL BE SAVED

1. But the fact that Jesus died for all men does not mean that all men will be saved. Cf. Heb. 5: 8, 9.

2. The word "author" in the passage just cited is significant; it literally means "cause." Jesus therefore *caused* or brings about the salvation of all them that obey him, or, to express the same thing in other words, the "procuring cause" of salvation resides in him.

3. In Heb. 2: 3 it is said that this salvation was first spoken through the Lord. Any salvation, that is, any plan of saving men which was not "caused" by the Lord, and first spoken through him, cannot be the salvation which men need today. Cf. Gal. 1: 6-9.

III. TO OBEY IS TO WORK GOD'S RIGHTEOUSNESS

1. Peter declares in Acts 10: 34, 35 that God is no respecter of persons; but in every nation he that feareth him, and worketh righteousness, is acceptable to him.

2. To fear God is to reverence or venerate him, and to work righteousness means to do that which is acceptable to him—that which he has ordained to be done. Cf. Psalm 119: 172; Matt. 3: 15.

3. Just here it should be emphasized that nothing will please the Lord except that which he has ordained; for he is the Sovereign Ruler of the universe, and no man has known his mind, that he should tell God that which is best to be done for the salvation of the soul. Cf. Isa. 55: 8, 9.

4. Jesus has been commissioned the Saviour of men, and it is only through him that one can find his way to God. See John 14: 6.

5. Ancient Israel endeavored to establish their own righteousness, but failed miserably. See Rom. 10: 1-3. The only way that any one can work the righteousness which is acceptable to God is, first, to learn that which God wants *him* to do, and then, to do it.

IV. WHERE IS GOD'S RIGHTEOUSNESS FOR US FOUND?

1. Paul, in Rom. 10: 4, tells us where God's righteousness for

people in this age is *not* found. No one today, therefore, can be justified before God by keeping the law of Moses. People now must believe in God *through Christ,* not through Moses. See 1 Pet. 1: 21.

2. But Paul just as clearly tells us in Rom. 1: 16, 17 where we can find that which God wants us to do. In Eph. 1: 13 the "word of the truth" is called "the gospel of your salvation," and Peter tells us in 1 Pet. 1: 22 that our souls are purified in our *obedience to the truth.*

3. Just before Jesus left the earth to return to the Father, he authorized his disciples to go into all the world, and preach the gospel to the whole creation. See Mark 16: 15. It follows, therefore, that no man who does not come into possession of the truth of the gospel can ever know that which the Father wants him to do. *Learning the gospel, then, is imperative in becoming a Christian.*

V. What the Gospel Reveals

1. One of the direct results of hearing the gospel is faith; for we are told in Rom. 10: 17 that faith comes by hearing the word of the Lord. When one learns of Jesus he must place implicit faith in him as the Saviour of men. Cf. John 8: 24; Heb. 11: 6. The New Testament, and especially that part of it known as the gospel records, was written for the express purpose of enabling people to believe that Jesus is the Christ, the Son of God; and that believing they may have life in his name. See John 20: 30, 31.

2. When one reaches the point where he has implicit faith in Jesus as the Saviour of men, he must turn his back upon every known sin and firmly resolve that he will walk the ways of sin no longer. This is repentance, and without it no one can be pleasing to God. See Acts 17: 30, 31.

3. The penitent believer must perform whatever acts of obedience that are required of him; for Jesus is the author of eternal salvation *only* unto all them that obey him. It is, of course, impossible for one to do that which the Lord wants him to do before he learns what the will of the Lord for him is. The question asked by Saul of Tarsus in Acts 22: 10 exactly expresses the frame of mind which always characterizes the penitent believer; and the Lord never fails to respond to such a mind as that, as may be seen by reading his answer in Acts 22: 16. The promise of salvation is vouchsafed to all who thus obey him. See Mark 16: 16.

4. When the people on the day the kingdom of Christ was established heard Peter's great sermon, "they were pricked in their heart, and said unto Peter and the rest of the apostles, Brethren, What shall we do?" The inspired answer, together with the results which followed, is found in the verses which follow. See Acts 2. 37-41.

Some Conclusions: Even a casual consideration of the teaching of the New Testament regarding the Lord's plan of saving people will reveal these simple conclusions:

1. The gospel is the Lord's sole means and method of bringing sinners to salvation. See Rom. 1: 16, 17.

2. No man was ever converted by the Holy Spirit, or any other direct means, separate and apart from the gospel. Cf. 2 Thess. 2: 13, 14.

3. The Holy Spirit is promised to obedient believers, and regardless of the figure which may have been used in expressing that promise, the Holy Spirit is promised *only* to obedient believers. Cf. John 7: 37-39; Acts 5: 32.

4. The Holy Spirit is nowhere promised to people who are out of covenant relationship with the Lord; and the quicker the people who have never obeyed the gospel find that out, the quicker they will cease depending upon a direct operation of the Holy Spirit for their salvation. See Gal. 4: 6; 1 Cor. 6: 19, 20.

5. The Christian's entire life is regulated solely by the New Testament, the law of the Spirit of life (Rom. 8: 2), the inspired word of God; and it is utterly preposterous for any one to think that the Holy Spirit would give a law, and then act independently of it or contrary to it. There is, therefore, no divine power whatsoever exerted upon or through the Christian, except that which is exerted through the word of God—the New Testament. See 2 Tim. 3: 16, 17; 2 Pet. 1: 3.

◆ ◆ ◆

THE CHRISTIAN ALTERNATIVE
2 Tim. 3: 16, 17

Introduction: 1. As you leave the halls of your *alma mater,* you are going out into a world which is torn asunder by controversy and strife. The great antagonists in this mighty conflict are Truth and Error, and you will be compelled, in the final analysis, to identify yourselves with one or the other. The final choice as to where you will cast your lot will, of course, be left up to you, but if you would be successful and free you must ever be mindful of the immortal words of Jesus, "The truth shall make you free." 2. As you take your places in life you will not always have the sympathetic understanding which your parents and teachers have manifested toward you. On the contrary, you will find determined opposition from many unexpected sources. But you must learn not to object to opposition; for opposition, in and of itself, is not always bad. It is only when the opposition becomes unfair and resorts to methods which are not right, that it becomes obnoxious. But regardless of where you take your stand, you will have God to reckon with. "Chinese" Gordon once said, "If you tell the truth, you have infinite power supporting you; but if not, you have infinite power against you." 3. There are people in the world today who, when they learn that they cannot fairly and successfully oppose your position or meet your argument, will resort to the all too common practice of endeavoring to counteract your stand by injuring your influence. Some of them may be honest in this, for Jesus said, "The hour cometh, that whosoever killeth you shall think that he offereth service unto God." (John 16: 1, 2.) They probably won't kill your body today; but whether it be body or influence, the principle is the same. But in studying this lesson, let us begin with

I. THE ISSUE STATED

1. The nation-wide controversy which has grown out of John T. Flynn's book, *The Road Ahead,* furnishes a very forceful illustration of the idea just suggested. Instead of meeting arguments on their merits and allowing the proponents of certain ideologies to express their own views and do their own reasoning, the opposition seeks to fasten some label upon those who differ with them— a label which will arouse prejudice in the minds of the uninformed.

2. Thus, if you are in favor of vital social changes, you will be labeled as a socialist or a communist; while if you are opposed to such changes, you will be classified as a capitalist or an antisocialist. And when once these labels have been applied to you, it will make little difference what you say; for all the average person will hear is the import of the label.

3. Such a viewpoint requires that every man must be made to fit into one of the isms of the day. It seems never to occur to those holding this philosophy that Christianity has anything distinctive to offer. With them there is no Christian alternative. They do not intend to look to Christianity for the solution of the many problems which vex this troubled world.

II. THE CHRISTIAN WAY

1. If this way of thinking is correct, then Jesus was wrong, for he taught that he was giving God's total answer to man's total need. See Matt. 6: 33; cf. James 1: 17; Phil 4: 19. The kingdom of God, here and now, is designed to meet every need of the human race, but its blessings are guaranteed only to those who are citizens of it.

2. This, of course, is complete totalitarianism, demanding total obedience in the total life, but it is a totalitarianism which, when fully obeyed, brings total freedom. The difference between this totalitarianism and the totalitarianisms of the world is the difference between total freedom and total bondage.

3. And isn't that what the human race is seeking for beyond the half-answers of our day—something that will command us totally, bring life into total coherence, and enable us to reach the supreme goal in the end? This is precisely what Jesus proposes to

do. But, let us ask, how does he propose to do it? This brings us to a consideration of

III. WHAT THE WAY OF CHRIST INVOLVES

1. It is interesting, as we read through the Book of Acts, to consider the passages which speak of *the Way* where a capital "W" is used. One will not go far in such reading before he sees that "the Way" is synonymous with the kingdom or church of Christ. Cf. Acts 9: 1, 2.

2. To be in the Way of Christ, then, is to be in his kingdom or church; for whatever Jesus does here on earth among men, he does it as the king of his kingdom, the head of his church.

3. What, then, does the Way of Christ involve?

(1) *A reconciliation with God.* Cf. Eph. 2: 3; Rom. 5: 10; 2 Cor. 5: 18-20. No one can please God while he remains in a state of estrangement and rebellion against him. The way of reconciliation may be learned from such passages as John 3: 1-5; Acts 2: 14-41.

(2) *The right attitude toward God and man.* Cf. Matt. 22: 35-40; Gal. 5: 14. The word for "love" in these passages does not denote a mere sentiment, but rather a feeling which will lead one to give himself up for the good of another, whether friend or enemy. Cf. Matt. 7: 12.

IV. THE LESSON PRACTICALLY APPLIED

1. The New Testament is the Lord's great law book for his people in this age, and no one can be successful today who does not seek to apply the principles set forth therein to the many problems which come before him.

2. To love God, of course, is to reverence him and keep his commandments, cf. Acts 10: 34, 35; 1 John 5: 3; and while it would be very profitable for us to study that phase of the question before us, we shall, however, because of the lack of time, devote ourselves to a consideration of the application of these New Testament principles with reference to our fellow men. We shall consider three questions here, questions which are sore spots in our society.

(1) *The bitter struggle between capital and labor.* With only a few exceptions, both sides are operating on a pagan basis—viz., "Thou shalt love thyself." What would happen if both sides should shift the emphasis and follow the teaching of Jesus. It seems that there would be a joint responsibility in the matter of management, and a division of both profits and losses. That certainly would put a new motivation into industry.

(2) *The ever recurring race question.* What would happen if we should follow the Lord's teaching with reference to loving our neighbor as ourselves? If any one wants to ask, "And who is my neighbor?" the Lord has the answer to that question too. He ap-

plied the word to a man of another race—a despised Samaritan. What, then, would it mean to follow the Lord's teaching with reference to men of other races? Would it not mean equality of opportunity? Not just equality; for that is something which society cannot give. Equality can only be earned by character and achievement. Furthermore, this economy of equal opportunity cannot be forced by legislation. The teaching of Jesus is the only way by which it can be successfully brought about.

(3) *The question of peace—personal, national, and international.* In dealing with each other, there are three levels on which we may operate: the demoniac, where we return evil for good and hate for love; the human, where we return evil for evil, hate for hate, and good for good; the Christian, where we return good for evil and love for hate. If acting upon the Christian level does not bring peace every time, it certainly will give the actor moral strength and bring him into the favor of both God and all right thinking people. Cf. 1 Pet. 3: 13, 14.

◆ ◆ ◆

CHRISTIAN CITIZENSHIP
1 Pet. 2: 17

Introduction: 1. A great part of the teaching of Jesus was devoted to the social obligations of the individual. Man is essentially a social being; and not only is he required by the principles of righteousness to discharge his duty toward his fellow men; he must also be willing, if he is to do his best, to give positive attention to creating the neighborly attitude. 2. We usually think of a citizen as a member of a state—one who owes allegiance to a government, and who is entitled to protection from it. It is possible, of course, for a citizen of a worldly state to meet its requirements without being governed directly by the teaching of Jesus. But if the citizen wishes to reach the highest degree of attainment possible in this relationship, he must order all his attitudes and conduct after the teaching of Christ. For convenience in speaking, the obligations of Christian citizenship may be divided into three groups—viz:

I. THOSE WHICH RELATE DIRECTLY TO THE STATE

1. See Rom. 13: 1-7; 1 Pet. 2: 13-17.

2. A simple reading of these passages and a few well chosen comments, based on them, should be sufficient to bring out and emphasize this phase of the subject.

II. THOSE WHICH RELATE DIRECTLY TO ONE'S FELLOW MEN

1. The text suggest two aspects of the Christian's relation to his fellow men—viz., to those who are not Christians and to those who are: "Honor all men." "Love the brotherhood." Cf. Gal. 6: 10.

2. The Parable of the Good Samaritan (Luke 10: 25-37) sets forth a concrete illustration of this principle which is unequaled in all literature. In dealing with humanity, as pointed out in this parable, one sees three outstanding philosophies or viewpoints of life. They are,

(1) Those who act on the principle that might makes right.

a. The robbers held the philosophy that what a man has the power to do, he has the moral right to do. Such people make their living by exploiting others.

b. People of this type do not know the meaning of philanthropy. They love money more than they love men; and they will kill a man in order to get his money.

c. The principle which actuates men on this level leaves death and destruction in its path; and should it gain supreme control in the world, human life would no longer be safe, and peace, happiness, and contentment would no longer be possible.

(2) The passive class in human society.

a. The character of a man cannot be adequately estimated until an opportunity for service is presented to him. No one could have foretold what the men of the Parable of the Talents (Matt. 25: 14-30) would do with their talents, until they were given a chance to use them. The priest and the Levite, in the lesson now before us, had such an opportunity in the wounded man. His condition presented a problem, the solution of which involved human duty.

b. Those of the passive class refuse to assume any responsibility for the condition of the unfortunate; and, consequently, feel no obligation to assist them. Other duties seem more important to them; but, whatever their thought may be, they pass up their opportunity, and leave the problem unsolved.

c. This class, unlike the first, does not actively harm society; but neither does it help. Such people will not kill a man for his money; but neither will they spend theirs to rescue him.

d. The philosophy of this class may be summed up in these words: What I have is mine, and I will keep it; I am under no obligation to use it in the interest of others.

(3) The good Samaritan.

a. Those of this class are nearest like God. Love and sympathy find their highest expression in them. When they see the needy, they ask no questions; but, being "moved with compassion," they immediately set about to take care of them, and endeavor to help them solve their problems. (There is a vast difference in simply giving a man something, and in seeking to help him solve the problems in which his condition has involved him.)

b. To such people, men, though strangers, mean more than money; and they are willing to invest, not only their means, but their time and influence as well in an effort to save the unfortunate.

c. Those of this class do not see in the teaching of Christ a list of distinct precepts, each of which is applicable to only one case, but rather a code of living principles of universal application; and, having a heart full of love for God and man, they have no trouble in finding occasions for their application.

d. Their philosophy is this: What I am and have belong to God, and I am willing to spend and be spent according to his pleasure and the needs of my fellow men.

III. THOSE WHICH RELATE DIRECTLY TO GOD

1. God must be first in the life of every Christian; and should there come a conflict between God's requirements and that which the state and other men require, the Christian must obey God first. See Acts 4: 18-20; 5: 27-29.

2. Some interesting and forceful examples: Dan. 6; the three Hebrew children, Dan. 3.

◆ ◆ ◆

MARKED-DOWN CHRISTIANITY
Prov. 30: 12

Introduction: 1. It is a very common thing to find marked-down merchandise in the business world, especially at this time of the year. One may look into the show-windows or on the counters of many stores and see items which have been marked down. For example, a suit of clothes may have been priced at $65.00; but a line has been drawn through that figure, and below it one sees $47.50, or some smaller amount. Just so with many other items of merchandise. 2. The implication is that the items so marked are out of season, inferior in quality, shop-worn, or affected in some other way. In either case, however, they are not as desirable as other merchandise, not similarly affected. It may also indicate that the merchant realizes that many people are looking for marked-down merchandise, and that they will not buy except at "bargain prices." There are many such buyers who will accept inferior merchandise, but they will not pay the regular price. They must find a bargain before they buy! 3. This attitude creates a situation for the merchant which must be met in some way. One popular way is to mark the item in question up and then mark it down, so that the buyers may find what they are looking for, namely, bargain prices! 4. Strange as it may seem, there are many people, both in the church and out of it, who are looking for "marked-down Christianity;" and they will not buy (cf. Prov. 23: 23) unless the price is reduced. And in order to meet this demand, there are churches on every hand with bargain prices always available. Thus, one may have what he wants at his own price and on his own terms. But in studying this lesson, let us observe that

I. CHRISTIANITY IS NEVER CHEAP

1. Christianity is the most priceless possession which man can

have and enjoy. It is expensive; but when rightly considered, it is cheap, even at the high price which one must pay for it. Cf. Phil. 3: 7, 8; Matt. 16: 26.

2. There are many people who would not think of doing without Christianity, but they are willing to accept an adulterated and corrupted form of Christianity, in order to get the price reduced. Cf. 2 Tim. 3: 1-5.*

3. Those who are not careful to do exactly as the Lord commands are not greatly concerned about the quality of the "Christianity" they get, so long as they get it at their own price and on their own terms. Cf. Matt. 7: 21-23; Luke 17: 10.

II. The Principles and Standards of Christianity Are Unchangeable

1. The testimony of the Scriptures: John 8: 31, 32; Matt. 7: 24-27; John 12: 48-50.

2. The Bible plainly teaches that God is no respecter of persons, and there is, therefore, one price to all. Cf. Acts 10: 34, 35; Gal. 1: 6-9.

III. Marked-Down Christianity Is a Cheat and a Fraud

1. The testimony of the Scriptures: Gal. 1: 6-9. "Too many people are like the small boy who insists that his hands and face and ears are perfectly clean, without looking to see. He simply does not want to be washed. He is not in the least concerned about the condition of his hands and face and ears." Cf. Prov. 30: 12; Acts 17: 11; James 1: 22-27.

2. What are some of the claims and practices of those who want marked-down Christinity? They insist, for example,

(1) That honesty be maintained, but they persist in cheating, defrauding, and taking advantage of others. Cf. Rom. 2: 22-24; 1 John 5: 17 (unrighteousness includes every breach of duty and everything that comes short of the requirements of justice); Heb. 2: 1-3.

(2) That truth be upheld, but they continue to lie, misrepresent, deceive, bear false witness, and malign their fellows.

(3) That the Lord's day be revered, but they flagrantly desecrate it whensoever they desire.

(4) That Christians should not forsake the assembly of the saints, but they do not hesitate to absent themselves whenever they desire to do something else.

(5) That the church should be strong and influential, but they

---

*The original word from which we have the term "form" (*morphosis*) signifies a mere form of semblance (Thayer), and implies that the people described profess to be religious. However, their religion is in their creed (what they claim to believe) rather than in their heart. They are not governed by what God says. Their cry is that the standards are too high, and the demands on their time, talents, and possessions are too great. Cf. Matt. 16: 24.

either practice, or do not do anything to hinder others from practicing, things which prevent the church from enjoying such influence. Such practices include bridge-playing, dancing, drinking, and many other social evils of our day. Leaders in the churches will tell a man that he will be lost if he engages in sinful practices, such as drunkenness, profanity, and the like; but they also tell him, in effect, that nothing will be done with him by the church if he is guilty of such sins. See 2 Thess. 3: 6; Acts 5: 13, 14, and the context.

(6) That the church be sound in the faith—make the teaching of Jesus clear and strong—and defend it against all error, yet they slip back and forth from one side to the other on questions of divine teaching on the basis of conditions under which they must take a position. They will take a stand, if public sentiment is favorable!

3. Such people are great Christians (?), so long as they can have their own Christianity, at their own price and on their own terms. They should learn, however, that it isn't enough to keep the price up on one or two aspects; it must be kept up at every point all the time. Cf. James 2: 10; 4: 17; Gal. 2: 20.

4. Each congregation of the Lord's people should endeavor to make the neighborhood in which it is located see that there is one church in the community that deals with divine things in a manner that is pleasing to God; and that seeks to see that the price which the Lord has fixed is the price which every one must pay.

◆ ◆ ◆

THE CHURCH AS AN EDUCATIONAL INSTITUTION
Eph. 3: 10

Introduction: 1. The "wisdom of God" is the greatest possible subject which can engage the attention of the created inhabitants of the universe. Numerous passages of scripture plainly state that this wisdom was hidden for ages. It remained for the church of the Lord Jesus Christ to become the medium through which the *much-variegated* or *many-tinted* wisdom of God should be made known. The church likewise was ordained to be the evangel of this infinite heritage. Cf. Mott. 28: 19, 20; Acts 2: 42; 8: 4; 2 Tim. 2: 2. 2. The primary reference of the text, in all probability, is not to men, but to angels. See 1 Pet. 1: 12; 1 Cor. 4: 9; Heb. 12: 22. However, the principle involved is the same, whether the reference is to men or to angels, or whether the "teaching" is done by observing the existence, purpose, and fortunes of the church, or by being instructed by it. But in studying this lesson, let us consider,

I. The Testimony of the Scriptures

1. The great commission, as recorded by Matthew. See Matt. 28: 18-20.

(1) The scope here contemplated is world-wide and age-lasting, and takes into consideration the whole range of teaching necessary for redemption and sanctification. Cf. 2 Tim. 3: 16, 17.

(2) The intentions involved are clearly seen when one considers the facts recorded in Acts 2: 1-42.

2. The supreme purpose of the church, as set forth by Paul. See Eph. 4: 11-16. In this passage, as may likewise be seen, the inspired penman refers to a system of teaching which supplies all that is needed for redemption and sanctification.

3. The will of God, so far as men are concerned, can only be known by teaching; and that process, therefore, is an absolute essential.

II. Reasons for the Necessity of Teaching

1. The wisdom and good pleasure of God require it. Cf. 1 Cor. 1: 18-21.

2. The nature and necessities of the case demand it. See Rom. 10: 14, 15 (this passage refers primarily to the original revelation by inspired men); John 6: 44, 45; cf. Rev. 22: 17.

3. The church has been constituted the pillar and ground of the truth. See 1 Tim. 3: 14, 15; Rev. 1: 20.

III. Ways and Means of Teaching

1. This study is concerned with the work of congregations and individual Christians in their efforts at making known the will of God.

2. The object in view is to win men to Christ and his way of thinking.

3. What, then, are some of the ways and means at their disposal for the accomplishment of this work?

(1) Individual or private instruction, by word of mouth, the printed page, etc. See Acts 8: 4, 26ff; 15: 22-29.

(2) The class method, evangelistic efforts, the radio, etc.

(3) The school, such as the Bible college and other similar institutions.

(4) The church library and a definite program consistent with its possibilities. This is, perhaps, one of our most neglected opportunities.

◆ ◆ ◆

THE CHURCH IN A WORLD AT WAR
2 Cor. 4: 1, 2

Introduction: 1. In the beginning of 1939, when the dark clouds of another world conflict were fast gathering, *Fortune,* one of the nation's leading business magazines, after charging that the church during the First World War merely repeated that which the people in general were saying, called upon the church, in the event of war, not merely to echo the voice of the world, but to speak courageously its own message. The war did come and how well the church met the issue is now a matter of history. 2. The reference, of course, was to the church in the denominational sense, but the statement of *Fortune* serves to illustrate the attitude which thoughful business men have toward the church, as it exists in the popular mind. 3. The church of the New Testament is a spiritual institution, with a definite mission to perform. It is in the world, but it is not of the world (cf. John 17: 14-16); and, whether in time of war or in time of peace, it must fulfill its mission, if it is to have the approval of God. 4. But in studying the duty of the church in a world at war, it should be observed that the duty of the church necessarily involves the duty of individual Christians; for the church is made up of individual Christians. But in studying this lesson, let us consider,

I. GOD'S PURPOSE IN THE CHURCH

1. The church is the medium through which the manifold, or much-variegated, wisdom of God is made known, in keeping with the eternal purpose of God. See Eph. 3: 10, 11. Much-variegated wisdom is wisdom manifesting itself in a great variety of forms. "The innumerable aspects of God's wisdom" (Weymouth); "the full sweep of the divine wisdom" (Moffatt); "the many-sided wisdom of God" (Goodspeed). "Manifesting itself in a great variety of forms" (Thayer). Cf. Joseph's coat of many colors, Gen. 37: 3. "Through the church God's wisdom in its infinite variety is to be displayed" (Vincent).

2. It is also the medium, along with Christ Jesus, through which God is to receive glory "unto all generations for ever and ever," or throughout all the ages to come. Cf. Eph. 3: 21.

3. Thus, it can be seen that the church transcends all time, places, and conditions which are related to the people of the earth; and it is for this reason that no situation can have any effect in bringing about a change in God's plan for his church. Cf. Heb. 12: 28, 29. ("Let us have *grace,* or *thankfulness,* margin; that is, let us be thankful that we have the opportunity of offering "service well-pleasing to God.")

II. SOME OF THE CHURCH'S OBLIGATIONS

1. *It is the duty of the church to preach the gospel. See Mark 16: 15.*

(1) This must be done in time of war, just as it is done in time of peace, that is, the full gospel must be preached at all times. Cf. 1 Tim. 3: 14, 15; 2 Tim. 4: 1-5; 1 Pet. 2: 9.

(2) The early church labored under conditions that were almost unbearable, but it was faithful to this trust. See Heb. 10: 32-35; Acts 8: 4; Col. 1: 23.

2. *It is the duty of the church to work for the unity of all Christians. See Eph. 4: 1-3; cf. Isa. 11: 6-9.*

(1) This diligence is especially needed in time of war; for it is a well known fact that many brethren have widely differing views regarding that which a Christian may or may not do under such circumstances. Note: The word *diligence* means *to exert one's self—to make an effort.*

a. There are some who hold to the view that it is never right for a Christian to support war in any form, and it is for that reason that they cannot participate in any activities that are directed by military authority.

b. There are others who contend that the decision in such matters lies wholly with the state; and that if the state calls them into active military service, they are not morally responsible for that which they do as soldiers. Those holding this view usually cite such passages as Rom. 13: 1ff. as authority for their stand.

c. There are some who believe that they are justified in doing anything they are called upon to do, so long as they are not required to violate that which they understand to be their higher duty to God. Cf. Acts 4: 19, 20; 5: 29.

d. There are some who are willing to participate in carnal warfare if they believe it to be a just war, that is, one that is waged in defense of freedom or on behalf of the victims of aggression.

(2) But regardless of that which one thinks about such questions, there is certainly something wrong with him if he manifests a bad spirit and makes ugly charges against his brethren who hold views which are different from his. Cf. Rom. 8: 9; Gal. 5: 22, 23; Matt. 7: 20.

3. *It is the duty of the church to do good unto all men. Cf. Gal. 6: 10.*

(1) There are many new opportunities for ministries of mercy during times of war, and the church must do its best in dealing with them, if it is to measure up to the full weight of its responsibility. Cf. Luke 10: 25-37; John 4: 9b.

(2) Regardless of that which one thinks of war and the participation of Christians in it, it is the duty of the child of God to do all he can for the welfare of needy humanity whenever and wherever he has the opportunity.

4. *It is the duty of the church to strive for peace. Cf. Matt. 5: 9.*

(1) The reference here is not to peaceable men as such, but to the active promoters of peace. Such people not only keep the peace themselves; they also seek to bring men into harmony with God and with each other.

(2) There is never a time in the life of any Christian when this work should not go on. Cf. James 3: 13-18.

III. How Can the Church Fulfil These Obligations

1. The church must *always* act by the authority of Christ. Cf. Matt. 28: 18; Eph. 1: 22, 23; Col. 3: 17.

2. The church must always act as the church, that is, it must not allow itself to become the agency of some other organization, such as the state, and thus be found endeavoring to do something which does not belong to its God-given work. The church, therefore, must not become,

(1) A recruiting station for military service.

(2) A bureau of propaganda for secular affairs.

(3) A bond-selling agency for a nation at war.

3. Such matters as those just named belong to the state, and no man has the right to ask the church to participate in anything beyond its divinely-authorized mission. It is never right for the church to assume obligations which belong to the state, and *vice versa.*

Let the church be the church and do its work!

◆ ◆ ◆

"COME AND SEE"*
John 1: 43-51

Introduction: 1. When Philip, one of the first disciples of Jesus, told Nathanael about finding "him, of whom Moses in the law, and the prophets, wrote, Jesus of Nazareth, the son of Joseph," Nathanael asked, "Can any good thing come out of Nazareth?" Philip's reply was both simple and to the point: "Come and see." 2. Although Nathanael was to some extent prejudiced against any one who lived in Nazareth, he was, nevertheless, willing to accept the challenge which Philip placed before him. He did as Philip suggested, and he was overwhelmingly convinced that Philip and his companions had indeed found the Son of God; the King of Israel. 3. No person should ever allow himself to get into a condition which makes him unwilling to consider the merits of any proposition involving the truth, and which vitally affects his eternal welfare. But in studying this lesson, let us consider,

I. THE LESSON BROUGHT DOWN TO DATE

1. This incident involving Philip and Nathanael is used in this study for the express purpose of suggesting to our neighbors and friends that they "come and see" that which we who claim to speak where the Bible speaks, and to remain silent where the Bible is silent, teach and practice, instead of simply taking that which others may say about us.

2. There are many honest people who misunderstand our position on many questions, because it has been misrepresented to them; and in some instances those who did the misrepresenting were themselves honest about the matter. It is easy for one to misrepresent a proposition when it is remembered that there is

*Or, Prejudice and Its Cure

only a short step between *misunderstanding* and *misrepresentation*. Cf. John 2: 18-22.

II. HONEST PEOPLE ARE FAIR AND OPEN-MINDED

1. But inasmuch as what the Jews *thought* that Jesus meant by the term "temple" was so seemingly impossible of accomplishment, the least that they could have done would have been to ask him what he meant by the expression, before they criticized and condemned him for that which he said.

2. Any fair-minded person, therefore, will readily admit that the enemies of Jesus were manifestly unfair to him when they used his words in John 2: 18-22, with a meaning which *they* attached to them, against him at his trial. See Matt. 26: 59-61. His enemies had reference to the temple in which people worshipped; but any thoughtful person knows that Jesus did not have that temple in mind; and to try to make it appear that he did, because of that which he did say, was utterly unfair to him and wholly untrue to the facts in the case.

3. Jesus declares in John 8: 32 that the truth shall make one free; but the person who is sincerely seeking for the truth must realize that it is just as necessary for him to be honest intellectually, as it is for him to be honest in the material things of life. Cf. Acts 17: 11, 12.

Of all human ambitions an open mind, eagerly expectant of new discoveries and ready to remold convictions in the light of added knowledge and dispelled ignorance and misapprehensions, is the noblest, rarest, and the most difficult to achieve.
—James Harvey Robinson

4. It is easy, by means of a few small alterations, or with a different meaning attached to one's words, to make it appear that he is teaching something different from that which was actually taught. People who do things like that nearly always try to state the other person's views in *their* words and with a meaning attached to his words which *they,* and not he, attached to them. They seldom ever use the speaker's or the author's own words, or ask, "What does *he* mean by that expression?"

5. The rules of interpretation which are of common acceptation among fair-minded students require that no expression which is not clear to the reader or hearer shall be made to mean something that is contrary to the general teaching of the author or speaker, unless *he* makes it plain that he meant to teach something that is different from and contrary to his known position.

III. SOME MISUNDERSTANDINGS AND MISREPRESENTATIONS

1. It has already been pointed out that where there is a misunderstanding it is easy to misrepresent; but if one is honest in his misrepresentations he will always be glad to consider the facts in the case, when they are called to his attention, and he will be

just as glad to correct the false impressions which he made, as he was to make them in the first place.

2. Those who claim membership in the New Testament church and who endeavor to speak where the Bible speaks, and to remain silent where it is silent, have frequently been misrepresented with reference both to their teaching and their practice. And inasmuch as the speaker stands indentified with these people, he shall speak in the first person (plural) of some of these misunderstood and misrepresented positions:

(1) *It has been said by some that we have discarded the Old Testament Scriptures altogether.* But if they are willing to come and see, they will learn that our position with reference to the Old Testament Scriptures is precisely the position of the New Testament itself. Cf. Rom. 15: 4; 1 Cor. 10: 11; Heb. 1: 1, 2; Acts 3: 22, 23; Matt. 17: 1-5.

The people of God during the age of Moses were God's church for that period (Acts 7: 38), and they had the Old Testament as their law; and in like manner, the people of God during the age of Christ are his church for this period (1 Cor. 15: 9; 1 Tim. 3: 15; cf. Heb. 3: 1-6), and we have the New Testament as our law. Read Gal. 3: 15-4: 7.

(2) *Others have said that we do not believe in the work of the Holy Spirit in conversion, thus leaving the impression that we teach against the work of the Holy Spirit in this respect.* We believe that every case of conversion is brought about by the Holy Spirit, but we do not believe that the Spirit operates directly in the matter of conviction and conversion, separate and apart from the written word of God. The Spirit always does such work through the divinely chosen medium, the revealed word of God. Cf. John 6: 44, 45; Rom. 1: 16; 1 Cor. 4: 14, 15; 2 Cor. 5: 18-20; 2 Thess. 2: 13, 14.

(3) *It has been urged by some that we do not believe in prayer.* This is a gross misrepresentation, for our practice plainly shows that we do believe in prayer. We do not, however, believe in asking God to do something for people which he has not promised to do—forgive alien sins in answer to prayer, for example. Cf. Rom. 1: 16; Prov. 28: 9.

Prayer is a blessed privilege which belongs to God's people (see James 5: 16), but one does not become a child of God simply through prayer. Saul of Tarsus and Cornelius both prayed before they became Christians, but they didn't stop there; they were told what to do in *words,* whereby they were saved. See Acts 11: 14; 22: 10, 16; cf. James 1: 21.

(4) *Some have charged that we do not believe in a change of heart or heartfelt religion, but that we teach that religion is cold, formal, ritualistic, and with no warmth of feeling in it.* But if any one who thinks this will come with an open heart and see for himself, he will learn that we not only believe in and teach

heartfelt religion, but that we teach that the *whole* heart must be changed.

a. The intellectual processes must be changed, Matt. 9: 4; Mark 2: 8; Matt. 13: 15; Rom. 10: 9, 10.   (These passages will give some idea of what the heart is.)

b. The emotional processes must be changed, Matt. 22: 37; 2 Sam. 6: 16; Psalm 33: 21; 2 Cor. 2: 4; 2 Sam. 15: 1-6.

c. The volitional processes must be changed, Acts 11: 23; 2 Cor. 9: 7; 1 Cor. 7: 37.

d. The conscience must be changed, Acts 2: 37; 5: 33; 1 John 3: 20, 21.

This is much further than most religious teachers are willing to go in discussing the change of heart or heartfelt religion.

(5) *It has been claimed by some that we deny the cleansing efficacy of the blood of Christ, and teach only a water salvation.* However, if those making this claim will come and see, they will learn that we teach that it is only through the blood of Christ that sins can be forgiven.   See Eph. 1: 7; Rev. 1: 5; Heb. 9: 14. But we further teach that it is only through obedience that one comes in contact with the cleansing blood.   Cf. Heb. 5: 8, 9; Rom. 6: 16-18; 6: 3, 4; Acts 2: 37-39.

Christ, indeed, died for all men (Heb. 2: 9), but who wants to affirm that all men will be saved?   Only the obedient will enjoy his salvation.   Cf. Matt. 7: 21-23.

❖ ❖ ❖

THE GREAT COMMISSION EXECUTED
2 Cor. 5: 18-20

Introduction: 1.   The Great Commission, or some phase of it, is set forth in a number of places in the New Testament; but it will only be necessary for our purpose here to call attention to some of the more prominent statements regarding it.   This will be done by reading the language of the inspired text.   2.   While the commission is set forth in full in the New Testament, it is, nevertheless, true that in no one place are all its various phases mentioned.   3.   Attention in this study shall be directed to five statements of the commission—one each by the four biographical writers, and one by the great apostle to the Gentiles.   As a beginning point in this study, then, let us ask,

I. WHAT DID JESUS COMMISSION HIS DISCIPLES TO DO?

1.   This question can be best answered by considering the five statements of the commission referred to in the introduction to this lesson.

(1) *Matt. 28: 18-20.*   The prominent features emphasized by Jesus in Matthew's record are:

a. His authority or right to give the commission. This also served as a motive for their unprecedented task.

b. The duty of those commissioned, that is, the preachers.

c. Not anything is said directly about the duty of the lost, or those to whom the preaching was to be done.

(2) *Mark 16: 15, 16.* In this record we find:

a. The duty of the preachers, including the subject matter to be preached, and the extent of the territory to be covered.

b. That which is expected of the hearers, together with the consequences which will follow their response, or non-response, to the gospel.

(3) *Luke 24: 46, 47.* Prominently mentioned in this record are:

a. The great fundamental or basic truths of the gospel. Cf. 1 Cor. 15: 1-4.

b. The fact that these things were foretold in the Old Testament Scriptures. Cf. 2 Tim. 3: 15.

c. The subject matter to be preached, together with their authority for preaching it, as well as the ground upon which sinners might expect the remission of their sins.

d. The beginning point and the territory to be covered. The first preaching was to be done in Jerusalem, thus making the first overtures of mercy to his murderers.

(4) *John 20: 21-23.* We find the following facts emphasized in this record:

a. As Jesus had been sent by the Father, just so were his disciples to be sent by him.

b. He promised them the Holy Spirit.

c. He made known to them the authority and the results which would accompany their preaching.

(5) *2 Cor. 5: 18-20.* In this passage Paul sets forth the following facts:

a. The grand Source of all things, namely, God.

b. The One through whom the work of redemption is accomplished—Christ.

c. Those to whom he entrusted the ministry of reconciliation —the apostles. *They were his ambassadors and the executors of his will.*

2. Once the work was committed to their hands, the Lord never spoke directly to the people of the earth regarding their salvation again. Cf. 2 Cor. 4: 7; Acts 22: 10.

3. The Lord made possible the salvation of every man (Heb. 2: 9); but the terms upon which salvation may be received must be learned from the apostles, or inspired messengers.

II. A GENERAL SUMMARY

1. Considering the commission as a whole, we find,

(1) That God is seeking to redeem the lost through his Son.

(2) That the Son was sent to the earth as the Father's special representative, and that by his death and resurrection the salvation of the human race was made possible.

(3) That the Son chose his apostles as his representatives, and commissioned them to make known to the world the terms of salvation, "beginning from Jerusalem."

(4) That they were told to preach faith, repentance, and baptism, and to promise salvation from past sins to all who would comply with these conditions.

(5) That they were forbidden to begin their work until they were clothed with power from on high. See Luke 24: 49. Acts 1: 8 and 2: 1-4 tell us when the power came.

2. These facts must be kept clearly in mind, if we are to understand and appreciate the work which the apostles and early disciples did in carrying out the terms of the Great Commission.

III. THE PROCESS AT WORK

1. The Book of Acts contains a record of the work of the apostles and early Christians in executing the commission. As has already been seen, their work was to begin in Jerusalem; and it is there that we must go, if we would know that which the executors understood and did about the Lord's charge to them.

2. Acts 2: 1-4 shows that the day of Pentecost, the first Pentecost following the Lord's resurrection, was the beginning date of this work.

(1) Pentecost was one of the three great annual feasts of the law of Moses, which all the men of the Jewish world were expected to attend; and since the gospel was to be preached to the Jews first (cf. Acts 13: 44-46; Rom. 1: 16), there was no better time nor place to begin preaching it than the one mentioned here. Cf. Acts 2: 5. Jesus had been condemned at the first of these annual feasts, and now he is to be vindicated at the second.

(2) The demonstrations which accompanied the outpouring of the Holy Spirit served to bring the multitudes to a place within hearing distance of the apostles; and it was to this great audience, those who had killed the Son of God, being, of course, unbelievers—that the executors first made known the terms of salvation.

3. With these facts before us, and keeping in mind the things which Jesus commanded them to preach, let us see that which they did on this memorable occasion.

(1) The first thing they needed to do was to induce their hearers to change their minds regarding Jesus, that is, become believers in him.

(2) Acts 2: 14-36 contains a record of Peter's sermon to them; and in it he pointed out the following facts:

a. The things which they were hearing and seeing had been foretold by their own prophets. See Joel 2: 28-32.

b. Jesus was approved of God unto them by the mighty works which God did by him in their midst.

c. Their inspired speaker charged his hearers with the Lord's crucifixion, but made it plain that death could not hold him, for God raised him up to sit on David's throne; and having received of the Father the promise of the Holy Spirit, Jesus was responsible for that which they saw and heard.

d. Peter then called upon them to "know assuredly," or *believe with confidence,* "that God hath made him both Lord and Christ, this Jesus whom ye crucified." Cf. Heb. 11: 6; John 17: 20; Acts 14: 1; Rom. 10: 17.

4. The effects of the sermon.

(1) Verse 37. These words clearly imply that the inquirers accepted as true that which Peter had said regarding Christ; and that they had changed their minds about him, that is, they were now believers in him.

(2) *Verses 38, 39.* Peter's answer, together with his sermon which had caused them to believe in Christ, clearly shows that the executors of the Lord's commission were doing exactly that which Jesus had told them to do, namely, preach faith, repentance, and baptism, and offer salvation, or the remission of sins, to all who comply with these conditions.

(3) *Verses 40, 41.* These newly made disciples, and those who were later converted to Christ in that city, were afterwards referred to as "the church which was in Jerusalem." See Acts 8: 1; cf. 5: 11.

(4) Referring to the events of Pentecost, Orchard, a leading Baptist historian, says, "This Christian assembly as it was the first, so it is the mother church in the Christian dispensation." (Vol. I, p. 7.)

5. Then, in various sections of the country, and following the plan outlined in Acts 1: 8, the disciples preached the gospel, people heard it, believed it, and obeyed it, and were, according to the Lord's promise, saved from their sins.

(1) In this way churches were established, which, in turn, continued to sound out the word (1 Thess. 1: 8) until Paul was able to say, about thirty years after the beginning on that first Pentecost, that the gospel had been "preached in all creation under heaven." See Col. 1: 23.

(2) Letters were written to many of these congregations, and several of them have been preserved in the New Testament.

(3) Concerning the work in Corinth, it is said, "And many of the Corinthians hearing believed, and were baptized (Acts 18: 8); and when Paul sent his letters to them, he addressed them, "Unto the church of God which is at Corinth" (1 Cor. 1: 2; 2 Cor. 1: 1).

6. A careful examination of the record will reveal that in every case the same gospel was preached; and that those who did as

the Lord wanted them to do believed it, repented of their sins, and were baptized in the name of Jesus Christ for the remission of their sins. Cf. Gal. 1: 6-9.

(1) It is a settled fact that Peter on the day of Pentecost, guided by the Holy Spirit, preached faith, repentance, and baptism to the great multitudes gathered there; and the record just as plainly declares that that was the plan followed by Paul in Corinth.

(2) Gal. 3: 26, 27 plainly shows that obedience to such preaching made the obedient the Lord's people; and when these facts are all considered in the light of Paul's statement in Gal. 1: 6-9, it is easy to see that which the Lord expects of people today. He will not countenance a change in his plan, as Gal. 1: 6-9 plainly declares.

◆ ◆ ◄

THERE WERE THREE CROSSES ON GOLGOTHA
John 19: 17, 18

Introduction: 1. One of the most familiar terms used to designate the place of our Lord's crucifixion is Calvary. Many sermons and songs in honor of Christ owe their inspiration to this well known and deeply loved name. Cf. songs, "On the Cross of Calvary" and "The Old Rugged Cross." 2. The term "Calvary," however, is not a New Testament word. It has come to us through the Latin *calvaria*. The original New Testament word is *Golgotha*, which means a skull, and was probably so-called because of the shape of the mound or hill on which Jesus was crucified. 3. There were, according to the text, three crosses on Golgotha, or Calvary, but we nearly always refer to *the* cross of Calvary, as if there was only one. Two others were crucified with Jesus, he being in the midst. The other two men were robbers, but the Roman governor who sentenced Jesus to die found no fault in him. Cf. Luke 23: 14; Matt. 27: 22-24. But since three men were crucified on Golgotha on that fateful day, let us look at the three crosses one by one.

I. ON ONE CROSS A MAN DIED *in* SIN

1. This man had lived as a robber, and he died as a robber. (It should be observed that the correct rendering of the original is *robber,* not *thief.* See Thayer, *in loco,* and cf. Trench, *New Testament Synonyms,* pp. 157-160.)

2. This man had lived in rebellion against the laws of both God and man, and as he paid the penalty for his crimes he remained bitter and impenitent to the end. The agony of death brought no softening to his hard heart; no word of regret to his lips; no tear of repentance to his cheek. Only bitterness, railing, and abuse characterized him in his dying hour.

3. Among the objects of his bitterness was Jesus himself. See Luke 23: 39. He wanted salvation from the cross, but he wanted

it on his own terms. That is still the spirit which characterizes many even today. Jesus, however, has not promised to save us *from* the cross, but *through* the cross, both his and ours. Cf. Eph. 2: 16; Luke 14: 27.

II. On Another Cross a Man Died *to* Sin

1. This man had also been a robber and was dying for his crimes, but he had come to himself and was pleading for mercy.

2. It is possible that he, for the first time in his life, was seeing things in their true light. At any rate, his thinking was straight as he hung there on the cross. This is evident, because,

(1) He admitted the justice of his own suffering and death, Luke 23: 40, 41.

(2) He called on Jesus for mercy, but made no demands, Luke 23: 42.

(3) He expressed no doubt regarding Jesus. In response to his humble cry of faith, he received an infinitely precious promise, Luke 23: 43.

III. On the Central Cross a Man Died *for* Sin

1. When we look at that cross, it is almost enough to make us ashamed that we are a part of the human race. At least, it ought to be enough to make us ashamed, not only for the sins of the race, but, and what is more to the point, our own sins.

2. Jesus died for *our* sins, and in a very true sense *we* spat upon him, *we* pressed the crown of thorns down upon his brow, and *we* nailed him to the cross.

3. But God is able to make the wrath of man praise him. He is able to make of the cross a means for our salvation. Cf. Isa. 53: 4, 5; 2 Cor. 5: 21; Rom. 3: 25, 26.

4. When Jesus prayed for the forgiveness of those who cruci-fied him, he was by his own death on the cross making possible the only means by which that prayer could be answered. If Jesus had not died as he did, all the penitence in the world could not have brought the dying robber, nor any one else, to Paradise.

Conclusion: Let us, therefore, re-emphasize and firmly fix in our minds the lesson of the three crosses:

1. The first one teaches that even the power of God cannot save the rebellious and unbelieving.

2. The second one teaches that the Son of God hears the weakest cry of the worst sinner in his great extremity.

3. But when we look at the central cross we see that "in none other is there salvation."

> When I survey the wondrous cross
> On which the Prince of glory died
> My richest gain I count but loss
> And pour contempt on all my pride.
> Forbid it, Lord, that I should boast,

Save in the death of Christ, my Lord;
All the vain things that charm me most,
I sacrifice them to his blood.
See, from his head, his hands, his feet,
Sorrow and love flow mingled down;
Did e'er such love and sorrow meet,
Or thorns compose so rich a crown?
Were the whole realm of nature mine,
That were a present far too small;
Love so amazing, so divine,
Demands my soul, my life, my all.

❖ ❖ ❖

"IN ALL GOOD CONSCIENCE"
Acts 23: 1

Introduction: 1. The term "conscience" is strictly a New Testament word. It does not occur at all in the Old Testament, but the idea which is conveyed by the word is found in practically all parts of the Bible. 2. Except for John 8: 9 (King James Version), the word does not occur in the gospel records. It is found twice in Acts and three times in First Peter. Paul used the term more than any other New Testament writer. If we regard Hebrews as his production, Paul used the word twenty-five times in his epistles (American Standard Version). He also spoke the word in both of its occurrences in Acts. 3. If one, therefore, would like to have a personal illustration of the teaching of the New Testament regarding the conscience, he can do no better than to go to the apostle Paul. 4. The average man today has no greater need than that of recognizing the place of conscience in his own life, and of cultivating a consideration of its demands at any cost. But in studying this lesson, let us ask,

I. What Is the Conscience?

1. It is not merely an intuition by which one determines right from wrong, nor is it an independent and unregulated source of law. If these things were so we would have no need for the Word of God.

2. Conscience is a part of the native equipment with which man is endowed. Some one has defined conscience as "the sense within us by which we approve or disapprove for having followed or failed to follow a moral standard known to us." Cf. Rom. 2: 12-15.

(1) If one is following this moral standard, he will have a *good,* that is, an approving conscience (Acts 23: 1; 1 Tim. 1: 5, 19; Heb. 13: 18; 1 Pet. 3: 16, 21). He will, as a result of this, have a *pure* conscience (1 Tim. 3: 9; 2 Tim. 1: 3), or a conscience *void of offence* (Acts 24: 16).

(2) But if one is not following this moral standard, he will have an *evil* conscience (Heb. 10: 22), or a *defiled* conscience

(Tit. 1: 15; 1 Cor. 8: 7). When one continues an evil course until he becomes insensible to all feeling, his conscience is *branded,* or *seared,* "as with a hot iron" (1 Tim. 4: 2).

II. The Determining Factor

1. It should be remembered, however, that it is the *judgment,* and not the *conscience,* which determines that which is right or wrong. The office of the conscience is not to judge, but to execute. It is a faithful monitor, or, to use a figure, it is the sheriff which faithfully carries out the decisions of the reason or judgment, "whether they be right or wrong; whether they be true or false; whether they be just or unjust."

2. It is the judgment which must determine that which is right or wrong, and this, in turn, will depend upon the standard which is adopted. One adopts a standard as the result of his surroundings and the influences which mold his thought (Prov. 23: 7), or what is properly embraced in the term *education.*

3. This explains why people can act differently regarding the same thing, and still have a good, or an approving, conscience. For example, baptism, the Lord's supper, the contribution, and many other similar questions. Cf. John 7: 17.

III. Conscientious Service Is Demanded

1. Paul lays down the law that a man should follow his own conscience, even though it be weak. If this is not done, moral personality will be destroyed. Cf. 1 Cor. 8: 10f.

2. But a good conscience alone will not suffice. Paul always had an approving conscience, because he always acted conscientiously; but he was, nevertheless, prior to his conversion, a very great sinner, due to the fact that his reason erred. Cf. 1 Tim. 1: 12-16.

3. No amount of conscientious service, therefore, will avail in the sight of God, unless it is based upon right standards. Cf. John 16: 1, 2; Matt. 7: 21-23; 1 Cor. 4: 2-4; John 12: 48-50.

4. All acceptable service must be properly motivated—it must be done with an aim to please God. See 2 Cor. 5: 9. It is not enough to be conscientious in one thing, and indifferent in another; we must endeavor to do all that which God commands. Cf. Matt. 28: 20a; James 2: 10; 4: 17.

IV. The Fruits of a Good Conscience

1. *A good conscience makes a high degree of spiritual enthusiasm possible.* To be dubious about the moral quality of a cause is to cut the nerve of one's enthusiasm for it; but a cause which has the approving conscience of its adherents behind it will have the assurance that the best they have will be put into it. Cf. Acts **8: 1-4.**

2. *It prompts a man to endeavor to be ready to meet every challenge which the world places before him.* Cf. 1 Pet. 3: 15.

3. *It helps a man to live down slander and gives him warmth to weather out every storm of unjust criticism.* Cf. 1 Pet. 3: 16. This would not be possible, if his conscience accused him of doing wrong.

> My good blade carves the casques of men,
>   My tough lance thrusteth sure,
> My strength is as the strength of ten,
>   Because my heart is pure.

> *—Tennyson*

◆ ◆ ◆

A HUMBLE DELIVERANCE
Judges 3: 31

Introduction: 1. The checkered history of Israel is interestingly set forth in the Book of Judges. Following the death of Joshua and his contemporaries, the people, because of their sins, were frequently subjugated by the nations about them; but when they repented and cried unto Jehovah, he raised up a judge who delivered them from their distress. 2. It is thought by some that the third of these judges was a humble ox driver; but, whatever his station in life, his sole weapon was an ox-goad, and God used him to lead the people to their freedom. 3. The name of this judge was Shamgar and he lived in a distressful period in Israel's history. Something of their deplorable condition may be learned by reading Judg. 5: 6-8; 1 Sam. 13: 19-22; 12: 9. They had forsaken God, and he, accordingly, had forsaken them. The people were afraid to walk in the highways, and their crops had been destroyed or taken away from them. Their weapons of warfare had also been taken away, and they had no chance to make any more. The morale of the nation had been broken, and they had lost confidence in themselves and faith in God. Their need for a righteous leader, therefore, was great. But in studying this lesson, let us consider,

I. SHAMGAR THE MAN

1. His name occurs only twice in the entire Bible, and there is not much said about him in those places. But, like many others who have served a righteous cause, it was not necessary that much be said about him in order for him to be a faithful servant of the Lord.

> Full many a gem of purest ray serene
>   The dark, unfathomed caves of ocean bear:
> Full many a flower is born to blush unseen,
>   And waste its sweetness on the desert air.

> *—Thomas Gray*

2. From the brief record which is given, one would naturally conclude that Shamgar's station in life was a humble one. There is no indication that he was a man of royal birth or military training—perhaps only an ox-driver.

II. Why Did God Choose Him?

1. Certainly not because of his disadvantages, but because he possessed those qualities which made it possible for God to use him for this great service.

2. What were some of the qualities which he possessed?

(1) *A noble spirit of discontent.*

a. Much of our discontent is ignoble, e. g., homes, automobiles, clothing, etc.

b. Some of our discontent is born of mere restlessness. We want to be entertained or going somewhere all the time.

c. There was no littleness in Shamgar's discontent. He saw the conditions in which his people were, and he was filled with a desire to improve them. It is bad enough to be in a deplorable condition, but still worse to be satisfied to remain therein. *The same is true of careless, indifferent, and sinful church members.**

(2) *He was a man of faith.* He could see their difficulties and weaknesses as well as others could, but he could also see the forces which make for conquest. It does not take much faith to say, "I believe that God uses men in his service," but it requires great faith to say, "I believe that God wants *me* to do this or that."

(3) *He dared to make a beginning.* When the enemy came upon him he ventured to fight, in spite of the littleness of his weapon. He could have refused to fight and have offered as his excuse that he was greatly outnumbered and that his opponents were all well armed. That, however, would not have been a valid excuse, and he, accordingly, did not use it.

---

*There is a story told of an eagle that was hatched along with a family of chickens. His fellow chicks laughed at this awkward, brownish bird. He looked very funny to them as he tried to pick up the little grains of feed in the barnyard with his great hooked beak. He seemed to those chickens strangely out of place. And, good to say, he seemed to himself still more strangely out of place. He did not know exactly what he was made for, but he was sure that he was not made for the barnyard. So day after day he stood the picture of discontent, the embodiment of wretchedness.

But one sunny morning a tiny speck appeared in the distant sky. Then there was a strange wild call from the heights. And this ridiculous "chick," which had been the laughing stock of the barnyard, looked up as if he understood the wild cry. The call came again and nearer, and then it seemed that fire suddenly began to glow in the lusterless eyes of that "barnyard" fowl. With that he spread his great brown wings and circled above the barnyard, and was soon off to the freedom of his mountain wilds. He was made for the cloudland and the mountain heights, and he could never, therefore, be content to scratch among the filth of the barnyard. Cf. Luke 15: 11ff.

III. WHAT WAS THE OUTCOME OF SHAMGAR'S EFFORTS?

1. He won the fight, as all men do who put themselves on the Lord's side. The lad with the loaves and fishes could not feed the multitudes, but he could do his part by bringing them to Jesus. If Shamgar used what he had and did his best, the result was up to the Lord.

2. Not only did he win deliverance for himself, but for his people as well. Not only was he blessed himself; he became a blessing to others.

Conclusion: What does the Lord mean to you at this moment? If you will do what you can now, you may expect greater opportunities in the future. Cf. Matt. 13: 12. No one who has an opportunity should wait for an easier time or place for service. The Lord will bless every one who does his part; and in that way he will not only be blessed himself; he will become a blessing to others.

❖ ❖ ❖

THE MAN WHO DISTURBED PEOPLE
Luke 23: 5

Introduction: 1. As one reads the news reports in the religious papers he is impressed with the number of preachers who are enjoying ministries which are both pleasant and peaceful; and when they decide to make a change it is nearly always due to their own "free will and accord," even though no plans for the future have been made. 2. Now every one must admit that such conditions are certainly desirable; but when one remembers what the New Testament says about the lives of Christ and his early disciples, he is made to wonder just how these undisturbed conditions can exist today in this sinful world, along with so much worldliness, indifference, and actual wrong-doing in the church. 3. No inspired man ever said that Jesus lived undisturbed or undisturbingly. He was, on the contrary, the great disturber of men. Cf. Matt. 10: 34-39. No gathering in which Jesus spoke remained comfortable, and those who loved ease and pleasant things considered him a troublemaker. His disciples were accused of turning the world upside down, and Paul, perhaps his most illustrious follower, had serious trouble in some of the churches which he established. 4. It should be observed, however, that neither Christ nor his disciples ever caused trouble simply for the thrill of it, or even to have their own way. It was their devotion to the truth which brought about the disturbing conditions for which they were responsible. *Loyalty to the truth is the only excuse which any faithful Christian is justified in offering for being considered a troublemaker or a disturber of the peace.* Truth and error are diametrically opposed to each other, and no person can

be loyal to the truth while winking at or compromising with error.
5. Furthermore, when one allows himself to get into a condition
in which, for the sake of peace and the goodwill of the people,
he is afraid to discuss any question which involves the truth, and
which vitally affects the eternal welfare of himself and others, it
cannot be correctly said of him that he is devoted to the cause for
which Jesus died. But in studying this lesson, let us ask, What
was there about Jesus that disturbed people?

I. THE QUALITY OF HIS LIFE MADE SINNERS UNCOMFORTABLE

1. Like the brilliance of the sun, showing up the dirt on the
window-pane, the transcendent life of Christ revealed the imper-
fections of men. Cf. Luke 5: 8. However, there was nothing
unusual about Peter's response to the amazing life and goodness
of Jesus. Even today when we evaluate our lives by the life of
Christ, our first impulse is a feeling of utter unworthiness. Like
Isaiah, we cry: Isa. 6: 5.

2. Wherever Jesus went he shocked people with the refulgent
beauty of his spirit; and men, even of rank and influence, were
disquieted by his incomparable attractiveness.

(1) Nicodemus was a teacher in Israel whose interests lay in
the orthodoxies of the ecclesiastical *status quo,* but after a memorable night with Jesus, he was later found with courage enough to
defend the common rights of Christ in the face of overwhelming
odds; and, after Jesus had been crucified, it was Nicodemus, along
with Joseph of Arimathea, who gave Jesus a respectable burial.

(2) The rich young ruler was a complacent young man, but
when Jesus challenged him to a daring venture, to part with his
property and join the spiritual movement which was to remake
the world, "he went away sorrowful."

(3) Zacchaeus was a tax-collector who was apparently content with his ill-gotten gains, but after a visit with the Lord he
found himself in trouble. After the searching personality of Jesus
had penetrated his conscience, he found it necessary to make some
drastic readjustments in his own life, which he did by announcing
his intention of giving half of his goods to feed the poor, and to
reimburse fourfold any from whom he had wrongfully exacted
anything.

(4) Then, too, the woman of Samaria was apparently at ease
on that day when, with waterpot in hand, she had come to Jacob's
well for some water, but after her talk with Jesus she was not at
ease. With five husbands to her credit, and the man she was
then living with not her husband, she found that she would have
to clear up that domestic mess, or never know another peaceful
moment. Indeed, she was in trouble.

II. Jesus Disturbed People with His Ideas

1. "Thoughts that breathe and words that burn" always characterized Jesus wherever he went. He did not hesitate to call in question and criticize the most revered practices and institutions of his day; but it was never simply for the sake of criticizing. He knew whereof he spoke; and when the people heard him they "were astonished at his teaching: for he taught them as one having authority, and not as their scribes."

2. The leader who stirs us up and causes us to think usually incurs our displeasure. It is difficult to break camp and set forth on new intellectual pilgrimages; and it is for this reason that we much prefer to be let alone.

3. But Jesus spoke words that set men on their feet—powerful and revolutionary words; and it is no wonder that the common people heard him gladly.

III. Jesus Disturbed People with His Ethical Considerations

1. He knew the ineffectiveness of an evanescent piety, and he did not, therefore, hesitate to condemn all ostentatious acts of devotion. See Matt. 6: 1ff.

2. With Jesus it was deeds, not words, that determined the real value of a man's religion. See Matt. 7: 21. Moreover, that which is done must be authorized by Christ. Just any deeds, however pious they may be, will not suffice. Cf. Matt. 7: 22, 23.

3. This young Galilean teacher uttered some very strange things, so far as the world was concerned, when he forbade all acts of retaliation and taught men to love their enemies. But Jesus was a teacher come from God, not from man.

4. Some one has said that the business of religion is to comfort the afflicted and to afflict the comfortable; and if we give ourselves wholly to Jesus, that is exactly what will take place in and through us. If we follow his teaching, he will show us the needs of the people; and if we are faithful to him we will obey his commands.

IV. Jesus Disturbed People by His Attitude toward the Cross

1. People then, as they are now, were seeking for a life of ease, but Jesus offered them a cross. Cf. Luke 9: 23.

2. The idea that one can be a Christian and go through this life undisturbed has no foundation in the teaching of the New Testament. Jesus never admitted any one into his fellowship without first informing him of the cost of discipleship. Cf. Matt. 16: 24-26; Luke 9: 57-62.

3. Any one, therefore, is sorely mistaken if he thinks that he can have the good life which leads to heaven on his own terms.

There are no short-cuts to God, and it ever remains true that "the way of the cross leads home." Cf. Matt. 11: 25-30; John 6: 44, 45; Rom. 1: 16; Mark 16: 15, 16; Acts 2: 42.

❖ ❖ ❖

DIVISION VERSUS UNITY
1 Cor. 1: 10

Introduction: 1. One of the cardinal doctrines of the New Testament is the unity of all believers in Christ. Jesus does not teach any conflicting doctrines; and no one can be pleasing to him who either teaches or adheres to such. 2. But it is next to useless to call upon the religious world to unite while those who claim to stand upon the Bible alone ignore its teaching regarding this question. 3. Many of the passages which are commonly used to condemn sectarian division, as that expression is generally understood, were written primarily for the purpose of correcting internal conditions in local congregations. But in studying this lesson, let us consider,

I. TWO ASPECTS OF DIVISION

1. There are divisions which result from doing the right thing. Cf. Matt. 10: 34-37. No one is justified in rejecting the truth, or even compromising any part of it, in order to have peace with those who are not in sympathy with the Lord's teaching, either because of their outright rejecting of it or because they fail to understand it.

2. There are divisions which result from wrong doing. Cf. Luke 17: 1, 2; 1 Cor. 11: 18, 19.

II. HOW DOES THE LORD REGARD DISCORD AMONG BRETHREN?

1. He hates those who by their unfaithfulness and disobedience bring it about. See Prov. 6: 16-19.

2. All such will be denied entrance into heaven, unless they repent. Cf. Gal. 5: 19-21.

III. APOSTOLIC EXHORTATIONS

1. All professed followers of Christ are exhorted to strive for perfect unity. See 1 Cor. 1: 10.

2. They are to avoid those who cause divisions, "contrary to the doctrine which ye learned." See Rom. 16: 17; Tit. 3: 10.

(1) "The doctrine which ye learned" does not refer to that which is learned from uninspired men; for even the best of them are sometimes mistaken. The reference is to that which was taught by inspired teachers—that which is now found in the New Testament—, when correctly understood. Cf. John 7: 17; Psalm 119: 99.

(2) "A factious man" is not one who contends for the truth in the face of opposition; for if that makes a man a heretic, then

every reformer, regardless of the correctness of his views, would be a factious man. A factious man is one who introduces questions and practices which are clearly out of harmony with the teaching of the New Testament. It isn't very hard to identify a factious man, even aside from his teaching; for his very disposition betrays him. Cf. 1 Cor. 11 : 16; 1 John 2 : 19; Matt. 18 : 15-17.

Some men endeavor to stop all investigation respecting everything on which they have pronounced. And, lest they should not be regarded as the end of all wisdom, they make every effort to destroy every hypothesis which in any way seems to call in question any position they have taken. Not every one who opposes such a spirit as that is a heretic, and it is a misuse of Titus 3 : 10 to brand him as a factious man.

IV. THE SAVIOUR'S PRAYER AND AN APOSTLE'S PLEADING

1. Jesus prayed for unity among his followers, and from that prayer we can learn what ideal unity is. See John 17 : 20, 21.

2. The Apostle Paul has plainly taught how this ideal unity may be attained. See Eph. 4 : 1-6. "The unity of the Spirit" is not merely a fraternal attitude which looks with favor upon divergent and conflicting views, but is the unity of which the Spirit is the author. The Spirit is a *teacher*, not merely an influence; and when people listen to him and follow that which he has revealed, as contained in the New Testament, they will be one.

> How blest and how joyous will be the glad day,
> When heart beats to heart in the work of the Lord;
> When Christians united shall swell the grand lay,
> Divisions all ended, triumphant his word!
>
> Come, brothers and sisters and join in the fight,
> Our Saviour and Captain has bidden us come;
> Then on with the armor, and dare to do right,
> Press on in the struggle till Christians are one.
>
> The pray'r of our Saviour impels us, move on,
> Its words are still sounding the call of our King;
> And Paul, in devotion, doth echo the song,
> "I beg you, my brethren, to speak the same thing."
>
> Be faithful and true till the warfare is o'er,
> Till factions are foiled and the vict'ry is won;
> And millions of voices shall blend on the shore,
> To welcome us enter our Father's glad home.
>
> —*M. C. Kurfees*

◆ ◆ ◆

FAITH IN A FALSEHOOD
2 Thess. 2: 8-12

Introduction: Faith is an essential condition to a life that is well-pleasing to God. Cf. Heb. 11 : 6. The reason why faith is so important is that a person's whole life will be affected by that which he sincerely believes to be true. Cf. Prov. 23 : 7. However, there is a world of difference when it comes to the proposition that is believed; for it is a well known fact that a false report, and the faith that is based upon it, may have the same effect upon a person that would have been produced, had the report been true. Cf. Gen. 37 : 1-36. And, too, the reception of a falsehood may unfit the mind for the reception of the truth. See Gen. 45 : 25-28. But in studying this lesson, let us consider,

I. SOME IMPORTANT EXHORTATIONS

1. "Take heed *what* ye hear," Mark 4 : 24. This should include,

(1) The nature of that which is heard. See Rom. 16 : 17, 18; Col. 2 : 8; cf. 1 Cor. 4 : 6; 2 John 9.

(2) One should never show disinterest in or contempt for teaching, until he knows from whence it comes. Cf. 1 Cor. 1 : 21; John 6 : 44, 45.

2. "Take heed therefore *how* ye hear," Luke 8 : 18. We must listen to God's word, whether it pleases us or not. Cf. Isa. 55 : 8, 9 and contrast Balaam's attitude (Num. 22 : 19) with that of Cornelius (Acts 10 : 33).

3. Take heed *whom* ye hear, Matt. 17 : 1-5. Cf. Luke 10 : 16; John 12 : 48-50; Acts 3 : 22, 23.

II. SOME BIBLE EXAMPLES AND RESULTS

1. Satan's lie, Gen. 3 : 1-24.

2. The ten spies, Num. 13 : 25-33; 14 : 1-45.

3. The false prophet's lie, 1 Kings 13 : 1-32.

III. AN INEVITABLE CONCLUSION

1. To reject the truth and believe a lie will result in eternal condemnation. Cf. John 8 : 31, 32; 2 Thess. 2 : 8-12.

2. What about people who are honestly mistaken? A few questions should help one to see the truth here:

(1) Do such people, that is, those who are considered honestly mistaken, desire, above everything else, to know and to do the will of God? See John 7 : 17.

(2) Do they make a sincere effort to learn the truth? Cf. Matt. 13 : 12.

(3) When any one tries to tell them the truth, do they carefully weigh that which is said? See Acts 17 : 11; cf. John 9 : 34; Acts 22 : 18.

3. An example and a lesson: 1 Kings 13 : 1-32; cf. Mark 16 : 15, 16. In view of the example of the conflicting voices in 1 Kings 13 : 1-32, what should be one's attitude toward a teacher who says that baptism is not essential to salvation? Cf. Acts 10 : 47, 48; 1 Pet. 3 : 21.

THE TRUE TEST OF FAITH
James 2: 22

Introduction: There is an infallible test of faith—it is always identified by its deeds. Like "a city set on a hill," it "cannot be hid." A man may not say much about what he believes, but if he is sincere his actions will declare his faith. The deeds of a man with an honest and good heart will make known, not only his faith, but the quality of it as well. But in studying this lesson, let us begin by considering,

I. THE TEST GIVEN BY JESUS

1. Jesus left us the acid test for faith and it must be applied to two phases of Christian expression—viz:

(1) John 8: 31, 32. Genuine faith in Christ compels faithfulness to his teaching. That which Jesus taught will be accepted as final in the realm of truth. The teaching of Christ will never be misapplied by any one who really believes in him. All that he said regarding himself, his mission to the earth, his church, and his plan for saving the lost will be faithfully taught by those who believe in him.

(2) John 14: 15. As Jesus used the term, love is not a mere sentiment or emotion. It is an active principle which motivates life; it is always measured in deeds. The true believer will always keep the commandments of Jesus, it matters not what they may be. He will not evade them, nor offer a substitute for them; he will keep them. Cf. 1 Cor. 4: 6; 2 John 9.

2. Faith in Christ is an unreserved acknowledgement that he is both Lord and Christ. As such he is invested with authority; and he must be heard and obeyed. John 3: 36; Acts 3: 22, 23. Faith only will never suffice. See James 2: 14-26.

II. FAITH AND WORKS

1. Some people have taken Paul's statement in Rom. 5: 1 to mean that he was teaching the doctrine of "salvation by faith only." This, however, is a misinterpretation of the passage. If one will take into consideration Paul's purpose in writing the Roman letter he will see that the apostle was directing his arguments against the Judaizers who were endeavoring to fasten the law of Moses upon Christians. In contrasting "faith" and "works," Paul was simply contrasting the two religious systems of Moses and Christ.

2. The law of Moses required acts of obedience which could only be done by conforming to statutory enactments. It was therefore a system of works; and since nothing but perfect obedience would count for salvation under that system, Paul was arguing that no one was ever saved by the law.

3. Jesus was the only one who ever kept the law of Moses

perfectly; and by his accepting the death sentence and dying under the law, he took "it out of the way, nailing it to the cross" (Col. 2: 14), and set up instead his own system of "salvation by grace," or forgiveness through obedience to him. Cf. Heb. 5: 8, 9.

4. Thus, when Paul was dealing with "works" in the Book of Romans he was not discussing right living as such, but a religious system; and in like manner, when he wrote of "faith," he was not referring to "faith alone," but to *another religious system,* whereby its adherents obtain salvation by faithfully following Christ.

5. Salvation is the free gift of God, through Jesus Christ our Lord, given to those who accept Christ as their Lord, and prove their faith in him by their obedience to him. Cf. Acts 16: 30-34.

III. WALKING BY FAITH

1. He who walks by faith walks by the guidance of another. He has not traveled that road before, and does not himself know the way. He cannot therefore walk by sight, but, having absolute confidence in the one whom he trusts to lead him, he is able to walk by faith. Cf. Heb. 11: 1. Edward Robinson translated this passage as follows:

Faith is confidence as to things hoped for; conviction as to things not seen.

2. The eleventh chapter of Hebrews gives the New Testament teaching on faith, both in its definition and application; and it will be seen in the study of that chapter that faith is more than mere intellectual assent. It is trust in God which will lead to unquestioning obedience to his will. Without obedience there is no true faith. Cf. John 3: 36; James 2: 22. Even doing that which God commands would not be acceptable, unless the action was the result of faith. See Heb. 11: 6.

3. Some examples of faith and obedience:

(1) Abel "offered unto God a more excellent sacrifice than Cain," because he offered that which God commanded. Cf. Rom. 10: 17. Cain disregarded God's word, and it was for that reason that he did not offer that which God commanded.

(2) Enoch, we are told, was "well-pleasing unto God," but the writer hastens to assure us that his walking with God was the result of his faith.

(3) Noah's salvation was ascribed to three things—viz., faith, ark, and water. See Heb. 11: 7; 1 Pet. 3: 20. Now, if salvation is by faith alone, how can it be by something else too? Not only was Noah saved by faith, but in his conduct we have a clear example of the strength of faith necessary to save, or when faith is strong enough to save.

Observe that, being warned of God, he was moved with godly fear. To what extent was he moved? His faith was strong enough to move him to do exactly that which God told him to do;

and as a result of his obedience he was saved. Does any one
think that Noah would have been saved if he had refused to do
that which God commanded him to do? One may search the entire Bible through, but he will not find any other principle upon
which men may be saved. Each one must believe God, and then
do that which God tells *him* to do.

(4) Abraham, Heb. 11: 8-10.

4. Rationally viewed, there is no conflict between being "justified by faith" and being "justified by works"; for faith includes
all the works which God requires, and, as has been observed by
Canon Wescott, "this simple formula contains the complete solution of the relation of faith and works." Justification is the reward of those who obey through faith. See Eph. 2: 8-10. The
true test of faith is in what it leads one to do. Cf. Mark 16: 15,
16.

◆ ◆ ◆

THE CONQUEST OF FEAR
2 Tim. 1: 7

Introduction: 1. One of the problems common to mankind
today is that of fear. But notwithstanding the fact that the Bible
frequently speaks of fear, comparatively little is said on the subject by the average preacher. Cf. Luke 12: 4, 5; Phil. 4: 6, 7, 13;
Heb. 13: 5, 6. 2. These statements do not mean that there is
no place in our lives for fear, and that we should try to eliminate
it altogether. Fear has been described as the elemental alarm
system of the human organism, being one of our primary and indispensable instincts. That condition is what keeps us from being
run over by automobiles, from disobeying doctors' orders, from
being contented with unsanitary conditions in our daily living, etc.,
etc. The fear of ignorance is one of the reasons why we endeavor
to get an eductaion; and the fear of foreign domination is a major
cause for the nation's unprecedented war effort. Thus, there is a
wholesome fear which runs all through life, not only guarding us
from danger, but positively driving us to constructive enterprises
of personal and public protection. This shows, of course, that in
dealing with this problem we are not to try to get rid of fear, as
such; but our efforts should be to harness it and thereby become its
master. 3. Then over against the ordinary meaning of the word
fear, we read that "the fear of Jehovah is the beginning of wisdom." (Psalm 111: 10). This does not mean that one is frightened
by the Lord, but that he is filled with reverent awe in his presence.
4. But how are we to bring about the conquest of fear? This
is a serious question and demands a straightforward answer, for
Jesus did not say, "Be not afraid," because he thought that there
was nothing to be afraid of. On the contrary, this is a dangerous
world in which we live, with actualities and possibilities on every

side which sane men will dread. It follows, therefore, that if we desire a fearless life—one which transcends fear, or gains a conquest over it—there are serious conditions which must be fulfilled. For example,

I. We Must Possess a Clean and Upright Moral Life

1. This fact is forcefully illustrated in the first wages of sin. See Gen. 3: 9, 10. Man was afraid after he had disobeyed God.

2. Some people plunge gaily into sin, saying that they are not afraid; but it is a solemn fact that they seldom ever experience another day free from fear. Cf. Prov. 28: 1; Psalm 53: 5. Their unhappy condition is described by Coleridge in *The Ancient Mariner:*

> Like one that on a lonesome road
> Doth walk in fear and dread,
> And having once turned round, walks on
> And turns no more his head;
> Because he knows a frightful fiend
> Doth close behind him tread.

3. As one continues to sin he faces a growing habit. Sin at first dresses itself in garments of liberty and says, "Be free"; but as the inexorable laws of habit take charge that illusory freedom turns out to be the bait to a trap of terrific tyranny. We were free to start, but we are not free to stop; and fears haunt us on every side.

4. Thus, man at his best does desire a life free from unholy fears; and what is there among men which brings more satisfaction than to be able to go out each morning unafraid of any mortal being?

II. We Must Have Great Faith Which Says, "I Can"; "I Will"

1. Another wide area of fear is caused by trying to face the strain of life without adequate interior resources. Cf. the experience of spending a windy night in a tent when one does not know how firm the stakes are, or how stout the ropes may be.

2. It is true that people are not directly responsible for some of the fears from which they suffer, and they cannot, therefore, be cured by anything which they alone can do. Such fears got a long start on them in early childhood from unfortunate accidents, unwise parents, and the like. They now need skilled assistance.

(1) We are told that a normal baby's fear instinct has only two expressions—viz: the dread of falling, and the dread of a loud noise. If that be true, then every other fear which we possess has been accumulated since childhood.

(2) Parents, therefore, have few duties more sacred than to see to it that their children do not catch from them, or from others, unnecessary and abnormal fears.

3. Most of our living, though, belongs to another realm. We try to face the heavy strain of life without adequate spiritual resources—faith, for example.

4. Paul was a fearless man, both intellectually and physically (cf. Gal. 1: 11-17; 2 Cor. 11: 22-27), and his secret is found in such statements as Phil. 4: 12, 13; Rom. 8: 28; 2 Tim. 1: 12.

5. There is something wrong with a man's faith, if it does not furnish him with adequate spiritual resources for life. When one is faced with trials and Fear complains, "I cannot stand that which I must endure," the voice of Faith replies, "Yes, you can." If we listen to either voice long enough its message will become more and more convincing. See 1 Cor. 10: 13; James 1: 2-8. Cf. the struggle which the prodigal son must have experienced before he finally resolved to return to his father.

III. WE MUST EXPERIENCE LOVE WHICH TAKES IN OUR ENEMIES

1. The testimony of the Scriptures: 1 John 4: 18.

2. What are some of the things which we fear today?

(1) We are afraid that some one is going to get ahead of us, or be preferred before us. Cf. Rom. 12: 10.

(2) We are afraid of other people's disapproval, if we do that which we know to be right. This is true both from the standpoint of right living, and of telling others that which they should know.

(3) Jealousy, envy, bitterness, and the like, are forms of fear.

3. What, then, is the cure for such fear? See 1 John 4: 18. This love harbors no dread or suspicion, and is described by Paul in 1 Cor. 13.

◆ ◆ ◆

THE FOREIGN POLICY OF THE CHURCH OF CHRIST
Col. 4: 5

Introduction: 1. A subject which is widely discussed today is that of foreign policy. Leading statesmen of the world are giving much thought to it; for it is becoming more and more evident that nations cannot live to themselves. Each country must realize its relationship and consequent obligations to other nations; and it must, if those relations are to be improved, formulate a foreign policy consistent with the principles of justice and equity. 2. Mr. Walter Lippmann's recent book, *U. S. Foreign Policy,* has attracted wide attention, and that which he says regarding this nation may be well used to illustrate the subject now before us. 3. Mr. Lippmann argues that any successful foreign policy must be based on the principle of bringing into balance commitments and power of enforcement; and that if this is done a sound foreign policy will follow, just as surely as a sound fiscal policy will result from the proper consideration of one's assets and liabilities. 4. Mr. Lippmann further points out that these foreign commitments involve obligations which may, in the final analysis, have to be met by waging war; and the power he refers to is the force which is necessary to prevent such a war, or to win it if it cannot be prevented. Neither of these factors can be ignored or neglected, if the country's foreign policy is to remain solvent. But in studying this lesson, let us consider.

I. THE CHURCH'S NEED OF A FOREIGN POLICY

1. In order to understand this subject, one must have a fairly clear idea of the relation between the church and the world about it.

2. The church is spoken of as the kingdom of Christ and a nation of God's people (Col. 1: 13; 1 Pet. 2: 9), while the world is referred to as the kingdom of Satan. Here, then, are two world powers—two kingdoms in direct contrast with each other.

3. Notwithstanding the fact that the church and the world are diametrically opposed to each other, the church must have some dealings with the world. Cf. John 17: 14-16; Matt. 5: 13-16; 1 Pet. 2: 11, 12. It is this relationship, along with the obligation of trying to win men for Christ, which requires a foreign policy.

4. The text makes it plain that wisdom is required in our attitude toward the world; and our every effort should be to win as many as possible from the rule of Satan to that of our Lord and Saviour, Jesus Christ. Cf. Mark 16: 15; Rom. 1: 14-16.

II. THE CONSTITUENT PARTS OF A SOUND FOREIGN POLICY

1. As in the case of a political state, there must be certain commitments or open declarations of adherence, involving obligations which must be met by those making the commitments. These commitments by the church, in the very nature of the case, will be antagonistic to the interests and desires of the kingdom of Satan.

2. The church, therefore, must have sufficient power to "liquidate" these obligations, thereby bringing into balance the commitments and the power necessary to carry them out.

3. These commitments, as has already been observed, must be made with the view of influencing men in the direction of Christ; and the power necessary to their fulfillment must be that which is supplied by the word of God. Cf. 2 Tim. 3: 16, 17; 2 Pet. 1: 3.

III. SOME COMMITMENTS THE CHURCH HAS MADE

1. We are committed to faith in Almighty God—that is, we have announced to the world that we are convinced that there is a God, and that we are confident that his way is the only safe way to live. Cf. Heb. 11: 6; Rom. 8: 28; Gal. 6: 7, 8.

2. We are committed to the fact that faithful church member-ship is essential to our ultimate salvation. See Eph. 1: 22, 23; 5: 23; John 15: 1, 2.

3. We are committed to the truth that division among the Lord's people is displeasing to him, and is therefore sinful. Cf. John 17: 20, 21; 1 Cor. 1: 10.

4. We are committed to the doctrine that forgiveness of sins is absolutely necessary to a life acceptable to God, both here and hereafter. See 1 John 1: 6, 7; 2 Tim. 4: 6-8. Paul would not have been acceptable to God, if sin had been charged against him.

5. We are committed to the belief that only that which leads to eternal life is really worth-while. Cf. 2 Cor. 5: 17, 18; Matt. 16: 26.

If these and other similar commitments are successfully handled, the effect on the kingdom of Satan will be devastating, and many souls will be won to the church of the Redeemer of men. The question now before us therefore is,

IV. Do We Have the Power Necessary to Back Up These Commitments?

1. The answer to this question is Yes, so far as God's part is concerned; but what about our part? Cf. 2 Pet. 1: 1-11. Are we using our God-given power, and are we making an honest effort to convince the world, by actual demonstration of daily living, that we really believe these things ourselves? As matters now stand, are we "liquidating" these commitments in a way that will please God and produce a wholesome effect upon the world? Let us consider them again, one by one.

(1) God has given us his promises to enable us to become like him (see 2 Pet. 1: 4; 1 John 3: 1-3), and has shown us time and again, both by that which is written and by our own experience, that we can depend upon him. It is therefore up to us to appropriate that power; and the question is, Have we done it? God is faithful; are we? See 1 Cor. 10: 13a; James 1: 5-8.

(2) The Lord, in like manner, has given us his commands and promises to instruct and encourage us in the matter of church membership. Cf. Matt. 28: 20; 18: 20; Heb. 10: 23-25. Do we have that within us which is necessary in order to be faithful in this respect? Cf. 1 Cor. 15: 58.

(3) Are we making an honest effort to see that there are no divisions in the body of Christ, and especially among those with whom we are associated? See Eph. 4: 1-3; cf. Prov. 6: 16-19.

(4) Have we freely forgiven those who sinned against us, thereby making it possible for God to forgive us? See Matt. 6: 14, 15. Have we made an effort to bring them to repentance, as God has with us? Cf. Rom. 2: 4; 12: 19-21.

(5) Are we really putting first things first? See Matt. 6: 33.

How many of us are allowing the things of this life to absorb our time and attention? Cf. Luke 8: 14.

2. In the light of the facts as they exist in our cases, how do you suppose the world feels about the sincerity of our commitments and our ability to carry them out? Cf. Rom. 2: 17-24. Are our friends and neighbors, and even our own families, taking us seriously? What effect are we having with those who say that the way of Christ will not work under all conditions?

3. A sound foreign policy is one which brings into balance commitments and the power of enforcement; one which demonstrates that we can and do live a life consistent with our profession as disciples of Christ.

◆ ◆ ◆

THE PROPER ATTITUDE TOWARD THE GOSPEL
Gal. 1: 6-10

Introduction: 1. No one can read the text now before us without being deeply impressed with the necessity of manifesting the proper attitude toward the gospel of Christ, both with reference to preaching it and the reaction of those who hear. The responsibility of both the preacher and the hearer should be carefully emphasized, but in our lesson today we want to give particular attention to the matter of preaching the gospel. But in doing this we shall not neglect to emphasize the necessity of responding favorably to the call of the gospel. Cf. 2 Thess. 2: 13, 14. 2. There is a dreadful responsibility resting upon every one who pretends to preach the gospel. This is made certain by Paul's use of the term "anathema." This is an anglicized Greek word; and, in its practical application, it refers to spiritual death. According to Paul, any one, whether he be angel, apostle, or ordinary man, who preaches any gospel other than the divinely authorized gospel of Christ, will be anathema, that is, absolutely, hopelessly, and irrevocably cut off from God. But, in spite of this terrible responsibility, the gospel must be preached; and in discussing this lesson, let us consider,

I. Some Reasons for Preaching the Gospel

1. It is the power of God unto salvation to every one that believeth, Rom. 1: 16, 17.

(1) The original word for power is *dunamis.* It is the same term from which we have such words as *dynamic, dynamo,* and *dynamite.* The gospel is God's "dynamite" unto salvation. It moves men in the direction of salvation by causing them to meet the conditions upon which salvation may be had.

(2) If the preacher, therefore, expects to have a part in saving souls, he must use God's power; for God will recognize no other method. Cf. Matt. 7: 21-23.

·2. It came directly from heaven, Gal. 1: 11, 12. Cf. 2 Tim. 2: 2.

3. The anathema of God will be the portion of him who does not preach it, Gal. 1: 8, 9. Cf. 1 Cor. 9: 16.

II. What is the Gospel?

1. Let us suppose that some one decides to preach the gospel, but after reading the text now under consideration he resolves first of all to find out what the gospel is, lest he incur the displeasure of God by preaching something else.

2. To aid him in this discovery, he obtains an English dictionary and a Bible concordance; and with careful and prayerful study he learns some interesting facts regarding the gospel. For example,

(1) He learns that the word "gospel" literally means "good news" or "glad tidings." Cf. Luke 2: 10, 11.

(2) He finds that the gospel is something which can and must be obeyed. See 1 Pet. 4: 17; 2 Thess. 1: 7-10.

(3) The dreadful curse set forth in the text was about to cause him to decide not to preach the gospel, but when he considered the passages concerning the fate of those who do not obey the gospel, he concluded that he had no other choice in the matter. Cf. Rom. 1: 4.

3. The gospel made known, 1 Cor. 15: 1-4.

(1) The gospel of Christ, therefore, when reduced to its basic elements, is not merely a statement of principles, but a record of facts—things which happened in this world of ours.

It is because of the great sacrifice of Christ upon the cross and his triumphant resurrection from the dead that makes it possible for God to offer salvation to all who will accept Jesus as the Christ. Cf. Rom. 3: 21-26.

III. How May the Gospel Be Obeyed?

1. It is obvious to any thoughtful person that no one can obey the gospel before he learns what is required of him. The words spoken by Saul of Tarsus on the Damascus road (Acts 22: 10) exactly express the necessary frame of mind which must characterize those who thus learn the truth. Cf. John 8: 31, 32.

2. The testimony of Jesus, Mark 16: 15, 16.

3. A concrete example, Rom. 6: 17, 18, 1-11.

IV. A Grave Warning

1. The testimony of the Scriptures, Gal. 1: 6-9.

2. The word "pervert" means to change, corrupt, to turn around so that the meaning will be changed. Goodspeed renders the passage as follows:

> I am amazed that you are so quickly turning away from
> him who called you by the mercy of Christ, to some differ-
> ent good news—not that there is any other, only that
> there are some people who are trying to unsettle you and
> want to turn the good news of the Christ around.

3. A practical test:

(1) The language of the New Testament: "And he said unto them, Go ye into all the world, and preach the gospel to the whole creation. He that believeth and is baptized shall be saved; but he that disbelieveth shall be condemned." (Mark 16: 15, 16).

(2) The teaching of men: "He that believeth is saved. He may be baptized later, if he so desires; but he is saved before and without water baptism."

4. In the light of these indisputable facts, which one of these statements will you rely upon? Cf. 1 Pet. 4: 11; 2 John 9.

◆ ◆ ◆

HADES AND THE JUDGMENT
Rev. 20: 11-15

Introduction: 1. Some of the questions which frequently re-cur in the human mind are, "Who or what is man?" "Where did he come from?" "Why is he here?" and, "Where is he go-ing when this life is over?" These are questions which cannot be ignored by thoughtful people—by those who have any regard for their eternal welfare. The Bible is the only book which can give the true answers to these questions. Neither science, nor philosophy, with all their storehouse of information, can, aside from revelation, tell us that which we should know about these things. Turning, then, to the Bible, let us consider,

I. THE THREE STATES OR CONDITIONS OF MAN'S CONSCIOUS EXISTENCE

1. These three states are the fleshly, the intermediate, and the eternal.

2. The testimony of the Scriptures: 2 Cor. 5: 1-8; Luke 20: 27-40 (although dead physically, all men live unto God); Matt. 17: 1-8 (all three states are here represented: the fleshly—the three apostles; the intermediate—Moses; the eternal—Elijah); Luke 16: 19-31.

II. THE FLESHLY STATE IS THE STATE OF RESPONSIBILITY

1. Every responsible person must make a choice between the right and the wrong when the cross is reached, or, which is the same thing, when the gospel is heard. Cf. Acts 13: 46; Heb. 4: 7.

2. While in the fleshly state man has the power of choice, and he may, of course, choose his own pathway. Cf. Matt. 7: 13, 14; Luke 16: 27-31.

III. HADES, PARADISE, AND TARTARUS

1. Two of these words, Hades and Tartarus, together with the word Gehenna, are, in the King James Version, translated by the single term "hell," notwithstanding the fact that they represent three distinct ideas. Gehenna always refers to the place of eternal punishment, Hades, to the intermediate state, between death and the resurrection, and Tartarus, to the place where the wicked are held in the intermediate state.

2. The American Standard Version draws a clear distinction between all of these terms. *Gehenna* is uniformly translated "hell"; *Hades* is always anglicized; and while *Tartarus* is translated "hell," the marginal reference shows that *"Tartarus"* is meant. *Gehenna* occurs twelve times in the New Testament; *Hades*, ten times; and *Tartarus*, one time (2 Pet. 2: 4).

3. Hades, according to Thayer, is the realm of the dead, or the common receptacle of disembodied spirits. However, it is very clear from the teaching of the Scriptures that the righteous dead and the wicked dead are not together in Hades. See Luke 16: 19-26.

4. Hades, therefore, is divided into two parts—one part for the righteous dead and one part for the wicked dead.

(1) The part for the righteous dead is called *Paradise*. Cf. Luke 23: 43; Acts 2: 27, 31.

(2) The part for the wicked dead is called *Tartarus*. See Luke 16: 22, 23, 26; 2 Pet. 2: 4.

5. Hades, at the last day, will give up the dead who are in it. See Rev. 1: 18; 20: 13.

IV. ALL RESPONSIBLE PEOPLE WILL BE JUDGED

1. It seems that many people have a mistaken idea regarding the character and purpose of the judgment at the last day. The judgment at that time is not for the purpose of determining whether or not one is acceptable to the Lord. Instead, it will be the time for meting out rewards and punishments. See Rev. 22: 12. (Cf. marginal reading for "reward" in the American Standard Version.)

2. The New Testament teaches that there are two judgments— viz:

(1) The one which is going on now, and which determines whether or not one is acceptable to the Lord. Cf. John 3: 16-19; 5: 24; 2 Tim. 2: 19.

(2) The judgment at the last day. See Heb. 9: 27; 2 Cor. 5: 10; Matt. 23: 31-46.

3. There are two facts which should be considered regarding the final day of judgment:

(1) The Judge and those who are to be judged, Acts 17: 30, 31; John 5: 28, 29.

(2) The standard of judgment. John 12: 48; Rev. 20: 11-15. The books to be opened include at least three: the books containing the deeds of all men; the book of life, containing the names of the saints of God (Phil. 4: 3); and the word of God itself.

◆ ◆ ◆

THE PRICE OF HAPPINESS
John 10: 10

Introduction: 1. Wonderful provisions have been made for a happy life, even in this world; but they were made at a great cost. Comparatively few people stop to consider the price that was paid for their happiness. Not only are they satisfied to enjoy the things which have been provided by others; it also seems that they do not realize that they themselves have any responsibility, respecting either the present or future generations. 2. Such an attitude is contrary to the spirit of Christianity; and it is the purpose of this lesson to try to set forth something which will have a tendency to help overcome that attitude. With these things in mind, let us begin this study by calling to our attention,

I. SOME THINGS WHICH CONTRIBUTE TO OUR HAPPINESS

1. Friends, homes, communities.
2. Wholesome reading material, especially religious, such as books, leaflets, periodicals, social heritage, and the like.
3. Spiritual blessings, such as salvation from sin, the blessings of the Lord's day, religious meetings, Bible classes, etc.

II. WHAT DID THESE THINGS COST AND WHO PAID FOR THEM?

1. Take friends, for example; how did we come to have them?
(1) In the first place, we would not want them if *they* did not possess certain admirable traits of character which *they* supplied before they became our friends.
(2) And, too, if *they* were not big enough and gracious enough to overlook many of our faults, we would not have them for our friends.
2. No normal person would be happy without the things mentioned above; but too many people are willing for some one else to pay for them.*

---

*A school teacher and one of his pupils, so the story goes, were walking out in the country, late one afternoon. As they went along, they saw an elderly man plowing in his field. He had removed his shoes, and they were left near the fence beside the road.

The young man saw them and said to the teacher, "Let's have some fun by hiding that man's shoes; and then we will hide ourselves and listen to him curse when he comes for them and fails to find them."

The teacher replied that he was willing to have some fun with the farmer's shoes, but that he was unwilling for the working man to pay for the fun which they would enjoy. He then suggested that he and the young

III. What, Then, Should Be Our Attitude toward Such Blessings?

1. It will probably be easier to answer this question if we will first consider some general principles, as they are applied to similar situations. See, for example, Matt. 18: 21-35; Rom. 1: 5, 14, 15; 15: 26, 27.

2. What should be our attitude toward,

(1) Friends, homes, communities? Cf. Matt. 7: 12; Rom. 12: 10. The original word for "preferring" in the expression "in honor preferring one another" occurs nowhere else in the New Testament. It literally means, according to Thayer, "to go before and show the way, to go before and lead, to go before as leader." Cf. Phil. 2: 3; 1 Pet. 2: 17; 5: 5. The honor in question is the honor due from each individual to others. Hence, leading the way in showing the honor which is due. See Vincent, *in loco*.

(2) Reading material and social heritage?

a. If some one else provides the reading material, so that we have access to it, it seems that it is only fair for us to be willing to help support the effort which is being made, in accordance with our ability, so that the program may be continued and others may enjoy the blessings

There are some who say that we do not need the help of others in improving our knowledge of God's word. In writing about this attitude, J. W. McGarvey said, "The man who attempts to gain a knowledge of the Bible by his own unaided powers, while the aid furnished by a multitude of learned and devout predecessors is at hand, seems to declare himself the equal in exegetical power of all who have gone before him. In no other department of human study do we reject the aid of our fellow students; why should we reject it in this?

b. Concerning social heritage, E. H. Cameron says, "Man preserves the learning of the past and is able to build upon this foundation for the future." *What advantages will the succeeding generations have as a result of our contributions?*

(3) Spiritual relationships?

a. No informed and thoughtful person can possibly be happy,

---

man each put a dollar into the shoes, and then hide themselves and see what the man would do when he found the money.

They did so; and when the farmer saw the money, he called out and asked who put it in his shoes. When no answer came he knelt down and thanked the Lord for the kind friends who had supplied the money with which to buy some medicine for his sick wife, whom he had been compelled to leave at home alone, while he endeavored to make a crop.

The young man, in this way, was taught that he should not go through life, trying to get others to pay for his happiness. The lesson he learned was a valuable one; and every Christian should try to make his life a channel of blessings to others, rather than one which is always looking to some one else for those things which contribute to his happiness. Cf. the Lake of Galilee and the Dead Sea.

in the true sense of that word, without the consciousness of the forgiveness of his sins. Cf. Acts 8: 39; Matt. 6: 14, 15.

b. The Lord's day provides us with opportunities for worship and spiritual refreshment; how, then, do we regard the day? See Rev. 1: 10; Matt. 22: 21.

c. Are we willing to let someone else assume the responsibility and do everything to keep the meetings going, including the paying of the bills? When it is necessary for us to be absent, do we think to send our contribution, or bring it the next time we come?

d. Do we expect to find things going on as usual when we return? Then some one must be on duty.

e. Would you be willing to dispense with any part of the program of the church?

◆ ◆ ◆

"A DULL HEAVEN AND A SPRIGHTLY HELL"*
Rev. 21: 23-27, 8

Introduction: 1. In a letter written a few months before his death, Irvin S. Cobb, the well known American humorist, set forth some of his views regarding God, religion, and the hereafter. Mr. Cobb died a few days ago (March 10, 1944); and the letter referred to above, and which was not to be opened until after his death, was released to the public through the medium of the Associated Press. *The Chattanooga Times* published the letter on March 11th, the day following his death; and from that report some observations are to be made. 2. The things said by Mr. Cobb have to do with some vital issue; and since his remarks reflect the views of many others, it is well to consider them here and now. We shall begin with,

I. "A CONSUMMATION DEVOUTLY TO BE WISHED"

1. Said Mr. Cobb: "When a man dies with his sins, let the sins die with the man. That's what I say and it sums up such speculations as I might ever have had touching on the future state, if any."

2. If that philosophy were true, it would bring to those who die without God the greatest blessing imaginable; for then they would be spared all future sufferings for their sins.

3. But as it is, man has an eternal spirit; and being a moral creature, he must either accept the mercy offered by the Lord, or suffer for his sins. One of the benevolent purposes of the Bible is to teach man that his sins do not and cannot die with him.

4. The testimony of the Scriptures: Rom. 14: 12; 2 Cor. 5: 10; Matt. 11: 20-24.

---

*Preached by the author to the Central Church of Christ, Chattanooga, Tennessee, March 19, 1944.

II. THE CHARACTER OF JESUS AND JEHOVAH

1. Mr. Cobb referred to Jesus Christ as "the first true gentleman of recorded history and the greatest gentleman that ever lived."

2. But of Jehovah he said, "All Hitler needed to do was to let his whiskers sprout and sit on a nest of thunderbolts and naked swords, thinking of plague and pestilence and rapine and slaughter and slavery for the vanquished, to be a fit understudy for the vengeful murderous Jehovah of the forepart of the Old Testament."

3. If one will only take the time to consider the facts in the case, as they are revealed in the Bible, he will learn,

(1) That Jehovah never punished nor destroyed any individual or nation, by whatever means employed, that was not done in strict harmony with the principles of justice and holiness which ever characterize him. Cf. Isa. 13: 11; Jer. 28: 16; Dan. 9: 13, 14; Hos. 13: 9.

(2) He has always made it plain that the sinner must suffer for his sins; and it is certainly not any worse to take an innocent child from a sinful environment, such as was done in Old Testament times, than for wicked parents or contemporaries to bring it to maturity, only to become an heir of eternal punishment.

(3) Instead of denouncing Jehovah for that which was done in olden times, people should endeavor to discover the sinful cause which brought on that terrible condition; and they should realize that what took place on earth, in the way of death and destruction, is only a faint picture of that which awaits those who die in their sins. Cf. Mark 9: 47, 48; Rev. 14: 9ff.

4. But could Jesus be a gentleman, if Jehovah is a revengeful murderer?

(1) The relation between Jehovah God and Jesus Christ is characterized by the following facts:

a. Christ called God his Father, John 5: 17, 18.

b. He said that he and the Father are in each other, John 10: 37, 38.

c. He said that the Father is greater than he, John 14: 28.

d. He said that he could do nothing of himself, but only as he received from the Father, John 5: 19, 30.

e. He said that the Father told him what to say, and what to speak, John 12: 49.

(2) If Jesus was a gentleman, then God is what he claimed to be; but if God is not what he claimed to be, then Christ was not a gentleman; for he solemnly testified that God is everything that he claimed to be. Cf. Matt: 5: 48.

III. THE BIBLICAL PREVIEW OF HEAVEN AND HELL

1. In speaking of the Word of God and heaven and hell, Mr. Cobb had the following to say:

In deference to the faith of our dear mother, who was through her lifetime a loyal, though never a bigoted communicant of that congregation, perhaps the current pastor of the First Presbyterian Church would consent to read the Twenty-third Psalm, which was her favorite passage in the Scriptures and is mine since it contains no charnel words. No morbid mouthings about corruption and decay and, being mercifully without creed or dogma, carries no threat of eternal hell fire for those parties we do not like, no direct promise of a heaven which, if one may judge by the people who are surest of going there, must be a powerfully dull place, populated to a considerable and uncomfortable degree by prigs, time-servers and unpleasantly aggressive individuals. Hell may have a worse climate, but undoubtedly the company is sprightlier.

2. Time does not permit a discussion of the integrity of the Word of God in this study, but suffice it to say that, whether one likes it or not, Jesus (whom Mr. Cobb referred to as "the first true gentleman of recorded history and the greatest gentleman that ever lived") declared that the word which he spoke would be a determining factor in the destiny of those who reject it. See John 12: 48.

(1) It might be interesting to those with views similar to those expressed by Mr. Cobb to know that the original word for "hell" (eternal punishment) occurs twelve times in the New Testament, and that it was used by Jesus himself eleven times out of the twelve.

(2) If Jesus was the type of man Mr. Cobb claimed for him, "the greatest gentleman that ever lived," then surely his word must have some weight with people like Mr. Cobb.

3. Who is going to heaven?

(1) According to Mr. Cobb's judgment, heaven will be "populated to a considerable and uncomfortable degree by prigs, time-servers and unpleasantly aggressive individuals."

(2) But the One who *knows* who will be there has left no doubt about the matter. Cf. Rev. 21: 8, 27; John 14: 1-3; Matt. 7: 21-23.

a. In another part of his letter, and by way of parenthesis, Mr. Cobb said, "One advantage of dying is that it affords a fellow opportunity to say a lot of things that have been curdling in his system all these years."

b. But from that which he said about the population of heaven, one would naturally conclude that Mr. Cobb didn't have a very high regard for "time-servers." Now, if Mr. Cobb wasn't a time-server himself, why did he have to wait until he died before granting permission to make known to the public the thing that had been curdling in his system all these years. Why didn't he say them in life, and then face the consequences? "Verily, they who live in glass houses should not throw stones."

4. The "climate" and "company" of hell.

(1) Something of the character of hell may be learned by considering some of the Bible expressions used to describe it.

a. "The blackness of darkness for ever," Jude 13.

b. "Fierceness of fire," Heb. 10 : 27.

c. "Eternal destruction from the face of the Lord," 2 Thess. 1 : 9.

d. "Unquenchable fire," Mark 9 : 43.

e. "Weeping and the gnashing of teeth," Mark. 25 : 30.

(2) The following terms indicate something of the suffering which must be endured by those who go to hell:

a. Sight, Luke 16 : 23.

b. Desire, Luke 16 : 24.

c. Memory, Luke 16 : 25.

d. Torments, anguish, Luke 16 : 23, 24.

e. Shame and everlasting contempt, Dan. 12 : 2.

f. Vile companionships, Rev. 21 : 8.

◆ ◆ ◆

THE TRIALS OF JOB
Job 1: 1-2; 13

Introduction: 1. The Book of Job is one of the most remarkable books in that great body of ancient literature known as the Hebrew Scriptures. Although rich in varied forms of expression, the literature of the Hebrews developed no great drama. Perhaps the nearest approach to the drama, especially in the Old Testament literature, is the Book of Job; but even then it is probably more accurate to speak of it as "a drama without action." 2. The interest in the book, however, is not simply its literature grandeur; its interest is a living interest. This is true because it deals with one of the greatest of all problems—that of human suffering. It should be quickly added, however, that the book is concerned with an even greater problem than that of human suffering as such; it deals with the problem of injustice in human suffering. Job's complaint was not so much that he suffered, but that he suffered unjustly. He well knew that he had lived a righteous life, but he was being treated by God as if he were unrighteous. His friends, too, regarded him as a sinner and insisted that he should confess his sins; but Job was not conscious of any sins that he should confess. 3. Instead of giving the answer that one might expect to the question, Why do the righteous have to suffer? the book shows that God can and does care for those who place their trust in him, and it endeavors to correct the current notion that misfortune and disaster are evidences of God's disapproval of one's sins, while prosperity and good fortune are signs of his approbation and favor. But in studying this lesson, let us begin by considering,

I. THE MAN JOB

1. No one knows for certain to which race or nationality Job belonged, or when he lived; and the best that one can say, with any degree of accuracy, regarding the location of the "land of Uz" is that it was in the east. All of this, however, is to our advantage, for Job stands out, not as a man of any particular race or age or land, but as man in the universal sense, facing life and grappling with suffering, destiny, and God. He was, however, an actual being, Ezk. 14: 14, 20; James 5: 11.

2. His family consisted of his wife, seven sons, and three daughters.

3. He was a man of great wealth. His property was listed as,

(1) Seven thousand sheep.

(2) Three thousand camels.

(3) Five hundred yoke of oxen.

(4) Five hundred she-asses.

(5) A very great household, that is, servants or slaves, all of which made him "the greatest of all the children of the east."

4. His piety was in proportion to his prosperity, as is indicated by his practice with reference to his children, following the days of their feasting. Cf. 3 John 2. Not every one's religious prosperity is commensurate with his material or physical prosperity.

II. HIS FIRST GREAT SERIES OF TRIALS

1. On one occasion when the sons of God came to present themselves before Jehovah, Satan also came; and after being asked regarding his whereabouts and receiving his answer, Jehovah said to him, "Hast thou considered my servant Job? for there is none like him in the earth, a perfect and upright man, one that feareth God, and turneth away from evil."

2. Satan replied by saying, "Doth Job fear God for nought?" Hast thou not made a hedge about him, and about his house, and about all that he hath, on every side? thou hast blessed the work of his hands, and his substance is increased in the land. But put forth thy hand now, and touch all that he hath, and he will renounce thee to thy face."

3. Whereupon Jehovah granted Satan power over all that Job possessed, "only upon himself put not forth thy hand."

4. The calamities which befell Job. It seems that all of these things happened to him in a single day—a day on which his sons and daughters were eating and drinking in the home of their eldest brother.

(1) The Sabeans seized his oxen and asses and slew the servants who were with them, except the one who came and told Job about what had happened.

(2) Fire from heaven burned up the flocks and the servants with them, except the one who came and told Job about it.

(3) The Chaldeans formed three bands and took away his camels and killed the servants, with the exception of the one who came and told Job.

(4) All of his children who were feasting in their eldest brother's home were killed when a strong wind struck the house and caused it to fall upon them. Only one servant was left to tell this sad story to Job.

5. Job's reaction to all these troubles: "Then Job arose, and rent his robe, and shaved his head, and fell down upon the ground, and worshipped; and he said, Naked came I out of my mother's womb, and naked shall I return thither: Jehovah gave, and Jehovah hath taken away; blessed be the name of Jehovah. In all this Job sinned not, nor charged God foolishly.

III. HIS SECOND GREAT SERIES OF TRIALS

1. On another day when the sons of God came to present themselves before Jehovah, Satan also came; and after being questioned regarding his whereabouts and receiving his answer, Jehovah said to him, "Hast thou considered my servant Job? for there is none like him in the earth, a perfect and an upright man, one that feareth God, and turneth away from evil: and he still holdeth fast his integrity, although thou movedst me against him, to destroy him without cause."

2. To this Satan replied by saying, "Skin for skin, yea, all that a man hath will he give for his life. But put forth thy hand now, and touch his bone and his flesh, and he will renounce thee to thy face."

3. Jehovah then granted power to Satan over the person of Job, specifying only that his life be spared. Death would have been a relief.

4. The blows which Job received at this time:

(1) He was smitten with "sore boils from the sole of his foot unto his crown."

(2) His wife, probably through scorn, although possible through pity, called upon him to renounce God and die. Job 2: 9, 10.

(3) He lost his reputation and good name among his friends. Job 2: 11-13.

5. Few men have ever suffered as Job did, but "in all this did not Job sin with his lips."

> As sure as ever God puts his children in the furnace, he will be in the furnace with them.—Spurgeon
> There hath no temptation taken you but such as man can bear: but God is faithful, who will not suffer you to be tempted above that which ye are able; but will with the temptation make also the way of escape, that ye may be able to endure it.—Paul

JOB'S FAITH AND ITS REWARD
Job 23: 10

Introduction: 1. No one can read the Book of Job without realizing that its chief character had felt the iron of suffering pass deeply into his own soul. He had been driven by the cold words of well-meaning, though mistaken and unsympathetic, friends into open revolt against the God of popular imagination. He had fought his way through despair and doubt, if not to clear light on the problem of human suffering, yet to a more genuine and nobler faith in the living God. Job opened his heart and gave utterance to the feelings which passed through his soul in the agony of his grief, until he again found rest in God. 2. As he continued to suffer under the load of accumulated sorrows, he came to regard death as the only possible release from his trouble. But as he gazed into the misty depths of Sheol, the unspeakable horrors of death seized him. Cf. Job 10: 20-22.

> But that the dread of something after death,
> The undiscover'd country from whose bourn
> No traveller returns, puzzles the will
> And makes us rather bear those ills we have
> Than fly to others that we know not of.

Sheol, therefore, contained no hopes for his vindication. But in his despair he began to wonder if there is not another life after this one. Cf. Job 14: 7f, 13f. 3. The sorely wounded sufferer endeavored to move his friends to pity by the spectacle of all his accumulated woes; and to us it would be difficult to find a more pathetic plea than the one he made in Job 19: 1-22. But his friends remained cold and pitiless, and it seemed to Job that God did too. In his desperation he turned to posterity for his vindication (Job 19: 23, 24), but since the desire expressed there was impossible, he turned again to Jehovah as his only Vindicator. Job 19: 25-27. But in studying this lesson, let us begin by considering,

I. JOB'S MENTAL CONDITION

1. In order to appreciate, in a measure at least, something of what must have been his mental agony, let us look again at his losses:

(1) He lost all of his property and all of his children by violent means in a single day.

(2) His entire body was afflicted by a loathsome and distressing disease. The fact that he scraped himself with a potsherd suggests that his affliction was accompanied with intolerable itching. The disease was at once humiliating, disgusting, and tormenting; and if, as thought by some, it was incurable by human skill, that fact would cast a pall over all the future of his life.

(3) Just at the time when he most needed sympathy and tender care, his wife apparently turned against him and urged him to renounce God and die. No one should have been closer to him then.

(4) He was harshly judged and unjustly condemned by his closest friends.

(5) It appears from Job 7: 13-15 that he was denied even such refreshment and recuperation as comes to the weary through sleep. His nights were hideous with nightmares, terrifying dreams, and apparitions which drained his diseased nerves of all their strength and left him prostrate when the next day's battle with excruciating pain came on.

(6) But worse than all, he felt himself abandoned by the God in whom he trusted. Cf. Job 30: 19-21. It must be remembered that Job was given up to Satan so that he might be tried in every possible way—only his life must be spared. The severest of all temptations therefore were allowed to come. The heavens were shut against him and every friend, both earthly and divine, forsook him. It was in vain that he called to God for help at this time. Cf. Mark 15: 34b.

2. It would be utterly impossible for any one today to give an accurate description of Job's mental anguish during the days of his suffering. When he cursed the day of his birth, he did not curse God, but he did, during the time of his great agony, seem to question the providence of God in his life. Cf. Job 19: 7-12; 23: 1-9.

3. But in all his trials Job never doubted his own integrity nor swerved from his firm belief in the reality of God and his ultimate justice. Cf. Job 13: 15. At times he was bewildered, confounded, and terrified; but he held fast his integrity and his faith in the living God.

> O for a faith that will not shrink,
> Tho' pressed by ev'ry foe
> That will not tremble on the brink
> Of any earthly woe.
>
> That will not murmur or complain
> Beneath the chast'ning rod,
> But, in the hour of grief or pain,
> Will lean upon its God.
>
> Lord, give us such a faith as this;
> And, then, whate'er may come,
> We'll taste, e'en here, the hallowed bliss
> Of an eternal home.
>
> —*W. H. Bathurst*

II. GOD'S ANSWER AND JOB'S REPENTANCE

1. "Then Jehovah answered Job out of the whirlwind." See chapters 38-41.

2. As already seen, Job had not cursed God nor denied him; but out of the depths of his suffering he had seemed to question his providence and had asked many difficult questions. For example,

(1) Why, being innocent and upright, had so great a calamity befallen him?

(2) Why, if he must thus suffer, was he not permitted to die?

(3) Why does Jehovah permit the righteous to suffer and the unrighteous to prosper?

3. Jehovah answered all these questions, but it is a singular fact that in answering them no direct reference was made to Job's questions. Instead, the Lord's answer was found in a series of questions addressed to Job—questions which humbled him and reminded him of the majesty and omnipotence of the Almighty. See Job 38: 1-3. Some of the questions which God asked Job were,

(1) Where wast thou when I laid the foundations of the earth? Declare, if thou hast understanding.

(2) Whereupon were the foundations thereof fastened?

(3) Where wast thou when the morning stars sang together, and all the sons of God shouted for joy?

(4) Who shut up the sea with doors, . . . and said, Hitherto shalt thou come, but no further; and here shall thy proud waves be stayed?

(5) Hast thou entered the treasuries of the snow, . . .?

(6) Canst thou bind the cluster of the Pleiades, or loose the bands of Orion?

(7) Canst thou lift up thy voice to the clouds, that abundance of waters may cover thee?

(8) Is it by thy wisdom that the hawk soareth, and stretcheth her wings toward the south?

(9) Canst thou draw out leviathan with a fishhook?

4. In the midst of these questions which belong to the natural realm, Jehovah asked Job, Wilt thou even annul my judgment? Wilt thou condemn me, that thou mayest be justified? Cf. Job 40: 1, 2.

(1) If Job knew so little about the ways of God in nature, why then should he question the Lord's way in his providential dealings with him?

(2) The Lord's questions humbled Job and brought him to repentance. He did not repent of the sins which his friends had rashly charged him with, for he was not guilty of them; but he did repent of his questioning the ways of God in his life. See Job 40: 3-5; 42: 1-6.

III. JOB'S RESTORATION

1. The Lord's attitude toward Job's three friends and his command to them. Job 42: 7-9.

2. "And Jehovah turned the captivity of Job, when he had prayed for his friends: and Jehovah gave Job twice as much as he had before." See Job 42: 10-17.

IV. THE LESSON BROUGHT DOWN TO DATE

1. See Rom. 15: 4.

2. The answer given to Job regarding the question of human suffering, and the seeming injustice of it, is the answer that we need today. Cf. 1 Cor. 10: 13; James 1: 2-8. Jehovah is to be trusted and obeyed, rather than argued with or about. Cf. Job 13: 15; 2 Cor. 12: 7-10.

3. Any one who is acquainted with the Bible knows that the Lord teaches that life is a probation, a trial; but the purpose of the trial is always good. There is, after all, nothing extraordinary or unique about the sufferings of Job. People have always suffered since sin entered the world, but the outcome of the suffering depends on the character of the person who does the suffering. Cf. Job 23: 10; James 5: 10, 11; Rom. 8: 28.

◆ ◆ ◆

THE TRIALS OF JOSEPH
Gen. 42: 21

Introduction: 1. The story of Joseph is one of those immortal narratives which have been of deepest interest to all classes of readers for more than thirty centuries, and there is every reason to believe that it will continue so as long as time shall last. With the sole exception of that of Abraham, the story of Joseph occupies more space than any other personal narrative in the Old Testament Scriptures. 2. One of the chief reasons for the unusual interest in the story of Joseph is the fact that his life contained all the elements of true greatness. The average person is not particularly interested in a life which is all sunshine, happiness, and success. True greatness does not come until one has experienced the fires of pain and his soul has felt the touch of iron. In the words of Edwin McNeill Poteat,

> He cannot heal who has not suffered much,
> For only Sorrow sorrow understands;
> They will not come for healing at our touch
> Who have not seen the scars upon our hands.

Youth, ambition, beauty, temptation, sorrow, suffering, jealousy, hate, forgiveness—in short, all the elements of a great story are part and parcel of the life of Joseph. 3. The whole story of Joseph, from the time we see him going to visit his brothers, as they were feeding their father's flock, and onward, is one of divine providence. No one can read this delightful narrative without seeing in it the hand of God as he cares for and develops his own, and endeavors through benevolent discipline to bring the wayward into the fold. But in studying this lesson, let us begin by considering,

I. THE TRIAL BY TEMPTATION

1. If all the world loves a dreamer, it is also true that the world conspires against the dreamer. It will do what it can to persuade the dreamer to forsake his dreams, or, which is sadder still, it will endeavor to make him unworthy of them.

2. Joseph had dreamed some lofty dreams, inspired, as they evidently were, by God himself; yet it is a historical fact that many diabolical efforts were made to prevent their fulfilment, or to make him unworthy of them.

3. Joseph was a blessing to those about him wherever he was and the story of his life would not have been complete without severe trials by temptation. Good in this wicked world is never allowed to continue unopposed.

(1) There is no wall high enough to keep out temptation from a man's life; and with those who are ready to enter the prime of life, as was Joseph, temptation has a determining influence.

(2) What a man does then, what he accepts or rejects, what he chooses or dismisses, will have its effect on the rest of his life.

4. The temptation which came to Joseph in the house of Potiphar was no ordinary temptation; for he was a red-blooded young man in his late twenties. It was not a temptation that came to him just once and stopped there; it was repeated day by day.

(1) Looking at the matter from the standpoint of the world, there were many reasons why he should yield:

a. There was the high rank of the woman who tempted him and the natural inclination to feel flattered by her proposal.

b. The way would be open for an easy life and further promotion in his master's service.

c. Then, too, there was danger in refusal, for

> Heaven has no rage like love turned to hate,
> Nor hell a fury like a woman scorned.

5. Notwithstanding the fact that so much was in favor of his yielding, he, nevertheless, did not yield, and the secret of his notable victory is plainly set forth in the text:

(1) His gratitude to and respect for his master who had done so much for him.

(2) His fear of and loyalty to God to whom he owed his very life and before whom he would have to give an account for "this great wickedness."

II. THE TRIAL OF ADVERSITY

1. Having survived the fiery trial which involved the tempta-

tion of the flesh, he was much better prepared to deal with other temptations which might come to him.

> Yield not to temptation, For yielding is sin;
> Each vict'ry will help you Some other to win;
> Fight manfully onward, Dark passions subdue,
> Look ever to Jesus: He'll carry you through.

2. Joseph's loyalty to God and to his own conscience resulted in his being cast into prison. That, apparently, was his only reward. One can well imagine something of what he must have thought as he spent his first night in the dungeon. Did he ask, Does it pay to do right? Cf. Gen. 39: 21.

3. But Joseph was not soured by his misfortune nor cast into despair by his adversity. On the contrary, he resolved to make the best of his lot and do what he could to help other prisoners. See Gen. 39: 22, 23.

4. In due time the opportunity came to him to be of signal service to a fellow prisoner (chapter 40); but when it was well with the chief butler whom he had befriended, he promptly forgot Joseph!

III. THE TRIAL OF PROSPERITY

1. At the end of two full years the chief butler remembered Joseph, but it appears that it was in order to raise himself in the estimation of Pharaoh, rather than out of gratitude to Joseph. The occasion of this "remembrance" arose when Pharaoh sought for some one to interpret his dreams.

2. Not long after this the test of prosperity came to Joseph. He was taken from the prison dungeon and made governor over all the land of Egypt, second only to Pharaoh himself. What will be the effect on him? Will pride rule his heart? or will he lose sympathy for his fellow men, forget his friends, and the God who had always blessed him?

3. From the names that he gave his sons and the attitude he took toward his ten brethren, when they came to buy grain, it seems that his heart was filled with resentment for them and his father, whom he evidently thought should have rescued him. But when the facts were unfolded before his eyes, he saw the hand of God in it all and promptly forgave the sin which his brothers committed against him and called his father to him. See Gen. 45: 5; 50: 15-21.

4. Here, indeed, was a dreamer who dreamed lofty dreams, and it is worthy of notice that the combined efforts of Satan and his agents were never able to turn him away from the goal toward which his dreams pointed or make him unworthy of them. The story of his life remains forever enshrined in the temple of God's eternal revelation, and it ever lives to point the way to certain victory over sin and temptation. Cf. 1 Cor. 10: 13; Rom. 8: 28.

Amid the trials which I meet,
Amid the thorns which pierce my feet,
One thought remains supremely sweet,
Thou thinkest, Lord, of me!

The cares of life come thronging fast,
Upon my soul their shadow cast;
Their gloom reminds my heart at last,
Thou thinkest, Lord, of me!

Let shadows come, let shadows go,
Let life be bright or dark with woe,
I am content, for this I know,
Thou thinkest, Lord, of me!

Thou thinkest, Lord, of me,
Thou thinkest, Lord, of me;
What need I fear when thou art near
And thinkest, Lord, of me?

◆ ◆ ◆

THE LAW THAT LIGHTENS THE BURDEN
Gal. 6: 1-5

Introduction: 1. The statements made in verses 2 and 5 of the text seem to present a contradiction; but when they are carefully considered and taken together, it will be found that they give a brief description of the essence of Christianity—a definition, in few words, of the spirit of the Christian life. 2. The Christian faith is based upon two great underlying principles, which, while not strictly original with it, are, nevertheless, in their higher expression, among the most precious of its gifts to man. They explain at once the mystery and comprehensiveness of its scheme of salvation for the individual Christian; and also the divine beauty and eternal reality of that great ideal of the church as the kingdom of God, a community of souls in which each individual member must bear his own burden, while all the members are bound together, bearing each other's burdens, and united in him who is the great Burden-bearer of humanity, and the head of the church which is his body. 3. It is impossible to obey one part of this law without obeying the other. No one can bear his own burdens without at the same time bearing the burdens of others; and neither can he realize the awful responsibilities of his own being without at the same time realizing the claims of his brethren. No one can find his own true life without giving up his own individual will, without merging his personal interests in those of the human brotherhood. But in considering this question we shall find that the subject matter is divided into three parts—viz:

I. THE INDIVIDUAL BURDEN—VERSE 5

1. When Paul says that "each man shall bear his own burden," he is speaking of the burdens which no one can transfer from himself to another.

(1) The word which he uses *(phortion)* carries with it this meaning. See Matt. 11: 30; 23: 4 (note the contrast between the burdens of these two passages) ; Luke 11: 46. Cf. Acts 27: 10.

(2) The idea expressed is that of a burden which one cannot get rid of. *No soldier on active service can transfer his equipment to another.*

2. When God created man he laid firm and deep the foundations of individual life and individual character. Every man, therefore, is responsible for his own being and destiny; and he must bear the burdens which belong to his individual lot. For example,

(1) There is the burden of *physical disability or disfigurement,* such as lameness, blindness, or deformity of any kind. Such a burden is always a grievous thing to bear, but it must be borne, nevertheless. Cf. 2 Cor. 12: 7, 8.

(2) The burden of *intellectual weakness.* Not all men have the same mental capacity. Some excel others in acquiring knowledge, or in the range of vision and foresight; and notwithstanding the diligent efforts put forth by the latter, they may find themselves outdistanced by those of keener intellect and greater foresight. They may think that this is a hard lot and it may be so, but they must bear the burdens of their own defects as best they can.

(3) The burden of some permanent or far-reaching *consequence of a former act of our own,* such as neglect, recklessness, or sin. The sin may have been forgiven, but the temporal consequence will continue. Cf. 1 Tim. 1: 12-15.

> I walked through the woodland meadows,
>   Where sweet the thrushes sing;
> And I found on a bed of mosses
>   A bird with a broken wing.
>
> I healed its wound, and each morning
>   It sang its old sweet strain,
> But the bird with the broken pinion
>   Never soared as high again.
>
> I found a young life broken
>   By sin's seductive art;
> And, touched with a Christ-like pity,
>   I took him to my heart.
>
> He lived with a noble purpose
>   And struggled not in vain;
> But the life that sin had stricken
>   Never soared as high again.
>
> But the bird with the broken pinion
>   Kept another from the snare;
> And the life that sin had striken
>   Raised another from despair.
>
> Each loss has its compensation,
>   There is healing for every pain;
> But the bird with the broken pinion
>   Never soars as high again.
>
> —*Hezekiah Butterworth*

3. The apostle does not say that the burden shall be lifted from the shoulder of the child of God, but the Lord has promised that he shall be sustained in carrying it. See 1 Cor. 10: 13; 2 Cor. 12: 9, 10.

II. The Mutual Burden—Verse 2

1. The original word for burden in this verse is *baros,* and it literally means *weight, load, trouble.* The bearing of burdens of this kind does not involve transference of the burden to another, but signifies lending a hand to help in lifting a heavy load.

2. The primary reference in the burdens of this verse, as the context indicates, is to moral infirmities and faults, and the sorrow and shame which they awaken in the offender.

3. Different temperaments, like different plants, require different atmospheres. It is sometimes necessary to "humor" some plants, if we would lure them into blossom and flower. Each one must be dealt with according to its temperament; and, too, it is often the case that the atmosphere must be medicated in order to provide the necessary conditions which will help the plants to deal with their enemies (insects) and throw off their burdens (parasites)! Thus, we create suitable conditions for each plant; and so with our fellows.

III. Fulfilling the Law of Christ

1. All acceptable obedience must be actuated by a worthy motive. The motive which must prompt the Christian in the case now before us is plainly stated by the apostle—"and so fulfil the law of Christ."

2. The law of Christ is preeminently the law of love. Cf. John 13: 34, 35; Matt. 7: 12 Rom. 15: 1-3.

3. The bearing of our own burdens in a Christian spirit prepares us for lifting the loads of others.

(1) Have you ever passed through a time when your own religious faith was at stake? Then you can tenderly enter into the mental struggles of others.

(2) Have you ever known the difficulty of trying to make both ends meet? Then you can sympathize with others under similar circumstances.

(3) Have you ever had to leave a loved one who was seriously ill and go to your work in order to make a living for your family? Then you can feel for others whose hearts are filled with sorrow.

> How sweet, how heav'nly is the sight,
>   When those that love the Lord
> In one another's peace delight,
>   And so fulfil the word;
>
> When each can feel his brother's sigh,
>   And with him bear a part;
> When sorrow flows from eye to eye,
>   And joy from heart to heart.

When free from envy, scorn, and pride
Our wishes all above,
Each can his brother's failings hide,
And show a brother's love.

Love is the golden chain that binds
The happy souls above;
And he's an heir of heav'n who finds
His bosom glow with love.

—*J. Swain*

4. While it is true that by bearing our own burdens we learn best how to bear those of others, it is also true that we are better fitted to bear our own burdens when we bear the burdens of our fellow men. *This is the moral paradox of our being.* If we are sinking beneath the weight of our own burdens, then let us courageously shoulder the burdens of our neighbor, and the two will be incomparably lighter than our own alone.

5. The measure of our love to each other must be the love that Christ showed to us. Cf. 1 John 3: 16; 4: 20, 21; John 3: 34, 35. With this in mind, no one can say,

(1) I have done enough for my fellow man.

(2) I have loved enough.

(3) I have forgiven enough. See Matt. 18: 21, 22; 6: 14, 15.

❖ ❖ ❖

THE LORD'S DAY
Rev. 1: 10

Introduction: 1. The religious importance of the first day of the week arose from the conviction that Christ came forth from the dead on that day. In speaking of the original word for "Lord's" as found in the text, Thayer says, "Relating to the Lord, the day devoted to the Lord, sacred to the memory of Christ's resurrection." 2. There is no historical fact which is attested by better evidence than that the early church constantly observed the day by intermission of toil and by religious exercises. 3. The Lord's day is an institution which belongs primarily to the reign of Christ among men; and no one can be pleasing unto him who does not endeavor to learn and do his will regarding it. But in studying this lesson, let us begin by considering,

I. THE RELATION BETWEEN THE JEWISH SABBATH AND THE CHRISTIAN'S DAY OF WORSHIP

1. The Bible clearly teaches that there is a difference between the Jewish and Christian dispensations. See Heb. 1: 1, 2; Matt. 17: 1-5; Acts 3: 22, 23.

2. There is an abundance of evidence in the New Testament which plainly shows that in and through the death of Christ all

the typical and ceremonial institutions of the previous age were abolished. Cf. Rom. 7: 1-6; 2 Cor. 3: 7-11; Gal. 3: 19-25; 4: 21-31; Col. 2: 14; Heb. 8: 6-13; Matt. 28: 18.

(1) Christ is the sole mediator for this age; and no one can go to God except in and through him. See 1 Tim. 2: 5; John 6: 44, 45; 14: 6.

(2) All worship and service, therefore, and all institutions which are now acceptable to God, must rest solely upon the authority of Christ. Cf. Eph. 1: 22, 23.

3. There is nothing in Christianity which could be commemorated by the observance of the seventh-day sabbath. Cf. Deut. 5: 15; the Fourth of July for the United States of America.

(1) No Christian insofar as any New Testament evidence is concerned, ever kept the seventh-day sabbath as an authorized act of obedience. On the other hand, they were instructed not to allow any one to judge them, that is, sit in judgment on them or decide such matters for them (see Barnes' Notes *in loco*), regarding the observance of things authorized by the law of Moses, including the seventh-day sabbath. See Col. 2: 16, 17.

(2) The edict of Constantine regarding the Lord's day was not for the purpose of changing the day of religious observance from the seventh-day sabbath to the first day of the week; he simply authorized his people to observe the day which the Christians were already observing.

II. THE LORD'S DAY IS A NEW INSTITUTION

1. The original word for "Lord's" occurs only twice in the entire New Testament. See 1 Cor. 11: 20; Rev. 1: 10.

(1) This word is peculiar to the New Testament, insofar as its early use is concerned. All the evidence points to the fact that it was coined by the Holy Spirit. Cf. 1 Cor. 2: 13.

(2) According to Liddell and Scott, it is used in the sense of "belonging to the LORD (CHRIST)." Cf. Thayer *in loco*.

2. When all the facts are considered, there is no doubt but that the reference in Rev. 1: 10 is to the first day of the week—a day set apart and peculiarly devoted to the Lord. See Barnes' Notes *in loco*.

3. The following reasons seem to contain sufficient evidence to justify this conclusion:

(1) It was on this day that Christ arose from the dead, making it possible for him to be the Saviour of the world, Mark 16: 2-9; 1 Cor 15: 13-20; Heb. 2: 9.

(2) Jesus met with his disciples after his resurrection on this day, John 20: 19, 26.

(3) The church which Christ promised to build was established on this day, Matt: 16: 18; Acts 2: 1-41; 11: 15. (Note:

Pentecost, the day on which the church was established, always came on the first day of the week, Lev. 23: 15ff; Deut. 16: 9ff.

(4) It was on this day that the Holy Spirit came to the newly formed church, as the abiding Guest, and to qualify the apostles for their work in carrying out the terms of the great commission, Acts 2: 1-4.

(5) The early disciples met for worship on the first day of the week, Acts 20: 7; cf. 1 Cor. 16: 1, 2.

(6) The testimony of the fathers:

a. Barnabas: "The *eighth* is the beginning of another world; and therefore with joy we celebrate the *eighth day*, on which Jesus rose from the dead."

b. Justin Martyr: "On the Lord's Day *all Christians* in the city or country meet together, because that is the day of our Lord's-resurrection; and then we read the Apostles and Prophets. This being done, the President makes an oration to the assembly to exhort them to imitate and to practice the things which they have heard, and then we all join in prayer, and after that we celebrate the Lord's Supper; then they who are able and willing give what they think proper, and what is collected is laid up in the hands of the President, who distributes it to the orphans, and widows, and other necessitous Christians as their wants require." (See *Mosheim's Ecclesiastical History, Vol. I,* p. 135, note 10.)

c. Irenaeus: "On the Lord's Day *every one of us Christians* keeps the Sabbath." (By the term "sabbath" he simply means a day set apart unto the Lord.)

d. Eusebius: "From the beginning the Christians assembled on the first day of the week, called by them *the Lord's Day*, to read the Scriptures, to preach, and to celebrate the Lord's Supper."

e. Mosheim: "Some learned men labor to persuade us that in *all* the *early* churches *both* days, or the *first* and *last* days of the week, were held sacred. But the churches of Bithynia, mentioned by Pliny, devoted but *one stated day* to their public worship; and beyond all controversy, that was what we call the *Lord's Day*, or the *first day* of the week."

III. How Should the Day Be Observed

1. The very name, or designation, which has been given to it shows, beyond all reasonable doubt, that it is the duty of every Christian to consecrate it wholly to the worship and service of the Lord.

(1) A thousand precepts like that of the Fourth Commandment of the Decalogue could not more clearly and specifically express God's *reserved right* to this portion of time than the name by which he has seen fit to designate it.

(2) That which belongs to one person does not belong to another; and that which belongs to God does not beolng to man, any further than God, the great Proprietor of all things, has delegated

to him the right to use it. Cf. The Lord's supper; Matt. 22: 21; Isa. 58: 13, 14; Ezek. 46: 1ff. (These prophetic utterances seem to refer to the time of the reign of Christ; and the name of the type was, it seems, metaphorically transferred to the antitype, as was done in the case of Christ when he was called a shepherd, door, lion, lamb, etc. Cf. Isa. 65: 17ff; 66: 22-24. The proper designation for the day, as given in the New Testament, is *the Lord's day.*

2. It goes without question that the public worship ordained for the first day of the week must be attended to on that day. Cf. Heb. 10: 25. The Lord's day worship includes,

(1) The Lord's supper, Acts 20: 7.

(2) Preaching and teaching the word of the Lord, Acts 20; 7; 1 Tim. 4: 13.

(3) Singing, 1 Cor. 14: 26; Eph. 5: 19; Col. 3: 16.

(4) Praying, 14: 15.

(5) Benevolent giving, 1 Cor. 16: 1, 2.

3. No one can observe the day in any worthy sense who does not enter into the spirit of the day. Cf. secular holidays. That seems to be the meaning of the expression "I was in the Spirit on the Lord's day," that is, John was in the proper spirit to observe the day. He could not have done as the Spirit directed without this being true.

(1) Inasmuch as the day is for our spiritual refreshment and development, we should seek to engage in those things which are in harmony with the spirit and purpose of the day. Cf. Acts 17: 11, 12; Matt. 6: 6; Heb. 10: 24; James 1: 27.

(2) There is no evidence which warrants the conclusion that the day is to be kept in the spirit of the Old Testament seventh-day sabbath. Instead, the *Christian test* should be applied to our use of the day. Cf. Mark 2: 27, 28. *The Lord's day should be used so as to make men more Christlike in spirit.*

(3) The followers of Christ should regard this day, not to be hedged in by prohibitions and shrouded by gloom, but in every sense a day of rest from worldly cares, and one of growth and joyous service for the Lord. Whatever, then, is in harmony with the teaching of the New Testament, and which will tend to make men better in God's sight (see Matt. 7: 20), is proper to do on the Lord's day. Cf. Matt. 12: 1-8.*

---

*One of the great evils of our day is the commercialization of Sunday. Thousands of young people on their one free day in the week are allured to spend money and time in so-called recreation resorts planned almost solely for the financial gain of the owners. The natural desire for pleasure is deliberately exploited for the sake of financial gain. No finer Christian service could be rendered than to plan for the recreation of youth on Sunday in ways which should have reference primarily to uplifting results in character. Another evil, which fortunately has aroused the Christian conscience, is the industrial slavery which has made a normal Sunday impossible for many men and women, and side by side with this the unem-

UNCONSCIOUS LOSS
Judges 16: 20

Introduction: 1. The story of Samson is one of the most singular and interesting narratives to be found in all the Old Testament. He was one of the line of judges, used by God for the deliverance of his people from their enemies; and his service in that capacity illustrates the power of God to deliver his people from their oppressors, without the aid of large armies and powerful military equipment. 2. But inasmuch as the things "written aforetime were written for our learning," we may expect to see in the incident of the text an application, not only to Samson, but to the Lord's people even today, as well. Let us, then, in studying this lesson, consider it from two points of view—viz., Samson's loss and the Christian's loss. We shall begin with

I. Samson's Loss

1. The simple statement of the text is that "Jehovah was departed from him." This, of course, implies that Jehovah had been with him, but had left him.

2. But what difference did that make to Samson? The answer can be found by looking at him from two points of view—before and after the incident of the text.

(1) Before the incident of the text.

a. His consecration. He was the only Old Testament character, except Isaac, whose birth was foretold by an angel. He was a Nazirite from his birth and he grew up in the belief that he was consecrated to God. This, of course, involved the belief that there was a definite, divinely appointed work for him to do, and that God would endow him with the necessary strength to accomplish it.

b. The heroic in him.

(a) What was it that made Samson the heroic man that he was? It was, in part at least, because he refused to accept the low, degraded standard with which his contemporaries were content. Although the Israelites still believed that they were the chosen people of God, there was, nevertheless, a glaring inconsistency be-

---

ployment which does not permit others to have any work from which to rest. This also does violence to the spirit of the religious commands about work and rest. It is a travesty on just and brotherly sharing at the same time that it leads to other evils, such as the loss of skill, damage to self-respect, want, and misery and with these an inevitable result in bitterness and social cleavage. At the same time the more fortunate tend to become hardened to the misfortunes of others. Christian sentiment will not only insist on the elimination of unnecessary work on Sunday; it will also help to provide normal opportunities for work, for leisure, and for the cultivation of the higher life.—Gerald Birney Smith, *Principles of Christian Living.* (Revised by Leland Foster Wood, and published by The University of Chicago Press, Chicago.

tween that which they professed to believe and the real condition in which they were.

(b) The other judges were backed by the people. The movements for freedom began with them individually, but the people rallied to their call. Samson, on the other hand, fought alone. He despised the enemy's armies; and when they sought to trap him in their walled cities, he carried away their gates and bars. His name, Samson, which means "Sunny," or "Little Sun," refers not to his strength, but to his disposition. Cf. his riddle, his carrying the gates of the city away, and the incident with the foxes.

(c) Not only did Samson deliver the land from the enemy without the help of the people; he did it in spite of them. Instead of flocking to his standard and helping him, they bound him and gave him into the hands of their enemies, bitterly complaining that he had brought them into trouble with their masters, and showing their willingness to buy their peace at the price of Samson's life. See Judges 15: 9-16; cf. John 11: 47, 48.

(2) After the incident of the text. There were two causes for the Lord's departure from him—an *inward* cause and an *outward;* and as is always the case, the outward cause was subordinate to the inward and depended upon it. Let us consider these causes.

a. The inward cause. See Judges 16: 17; Num. 6: 1ff. The vow of the Nazirite was essentially a vow to abstain from fleshly lusts. He was to hold himself pure as God's instrument, yielding his members to no evil. Strength for duty will always come to such a person. The implications are that Samson never rose to the real spiritual significance of that vow; and it was here that the seed of defection were sown, which ultimately reached his outward life.

b. The outward cause. When his inner life was thus weakened, it was then that he was made an easy prey for his enemies. See Judges 16: 4-17; cf. James 2: 10.*

3. And what was the result? His yielding meant the loss of

---

*It seems to be a trifle whether a man's hair was to be permitted to grow, or was cut off. In itself it was a trifle—infinitely unimportant. But it was not a trifle in the light of its associations. Samson knew that it was no trifle: he had no mind to betray to Delilah what he knew to be the secret of his strength. Behind the commonest acts in life, it often happens, there cluster infinite issues; a whole moral world may be at stake: heaven or hell may await us behind a deed done, a word spoken, a consent or a refusal,—and these petty acts at once become momentous; their importance is measured by their results. What could matter less in itself than whether a man was or was not circumcised? "Neither circumcision availeth anything," said the Apostle, "nor uncircumcision." But let circumstances change: let it be maintained by a powerful school in Galatia that no Christian can do without circumcision, and the meaning of that act changes too: "Behold, I Paul say unto you, that if ye receive circumcision, Christ will profit you nothing" (Gal. 5: 2).—H. P. Liddon.

his power, but he did not know it until the strain came.   See
Judges 16: 20, 21.**

II. THE CHRISTIAN'S LOSS

1. The loss here contemplated is that which comes to the
Christian as the result of backsliding.***

**The constant message of every poet, prophet, and seer, of every
leader and guide of Hebrew history, is that only as God dwells in the
nation can the nation be great.   The chosen race go into the wilderness
a mere band of fugitive slaves; they become a great nation because God
is with them.   They go out to battle against mighty enemies, and a little
one puts to flight a thousand, because God marches with the host; They go
to battle without God and the process is reversed—they go out one way
and flee seven ways.   Prophets like Elijah defy kings like Ahab; men
untrained to arms like Gideon put trained armies to flight; Elisha, lonely
and forgotten, counts those who be with him more than those who be with
his foes, because he sees the chariots and horsemen of God moving in the
clouds; David, the shepherd boy, is stronger than Goliath; Daniel, in his
purity and piety, is much more than a match for the tyrannous king who
holds him in his power; and the simple explanation of every such triumph
is that God is with those heroes of faith and action.   We may say, if we
will, that the heroism of those men was but the reflex action of their
faith; it does not alter the facts.   Something made them great, some power
moving in and through them, which begot faith, and courage and high
ideals, and noblest heroism.   "The Lord was with them," is the explanation
afforded us in the Scripture.   He was with them of their own consent,
working through their own obedience and consecration.   They were his
vehicles, his instruments, the media of Divine manifestations.   And if
they had withdrawn from God, or if God had withdrawn from them, then
had they been as other men; they would have awakened as Samson did, to
know their strength departed and the fountains of their virtue dry.—W. J.
Dawson.

***What is backsliding?   It is a falling from grace.   But let us look
at it psychologically.   The man has been "born again," and the new-born
soul is feeling its way along a course absolutely new to itself.   It faces a
trackless area, and everything is strange.   Under these conditions of inex-
perience, evil meets the new life in countless guises.   It often comes suddenly with no time for deliberation.   It comes, many times, at an inop-
portune moment, when the new life is not at its strongest.   That life is
surprised and taken off its guard.   It does not take in the gravity of the
situation.   The seriousness of the consequences is not comprehended, and
the yielding is often almost imperceptible.   Yet, notwithstanding all palliat-
ing conditions, the yielding is sin.   Darkness again suffuses the soul; condemnation spreads its gloom over consciousness, and sin, once getting a foot-
hold, however slight and brief at first, in the regenerated heart, brings back
the old tendencies which, prior to regeneration, have dominated the psychical being.

The consequence is that there takes place in consciousness an oscillation
between victory and defeat.   Now the new life is victorious; and now the
old tendencies conquer.   But such psychical fluctuations, from the very
nature of the psychical structure, cannot be perpetual.   Resilience gradually
and imperceptibly grows less.   The movement now swings positively in one
of two ways.   Weary of vacillation, disheartened by repeated failure, vanquished by continuous defeats, the heart may swing completely back into
the old grooves of action.   The rebound from sin then ceases; the recoil
from condemnation ends.   The life then remains under the domination of
sin; in common terminology, it is "backslidden."—H. E. Warner, *The
Psychology of the Christian Life*, p. 127.

2. Backsliding may be, and often is, unconscious.

(1) Many people seem to imagine that once saved, they are always saved; and since they are not conscious of any break with the church, they take it for granted that they are still in the Lord's favor. Cf. Luke 15: 25-32; Matt. 25: 1-13. The "elder brother" never left his father, but it is obvious that he was not in harmony with him and did not respond to his entreaties. The "five foolish virgins" remained with the wise ones all through the parable, until the bridegroom's coming was announced, but they were denied entrance into the banquet hall.

(2) But in many instances a change *has* passed over their lives. Associations and practices which at one time they would have scrupulously avoided are now admitted for "business" reasons, "legitimate" pleasures, or because of a "broader" knowledge of the world. Alexander Pope expressed this attitude in these words:

> Vice is a monster of so frightful mien,
> As to be hated needs only to be seen;
> Yet seen too oft, familiar with her face,
> We first endure, then pity, then embrace.

3. The degradation of character, therefore, may continue quite unconsciously; and it is only in the time of some crisis in a man's life that he becomes aware that his moral strength has departed from him.****

4. If any one would like to make an estimate of himself, there are two things which clearly tell him what he is—viz., what he wants and what he does. Let us consider them.

(1) *What he wants.* It is true that as the will is, so is the man. What, then, is the direction of the currents of your desires? If one will only watch the flow of his desires, he can be sure as to whether his religious life is ebbing or rising.

(2) *What he does.* The clearest outward test of a man's

****He is like a man who has crossed the boundary between manhood and old age; and who has not discovered the effects which the lapse of years has had upon him. He only becomes aware of the fact of his utter helplessness in the face of some critical emergency.

I remember a great elm tree, the pride of an avenue in the south, that had spread its branches for more years than the oldest man could count, and stood leafy and green. Not until a winter storm came one night and laid it low with a crash did anybody suspect what everybody saw in the morning—that the heart was eaten out of it, and nothing left but a shell of bark.—A. Maclaren.

We are told that if a frog is put into a bowl containing cold water, and the water is then brought up slowly to the boiling point, the frog is so unaware of the gradual change in its condition that it is boiled to death when, at any moment, it might have jumped out. Thus, the depreciation of one's moral character goes on unsuspected.

heart is seen in that which he does. Conduct is the brightest illu-
mination of character, especially one's own character.*****

5. *A note of hope.* While it is true that a mis-spent life can
never be that which it might have been; yet, if such a man will
turn to God, he may be sure that the Lord will again hear him and
give to him his blessings. Cf. Judges 16: 22-30.

> I walked through the woodland meadows.
>   Where sweet the thrushes sing;
> And I found on a bed of mosses
>   A bird with a broken wing.
>
> I healed its wound, and each morning
>   It sang its old sweet strain,
> But the bird with the broken pinion
>   Never soared as high again.
>
> I found a young life broken
>   By sin's seductive art:
> And, touched with a Christ-like pity,
>   I took him to my heart.
>
> He lived with a noble purpose
>   And struggled not in vain;
> But the life that sin had stricken
>   Never soared as high again.

*****A Christian may be in a society where the tone is agreeably
worldly. And he finds it a little hard to maintain the distinctness of the
Christian life. It is pleasant to him to stand well with his unconverted
friends. And the temptation springs up in his heart to conform. It comes
in the subtle form of presenting to his friends a Christianity void of all
that even the world may call narrowness or fanaticism. He hopes that by
mingling as far as possible with those who are undecided, in their recrea-
tions and the pursuits that may be common, he may gain an influence over
them that may be used for God; but it leads him to compromises, until
the process of levelling down has gone so far that the distinctive attitude
of the Christian life has gone. Now, just so far as this has taken place,
a man's influence with others is killed. All the while that he was fondly
imagining he was presenting to his friends the type of a Christianity shorn
of all acerbities and angularities, his power over them has been quietly slip-
ping away. And the awakening to this consciousness is an unpleasant experience. Some one of his careless, light-hearted acquaintances has become
more serious—the breath of God's Spirit where it listeth has awakened a
new longing in his soul; and his life, so self-centered, so agreeably undisturbed before, has become to him poor and miserable without Christ. He
wants direction, he wants communion; he wants to hear the man speak
who can tell the reality of these things to his own heart. And to whom
does he resort?—to the Christian who has lost his Christian savour and
become worldly? No; but to the man about whom his Christianity is the
most distinctive thing, who has not been engaged in minimizing this difference between himself and the world, and paring down the dimensions
of that, but who has longed—and has got some part of that for which
he longed—to be "transformed by the renewing of his mind." Why,
thinks the Christian who has lost his influence, did my friends not come
to me?—James Hastings.

But the bird with the broken pinion
Kept another from the snare;
And the life that sin had stricken
Raised another from despair.

Each loss has its compensation,
There is healing for every pain;
But the bird with a broken pinion
Never soars as high again.

—*Hezekiah Butterworth*

❖ ❖ ❖

A MAN WHO TALKED TO HIS SOUL
Luke 12: 13-21

Introduction: 1. Christ was in the midst of delivering a very solemn charge to his disciples, in the hearing of great crowds of people, when a man out of the multitude interrupted him and said unto him, "Teacher, bid my brother divide the inheritance with me." As we view the matter, this was a rude interruption and was actuated by a very selfish motive. However, there is nothing unique about it; for if all the thoughts in the average congregation should suddenly become vocal as the preacher is speaking, there would indeed be some strange interruptions. 2. The answer which Jesus gave this man plainly showed that the Lord disapproved his request: "But he said unto him, Man, who made me a judge or a divider over you?" Jesus, therefore, deliberately refused to exchange his position as a teacher of the great principles of life for that of an arbitrator; and those who preach the word today should be very careful not to become unduly involved in social and political disputes. Their business is to preach the word, proclaim the eternal principles which will point to the way in which justice will be done to both sides. 3. Although refusing to leave his position as a teacher for that of an arbitrator, Jesus did make use of the interruption as an occasion for delivering a powerful lesson on the supreme values of life. He did not stop to investigate the claim of the man against his brother, but he did point out the fact that there is danger of a greater loss than that of this world's goods. See Luke 12: 15-21. Here is a lesson of universal application, and in studying it let us begin by considering,

I. THE STATUS OF THE RICH MAN

1. He was a successful farmer and that, in and of itself, is always an asset to any community. It is encouraging to see a man take pride in his farm, and who endeavors to make it produce that which it is capable of producing.

2. There is no indication that he came into possession of his wealth through fraud or other dishonest means. Nothing is said about his being unfair to any man who may have worked for him.

3. But with all his success in the material things of this life, he failed to place the emphasis on that which really counts.

II. WHY DID THE LORD CALL HIM A FOOL?

1. Because he left God out of his plans. Cf. James 1: 17; Acts 14: 17; Psalm 127: 1.

2. Because he did not consider aright his fellow man. See James 1: 27; Gal. 6: 10; Matt. 25: 31ff.

3. Because he placed the wrong emphasis on material wealth. Cf. Matt. 6: 19, 20; 1 Tim. 6: 10, 17-19; Matt. 16: 26. Here is what money, which has such marvelous possibilities for good or evil, says to us all:

> "Dug from the mountainside, washed in the glen,
> Servant I am or the master of men,
> Earn me, I bless you; steal me, I curse you,
> Grip me and hold me, a field shall possess you.
> Lie for me, die for me, covet me, take me;
> Angel or devil, I am what you make me."

4. Because he lived for time and time only; he did not take eternity into consideration. Cf. 1 Cor. 15: 32b; 2 Cor. 5: 10; Luke 16: 9-12.

III. THE LESSON ILLUSTRATED

1. Tolstoi, the great Russian novelist, has a moving story of a young Russian who fell heir to his father's small farm. As soon as he received possession of it he began to dream of how he might add to it. One morning as he was standing near the old homestead a stranger approached him and told him that he could have for nothing all the land which he could walk around in one day. But he warned him that he must be back at the very place from which he started by sundown. Pointing to the grave of the young man's father, the stranger said, This is the point from which you are to start, and to which you must return by the time the sun goes down.

2. The young man eagerly looked over the rich fields in the distance, and, throwing off his coat, and without waiting to say a word to his wife and children, he immediately started out across the fields. His first plan was to cover a tract of land six miles square; but after he had walked the six miles he decided to make it nine, then twelve, and then fifteen, which would give him sixty miles to walk before sundown. He covered two sides of the square, or thirty miles, by noon; but in his eagerness to cover the remaining distance of thirty miles, he did not stop for lunch. An hour later he saw an old man drinking water at a spring, but in his thirst for more land he brushed aside the cup which the old man offered him and rushed on in his quest for possession of the land.

3. As he approached his goal he was worn down with fatigue. When he was only a few hundred yards from the line he saw the

sun nearing the western horizon, and he realized that he had only a few minutes left. Hurrying on, and almost ready to faint, he summoned all of his energies for one last effort and managed to stagger across the line just as the sun was setting. But as he crossed the line he saw a cruel, cynical smile on the face of the stranger who had promised him the land, and who was waiting for him there at his father's grave. Just as the young man thought himself master and possessor of fifteen square miles of rich farming land, he fell dead at the stranger's feet. Then the stranger said to the servants, I offered him all the land which he could cover and you can see what it is—six feet long and two feet wide; and I thought that he would like to have the land close to his father's grave, more than anywhere else. With that the stranger, who was Death, vanished, saying as he went, I have kept my pledge. And the things which he so earnestly coveted, whose shall they be?

4. The rich man of the Lord's parable was a fool because he counted on time; and time, as it always does in such cases, betrayed him. He had doubtless expected several years at least in which to enjoy the fruits of his labors, but God said unto him, Thou foolish one, this night is thy soul required of thee; and the things which thou hast prepared, whose shall they be?

"So is he that layeth up treasure for himself, and is not rich toward God."

❖ ❖ ❖

THE SIN OF MEROZ
Judges 5: 23

Introduction: 1. The first period of the history of the judges closed with Israel's struggle against the Canaanitish king, Jabin. The central figure in the struggle was the prophetess Deborah, the one who spoke the words of the text. Her natural ability made her an outstanding woman; but when her prophetic powers are added to her natural endowments, she becomes one of the great women of history. 2. Little is said of the condition of Israel during Deborah's time, except that Jabin mightily oppressed them for twenty years. As these years drew to a close, Deborah delivered Jehovah's commandment to Barak. This commandment instructed him to take ten thousand soldiers and proceed to mount Tabor, adding, "And I will draw unto thee, to the river Kishon, Sisera, the captain of Jabin's army, with his chariots and his multitude: and I will deliver him into thy hand." But Barak refused to go, unless Deborah would go with him. She agreed to go, but assured him that the undertaking would not be for his honor: "for Jehovah will sell Sisera into the hand of a woman." The army was then assembled, and the ensuing battle resulted in the complete defeat of the forces of Sisera. 3. The closing part of the narrative tells of Sisera's flight and death, and the complete over-throw of Jabin's rule over Israel. Deborah's victory song follows next; and in the midst of it the words of the text are found. The inhabitants of the village of Meroz, for some reason, failed to respond to the call of Jehovah, and were, accordingly, made the victims of the curse of Jehovah, pronounced by Deborah. But in studying this lesson, let us ask,

I. What Was the Sin of Meroz?

1. *The neglect of a plain and positive duty.* There is no other mention made of Meroz in the entire Bible, and from what is said here we naturally conclude that its inhabitants were neutral, impassive, and useless. Their curse, as was the case of the people of Chorazin, alone preserves them from oblivion. They are not remembered because they conspired to betray their country into the hands of her enemies, but because they failed to assist her in the time of her crisis.

(1) The question concerning the sin of Meroz involves a vital principle; for there are people in practically every community who are to the Lord's work now what the inhabitants of Meroz were to it then. Cf. Matt. 7: 21; 12: 30; James 4: 17.

(2) However, before one can do his full duty in the Lord's service, he must have a clear understanding of what the will of the Lord is, and this can only be had by a careful study of the Bible. See Col. 3: 17; 2 Tim. 3: 16, 17; Psalm 127: 1; Matt. 15: 13; John 7: 17.

2. *It was the sin of lukewarmness.* To be lukewarm is to be indifferent toward or manifest a lack of interest in the Lord's work. See Rev. 3: 14-16. There is a continual struggle between right and wrong; and the Lord's people should always take a stand for the right and against the wrong, that is, they should be for everything the Lord is for and against everything he is against. To attempt to be neutral or indifferent is to identify one's self with that which Christ opposes. Cf. Matt. 12: 30.

3. *The sin of failing to take hold of an opportunity.* The fact that they were condemned for their inaction is proof that they had an opportunity to have part in the conflict.

(1) Today when truth is at stake many professed followers of Christ attempt to wash their hands in Pilate's basin of weak neutrality, but they only soil the water without cleansing their hands, and are guilty of failing to take hold of an opportunity of witnessing for the truth.

(2) Not only can people refuse to come "to the help of Je-hovah," they can even take an antagonistic stand against his work. Cf. Acts 5: 33-39; Phil. 3: 18.

II. Some Reasons for Their Sin

No reason is assigned in the Scriptures for the attitude of the people of Meroz, but we can both state and consider some of the reasons men give today for their failure to come "to the help of Jehovah."

1. *God does not really need help. He will do that which he sees is best, whether we help or not.* That is doubtless true, but the question is, Does he will to excuse us on that ground? If it is his will that we be his agents, can we wisely disobey him by pleading that we have too much reverence or too much faith to do what he commands? Cf. Mordecai's answer to Esther, Esth. 4: 13, 14.

2. *False humility.* Humility may be both good or bad. It is good when it stimulates the man who feels his weakness to a greater determination to use all the strength he has. It is bad when it paralyzes the active powers of a man and causes him to believe that it makes no difference whether he works or not. Cf. the one-talent man, Matt. 25: 24-27.

3. *Fear, or simple cowardice.* We all should be lovers of peace, but peace at any price is not taught in the Bible. *Right* is higher than *peace,* and it often happens that both cannot be had at the same time. He, therefore, who fears to offend the wicked is not right before God. Cf. Rev. 21: 8a (said "of Christians who through cowardice give way under persecution and apostatize"— Thayer). The garments of such a person may be faultless on a dress parade, but people usually save their cheers for those who are stained and scarred by battles. Cf. Matt. 5: 9. The reference here is to *peacemakers,* not just *peaceable* people.

4. *Indolence, or mere laziness.* This is one of the greatest sins among so-called Christians today. The five foolish virgins— those who make such preparation as their own indolence and indifference regard as sufficient, knowing all the while that they run some risk of being lost—furnish a classic example of this sin. See Matt. 25: 1-13.

III. THE CURSE PRONOUNCED UPON MEROZ

1. *Was this curse ungodlike and would such be unchristian today?* The wording of the text makes it evident that this curse was not the mere language of Deborah, spoken in the heat of exultation and vengeance—"Curse ye Meroz, said the angel of Jehovah." Such words would be wholly out of place upon the lips of fallible men, but they represent the exact attitude of Jesus. Cf. Matt. 25: 28-30.

2. *The principle of this curse is still in evidence today.* No audible voice is heard by those who consciously decline to do that which they recognize as their plain duty; but no such voice is needed. The process which leads to this moral and spiritual decay is usually, if not always, gradual. Such people go from one lost opportunity to another until their fate is sealed and the curse is pronounced, just as truly as if it were spoken in audible tones.

3. *The curse of Meroz is the curse of uselessness.* Such a con-

dition, as has already been observed, comes from false humility, fear, and indolence; and nothing but the power of Jesus can remove these stones which lie upon the sepulchres of vigor, energy, and work for God. When one realizes that he has been redeemed by Jesus, his soul leaps up in love and he desires to serve the Saviour who redeemed him from sin. Cf. Phil. 3: 7-14.

◆ ◆ ◆

A MOTHER IN ISRAEL
Judges 5: 7

Introduction: 1. Ordinarily, the voices which speak to us out of the past are those of men. It was God's will from the beginning that men should have the responsibility of leadership; but it is true that they have not always been faithful to that trust. It sometimes happens that women are compelled to do that which men should have done. 2. In our lesson today we are to listen to the voice of a woman:

> The rulers ceased in Israel, they ceased,
> Until that I Deborah arose,
> That I arose a mother in Israel.

The life of Israel at that time was at a very low ebb—politically, morally, and spiritually. The people were groping their way in darkness for the lack of leadership. Their situation was succinctly described by a statement found in Judg. 17: 6.

> In those days there was no king in Israel: every man did that which was right in his own eyes.

3. It was in a time like this, when the leaders failed, that a woman stepped into the breach; and as a result the political channels of the nation's life were cleansed. The enemy, both from within and from without, was beaten back. The people gained their self-respect, and hope took the place of despair. In the words of James Russell Lowell,

> When a deed is done for Freedom,
> Through the broad earth's aching breast
> Runs a thrill of joy prophetic,
> Trembling on from east to west.

When leaders failed and men were side-stepping their responsibility, a woman, a mother in Israel, stepped into the breach, and repaired it. But in studying this lesson, let us begin by considering the fact that

I. DEBORAH WAS A LEADER IN HER OWN HOME

1. She arose, she said, not an educator, stateswoman, or religious dignitary, but a *mother* in Israel. She evidently took pride in the noblest of all vocations, that of motherhood.

2. There are many of us today who have a tendency to wax sentimental on Mother's Day, and it is well that we should; but this attitude toward our mothers should not be confined to a special day—it should be extended to include all of our days.

3. No one can read the Bible without reaching the conclusion that woman's primary sphere is in the home. Cf. Tit. 2: 1-5. It is true, as some one has said, that "there is no influence in the world today like the influence of a Christian mother."

(1) We all agree with Lincoln when he said, "All that I am or ever hope to be, I owe to my angel mother."

(2) The most influential member of any home is mother. Her influence may be for good or bad. In the home, a mother's personality permeates the atmosphere and indelibly stamps itself upon the children. No mother who loves her home and her family would exchange places with any other woman. Her calling is so high, so sacred, that she has no higher aspirations. In the children entrusted to her, she is handling the Lord's most precious jewels, and will be held accountable for the shaping of their lives. Mothers are making or unmaking civilization; they are promoting or holding back God's kingdom upon the earth; they are doing this whether they will it so or not. The young life is plastic, and takes the shape of that with which it comes in contact. Therefore, let all mothers try to appreciate the power of their influence. There is no other person from whom the child receives so many ideas, impressions, and habits, which are so abiding. (Metta N. Thomas.) How true is the proverb found in Ezek. 16: 44!

4. When the day arrived, therefore, on which many mothers of our country sought careers outside the home, and gave over to others the rearing of their children, it was then that the first line of defense was placed in jeopardy. There is absolutely nothing that can take the place of a mother's influence in the home and with her family.* Cf. Jochebed, the mother of Moses; Hannah, the mother of Samuel; Elizabeth, the mother of John the Baptist; Mary, the mother of Jesus; and Lois and Eunice, the grandmother and mother, respectively, of Timothy.

> They say that man is mighty,
>   He governs land and sea,
> He wields a mighty scepter
>   O'er lesser powers that be;
> But a mightier power and stronger
>   Man from his throne has hurled,
> For the hand that rocks the cradle
>   Is the hand that rules the world.

—Wm. Ross Wallace

---

*But woman reaches her height of glory as wife and mother, as the ministering angel of the home. . .

The story is told of a woman who was rather given to public enterprises and looked down on the mothers who gave their very life to build

II. DEBORAH POSSESSED A FLAMING, MILITANT CONSCIENCE

1. The record shows that when Deborah's conscience was aroused the result was revolutionary changes in a corrupt society.

2. It is true, as has already been pointed out, that woman's primary sphere is in the home; but, as both the Bible and human experience show, her influence is not limited to the home. It will eventually reach every sector of community life.

3. Men, of course, should take the lead in these wider fields of moral and spiritual influence, but it often happens that while they are wringing their hands in futility, or are indifferent to entrenched evil, that women do something about these problems. Cf. Florence Nightingale; Frances E. Willard; and Harriet Beecher Stowe.

4. No one should offer any apology for Deborah's action in judging Israel and taking a leading part in the battle against the enemies of her people; for the context indicates that she acted under Jehovah's authority and with his approval. She endeavored to get Barak to take the lead; but even after his refusal, she never went beyond "womanly modesty" in seeking to direct the affairs which properly belonged to men.

III. THE UNITED EFFORTS OF MEN AND WOMEN

1. It was the united effort of Deborah and Barak which brought about the great victory and deliverance of Israel. This sort of united effort is implied in such New Testament expressions as, "Salute the church that is in *their* house." (Rom. 16: 5.)

---

up the home, that she one day put the question to one of those blessed home-women: "What literary work are you interested in?" She answered modestly: "I am engaged at the present time in writing three books." When the visitor plainly showed her interest and asked to see her product, she gladly consented; and, opening the door to an adjoining room, she called her three children and pointing to them she said: "These are my three books. I am trying every day to write something in the hearts and lives of my children which will make them better men and women and fit them to meet and to solve the problems of life." The literary visitor left that home thoughtful; that home-woman had taught her one of the greatest lessons of life.

There are women who have been the inspiration in the lives of their husbands without openly taking an active and leading part in their endeavors. Many of the world's greatest orators, statesmen, editors, and preachers owe their success in life to the help and the inspiration they have received from their wives. The wife has often furnished the thoughts, and the husband has expressed them. A wife should walk through life with her husband in that spirit, encouraging, inspiring, and always pointing him to yet greater heights of service and usefulness. Happy the man to whom God has given that kind of a woman! If she is not interested in his work, she neglects one of her first duties, and her husband will not wield the influence which might have been his with her at his side. His success is hers, and his failure is her failure. (A. T. Lundholm.)

2. No faithful Christian woman is contented to wage the battle single-handed. It is when the parents and children in a given home have a working relationship with the church that the best chance of happiness and success is seen.

3. The home is the unit of society, and we have no right, therefore, to expect a better society than the home. If we want society to be better, then we must improve the home; and this improvement must begin with the parents, and especially the mother. Cf. Prov. 22: 6; Eph. 6: 1-4.

4. There are few pictures which are more beautiful than the one which is painted in Prov. 31: 10-31; and as then, so now,

> Her children rise up, and call her blessed;
> Her husband also, and he praiseth her, saying:
> Many daughters have done worthily,
> But thou excellest them all.
> Grace is deceitful, and beauty is vain;
> But a woman that feareth Jehovah, she shall be praised.
> Give her of the fruit of her hands;
> And let her works praise her in the gates.

◆ ◆ ◆

"NEVER MAN SO SPAKE"
John 7: 46

Introduction: 1. Almost every one is interested in hearing the words of great men. Fortunate, indeed, were those who heard Moses' farewell address, Paul's defense before Agrippa, or Jesus' sermon on the mount. The words of Jesus always had a charm for those who heard him, whether friend or foe. The literature of the world may be searched, but the words of no man will be found which surpass, or even equal, the words of Jesus, especially when one considers their import. 2. The author of the Fourth Gospel had a definite purpose in view when he wrote his record—the purpose being to bring others to share his conception of Christ, to convince them that the historical Jesus of Nazareth was one—the only one—of whom it could be said, "We beheld his glory, glory as of the only begotten from the Father." 3. Looking to the fulfilment of his purpose, he accumulated evidence of the overpowering impressions of the greatness of Jesus that were left in the minds of those with whom he came in contact—from the testimony of the guileless Nathanael down to that which was borne by the officers who were sent to arrest Jesus, but who were so awed by his personality that they returned to those who sent them without having accomplished their mission. But in studying this lesson, let us consider,

I. Some References to the Speech of Jesus

1. Luke 4: 16-22; Matt. 7: 28, 29; Mark 12: 37; John 7: 45, 46.

2. It should be kept in mind, when considering this question, that the people who heard him on the occasions referred to did not know him to be the Son of God as we do; but, in spite of that, the verdict was, "Never man so spake."

II. In What Did the Charm of His Speech Consist?

1. Was it rhetoric, his choice of words, pleasing allusions, or delightful stories?

2. It is certain that the officers who reported his speech did not have in mind his oratory; and it is equally certain that the common people heard him gladly because he always had something to say.

3. There is a great difference in *having something to say* and in *having to say something*. Frequently, instead of fighting for some great cause, we find ourselves just uttering words, it may be beautiful words, but, nevertheless, words which are powerless to convict those who hear.

III. The Uniqueness of the Speech of Jesus

1. *Never man so spake of God.* He never argued the fact of God's existence, but spoke of him as a loving heavenly Father. See Matt: 6: 24ff and cf. 2 Pet. 3: 9.

2. *Never man so spake of man.* He knew what was in man (see John 2: 25), that is, his possibilities for good or bad. His words were such as to encourage the good and defeat the bad.

3. *Never man so spake of women and children.* Cf. John 4: 1ff; 8: 1ff; Matt. 18: 1ff. Notice the sphere to which he elevated them.

4. *Never man so spake of salvation.* Cf. Heb. 2: 1-3. Man has a threefold relation to sin—viz., love for, practice, and guilt of sin; and Jesus, accordingly, revealed a threefold method of salvation from sin:

(1) Faith to save from the love of sin.

(2) Repentance to save from the practice of sin.

(3) Baptism to save from the guilt of sin.

a. That the guilt of sin remains after one believes and repents is evident from the words that were addressed to the believing, penitent Saul of Tarsus. See Acts 22: 16: "wash away *thy* sins."

b. These words were spoken to him three days after he became a penitent believer. See the context.

5. *Never man so spake of a life beyond the grave.* He did not attempt to prove the fact of immortality; and who but he could say, "I am the resurrection, and the life," and leave the impression on his hearers that he knew that about which he was talking? Cf. John 11: 21-27.

Conclusion: " 'Never man so spake.' The bewildered officials who were sent to arrest him brought in the only verdict possible.

He spake uniquely, he spake divinely. Jesus Christ is God's speech to the world, his epic poem, his autobiography." (Edgar Dewitt Jones.) Cf. John 1: 1; Heb. 1: 1, 2; Matt. 17: 5.

❖ ❖ ❖

THE KING'S MARCHING ORDERS
Matt. 28: 18-20

Introduction: 1. One of the greatest needs of our day is a recognition of the authority of Jesus. No one can please God or make any real progress until this is done. 2. The purpose of this lesson is to stimulate greater activity on the part of the disciples of Christ by impressing upon them the significance of his final command to them. But in studying this lesson, let us observe, first, that

I. ALL AUTHORITY HAS BEEN GIVEN UNTO JESUS

1. *Authority:* "The right to command and to enforce obedience." (The New Standard Dictionary.)

2. *Primary and delegated authority:* Primary authority resides alone in God. Cf. Heb. 1: 1, 2; 2 Cor. 5: 18. But God has delegated authority to his Son (Matt. 17: 5; John 7: 16, 17; 12: 48-50); and Christ, in turn, delegated authority to his apostles (John 20: 21-23).

II. THE MARCHING ORDER WAS "GO"

1. Filled with the Holy Spirit and in possession of the truth, the disciples began their work on the first Pentecost following the Lord's ascension. Note the first few years of their activities. It might have been difficult to find the meeting place, but not the church!

2. The church has the same obligation today, if the Bible is still sufficient for our needs. Cf. 2 Tim. 2: 2; 3: 16, 17.

III. "MAKE DISCIPLES OF ALL THE NATIONS"

1. The religion of Christ is suited to the needs of all men the world over, and for all time. It appeals to the *whole* man, and not merely to his intellect or feelings.

2. Disciples were made by presenting facts to be believed, commands to be obeyed, and promises to be enjoyed. There are no greater motivating forces than the promises of the gospel. Cf. 2 Pet. 1: 4; 2 Cor. 7: 1.

IV. "BAPTIZING THEM"

1. Observe how the apostles and early Christians understood this command. Cf.. Acts 8: 38; Rom. 6: 3, 4.

2. Affusionists claim that the church had the right to make changes in the *form* of baptism.

Whether the person baptized is to be wholly immersed, and that whether once or thrice, or whether he is only to be sprinkled with water, is not of the least consequence. Churches should be at liberty to adopt either according to the diversity of climates, although it is evident that the term baptize means to immerse, and that this was the form used by the primitive church. (John Calvin, *Institutes, Vol. III*, p. 344)

"Wherefore the church did grant liberty to herself since the beginning to change the rites somewhat, excepting the substance. It is of no consequence at all whether the person that is baptized is totally immersed or whether he is merely sprinkled by an effusion of water. This should be a matter of choice to the churches in different regions. (Op. Cit., *Vol. IV*, Chapter 15.)

But where is the New Testament authority for such a claim? Cf. Eph. 1: 22, 23; Matt. 16: 19; Gal. 1: 6-9.

V. "TEACHING THEM TO OBSERVE," ETC.

1. The disciples must continue in the apostles' teaching and the fellowship, in the breaking of bread and the prayers. See Acts 2: 42.

2. The Lord has promised to be with his disciples, and he has never failed in a single promise which he has made unto them. Cf. Phil. 4: 13.

◆ ◆ ◆

CHRISTIAN PEACEMAKERS
Matt. 5: 9

Introduction: 1. Someone has asked, Would anyone undertake to measure the heartaches in the world today? And if anyone could, is there a man who thinks that he would be strong enough to carry that knowledge? Surely it would be a tremendous load; for it is doubtful if the human race has ever suffered so much from every conceivable ailment of body, mind, and spirit, as they are suffering now. 2. We may be sure that Jesus is "touched with the feeling of our infirmities;" and no one can read the New Testament aright without being convinced that the Lord expects his people to assume some responsibility with reference to these things. See Gal. 6: 10; Matt. 25: 31-46. 3. The tragedy of the modern world is too confused, vast, and terrible to be understood by the average person; but that fact does not relieve us of the responsibility to seek for as clear an understanding of its problems as is possible. 4. It would, of course, be good to consider all the problems of this sin-sick world at this time; but since that is impossible, we shall confine our study to a single phase of the question—viz., that of peacemaking, peacemaking from the Christian point of view. This, naturally, implies a peacemaker, and our first question is,

I. What Is a Christian Peacemaker?

1. To be a peacemaker, according to the Lord's meaning of the term, means something more than merely being peaceable, or amiable, or kindly in one's own personal relationship. It means to make peace between God and man, and between man and man.

2. Jesus pronounced a wonderful blessing upon peacemakers when he said that they shall be called sons of God; but it does not take a very close observer to see that many who undertake this great work today are called nearly everything else but sons of God by their contemporaries.

3. When one begins to study this question seriously he will find himself surrounded by a ring of probing questions. For example:

(1) Am I qualified to be a peacemaker as the Lord means that term?

(2) Am I willing to put forth the effort that is necessary to qualify myself for a real peacemaker?

(3) If I am forced to admit that I am not doing much in the direction of peacemaking, or in my preparation for that work, then let me ask, What, in God's name, am I doing which I think to be more important than this work which the Lord has authorized and encouraged his people to do?

4. The business of being a peacemaker in this modern world is often both difficult and dangerous. One who would bring about peace must be willing to labor long and hard, endure pain and misunderstanding, and even die if necessary. Jesus is the Prince of Peace, and that was the route that he traveled.

II. The Growth and Development of Christian Peacemakers

1. No one is qualified to be a peacemaker until he himself is at peace with God. If therefore he would be a Christian peacemaker, he must first of all find his own peace with God. This involves certain definite requirements—viz:

(1) He must accept God as the basic Fact and Factor in human life and history. See Heb. 11: 6.

(2) He must accept Jesus Christ as the one mediator between God and men. Cf. 1 Tim. 2: 5; John 14: 6; Rom. 5: 1.

(3) He must accept the will of God as his will. In fact, peace is found only in God's will, and he must learn to say, "Not my will, but thine, be done."

(4) He must actually do that which the Lord commands in order to become a child of God and live the Christian life. Cf. Acts 2: 14-41; 2 Pet. 1: 5-11.

2. He must find peace with himself.

(1) He lays a firm foundation for this when he does that which results in his finding peace with God.

(2) In finding peace with God he gives himself to God as the only sensible thing to do. To drift along without plan or purpose is to be guilty of gross neglect. Cf. Heb. 2: 1-3.

(3) God can do more with his life than any one else. To deny that God has a claim on his life is to assert that the Creator has no rights to or in his creature.

> Thou hast made us for thyself and our heart knows no rest till it rests in thee.
> —*Augustine*

(4) Having resolved to give himself unreservedly to God, the one who aspires to be a Christian peacemaker seeks to become a positive instrument of the Divine purpose and will. His greatest desire is for God's will to assert itself through him.

3. He must *endeavor* to find personal peace with others.

(1) No man can long remain at peace, either with God or himself, while enmity toward others is in his heart.

(2) If he is not at peace with others, it must not be *his* fault. See Rom. 12: 18.

(3) The futility of trying to worship God while one is not at peace with his brethren, due to some fault of his, is forcefully set forth by Jesus himself in Matt. 5: 23-26.

a. If a difference is thought to exist between brethren for which there is no foundation in fact, nothing will be settled by trying to compel the supposed offender to admit that he said or did that of which he is accused.

b. No one with the spirit of Christ will want to try to convict his brother of a wrong which he stedfastly denies and about which there is a doubt. He will endeavor to come to terms with him.

(4) The one who aspires to be a Christian peacemaker will want to be at peace with others; he will take the initiative in peaceful attitudes and actions; he will risk rebuff; and he will seek for and find the strength necessary for indefinite efforts on his part, until he is successful, or until he is convinced beyond a reasonable doubt that it is impossible to win his objective. There is no other way by which he can successfully storm the citadel of another's soul. Cf. Rom. 12: 17-21; Luke 23: 34. If he must disagree with his adversary, he will do so without being disagreeable.

4. Having found peace with God and himself, and having earnestly and faithfully tried to find personal peace with others, the one who aspires to be a Christian peacemaker is now equipped to be an instrument in peacemaking between others.

(1) This is because he has acquired certain characteristics which are essential to this, the highest as well as the hardest kind of peacemaking.

(2) He will be trusted by others because he is trustworthy.

The entire tenor of his life is set against inflicting harm; therefore he will not be feared.   He will never be guilty of double-talk, the kind of talk which discourages friends and stimulates enemies. Cf. James 3: 13-18.

III. Dangers and Obstacles in the Way

1. The very integrity of the Christian peacemaker will be a danger to him because selfish and hateful men among the disputants will want to secure his name and influence for their cause. They will tempt him with flattery, threats, and solemn warnings; but, remembering the lessons which he learned in his own struggle for peace with himself and others, he will know how to deal with all such matters. He will always remember that his mission now is that of a peacemaker.

2. But it is obvious that even the Christian peacemaker will not be permitted to intercede and set in motion the process of conciliation and reconciliation, in many instances, until one or both of the estranged and antagonistic parties has tried all the known or available means of imposing his will on the other. Such people will first have to be made to realize the end to which they are going before they are willing to listen to the Christian peacemaker.

3. One of the hardest tasks that confronts the Christian peacemaker is that of preaching the gospel of love and brotherhood to those who are filled with hatred toward each other. But that is his task and he must never waver or lose heart; for as his days, so shall his strength be.

◆ ◆ ◆

UNPOSSESSED POSSESSIONS
Obadiah 17

Introduction: 1.   The book in which our text is found is the shortest book in the Old Testament. It occupies but a single page in our Bible and contains only twenty-one verses. But, though brief as it is, the book contains some valuable information; and in the midst of the record are found these provocative words: "And the house of Jacob shall possess their possessions." What does that statement mean?   2.   For one thing, the words clearly indicate that it is possible for people to have possessions which they do not possess; and that it is a great day in the life of any people when they really come to possess that which they own.   3.   The story is told of a woman with plenty of money who went into a book store, and ordered three yards of books in brown bindings to match the color scheme of her living room. She got the books all right, and they were legally hers; but it is obvious that she was not the kind of person who could possess those possessions. But in studying this lesson, let us consider,

I. The Contrast between Physical Ownership and Spiritual Possession

1. Take, for example, the books in our private libraries and the pictures on our walls. They are ours, of course, by right of title, but how many of them really and truly belong to us?

2. There are multitudes of people who have children in the purely physical sense; but there are few people who *really* have children. For the latter there has grown up, like a flower from its bud, a spiritual comradeship, lovely and enduring. They, indeed, possess their possessions.

3. The characteristic American emphasis has long been on extrenal ownership and legal title. We have been saying, "Get more possessions, if you would enrich your life"; but now we are saying that there are two ways to enrich life—viz:

(1) Acquire more things. That is both legitimate and important.

(2) Really come into possession of them; own them in a truly spiritual sense. This last view requires that we turn our attention from the mere acquisition of material possessions to the quality of our souls.

(3) Because of our failure to put the emphasis where it really belongs, the result is that we have houses, but not homes; children, but not companions; books, but not wisdom; acquaintances, but not friends; money, but not happiness; and churches, but not Christ. Consider what the result would be if we really possessed our possessions.

4. Jesus had very little, so far as material things were concerned. He was born in a stable and reared amid very humble surroundings; but he was able to make the beauty of the flowers of his native hillsides; the loveliness of little children; and the unrealized possibilities of the common people his own.

However, this private and personal view is only the gateway to our real aim in this study. Let us consider next,

II. The Contrast between Inheriting Something from Our Ancestors and Really Owning It Ourselves

1. The attitude that one should have regarding this question is aptly expressed in the following words by Goethe: "The possessions which you have inherited from your ancestors—earn them in order truly to own them."

2. We frequently think that we have something because we have inherited it—a good name, for example. A name that has been spoken with honor in one's community is a grand thing to inherit; but every thoughtful person knows that it is impossible for him to hand down to his children the best he has without their cooperation. *One can inherit a house, but not a home.*

3. The same thing may be said of other great blessings which

have been handed down to us, such as the institutions and traditions of democracy. For example,

(1) Free people are at liberty to think and speak for themselves; free schools are at liberty to seek for the truth; free churches are at liberty to obey God rather than man, although all of them do not do that; and free minorities are at liberty to be convinced of truth and error, and free to maintain a loyal opposition.

(2) Such great traditions as the Fourth of July, Thanksgiving Day, et al., can become mere empty shells from which all vitality has vanished, unless each succeeding generation puts new life into them.

III. THE CONTRAST BETWEEN WHAT WE HAVE AND WHAT WE USE

1. A few years ago the newspapers carried an account of the death of a seventy-eight year old man who had gone to school all his life. When he was a boy he received a bequest, giving him an allowance of $2,000 a year as long as he should continue in school. With that arrangement, he never stopped going to school. In all, he took eleven degrees—in law, economics, engineering, medicine, business, etc., etc. That was a mass of information, but did he really have it? He never used it. He never really owned what those degrees stood for. He never truly possessed his possessions.

2. But if one wants to place the emphasis upon the spiritual assimilation of values which he has outwardly acquired or inherited, so that he may really possess them, at least two things are necessary. They are,

(1) *Appreciation.* This is obvious; for almost every one is wishing for things he does not have and for situations which are not his. However, if we only had the vision of appreciative eyes, we could readily see that in our unappropriated blessings we have many such enrichments unenjoyed and many such opportunities which we do not recognize.

(2) But, however great our appreciation, we never truly have that which we do not use. For example,

a. We have the Bible, but do we really possess it? Cf. John 8: 32.*

b. We have the Lord's day, but what does it mean to us? See Rev. 1: 10; Matt. 22: 21.

---

*The story is told of an old man in New Jersey who discovered about five thousand dollars in bank notes in an old family Bible. It seems that his aunt died when he was just a young man. One clause in her will read, "To my beloved nephew I bequeath my family Bible and all its contents, with the residue of my estate, after funeral expenses and my just debts are paid."

The estate amounted to only a few hundred dollars, which he soon spent. He then lived in poverty for thirty-five years. But one day, while packing his trunk to move to his son's home, where he expected to

c. We have Christ—chastener of our pride (Prov. 16: 18);
light to our way (John 8: 12); guide to our conduct (Matt. 16:
24; John 14: 6); friend in our need (Prov. 18: 24); but how
seldom do we appropriate these blessings!

IV. OUR NEED TO POSSESS THESE POSSESSIONS

1. There is, for example, nothing private and peculiar in
nature's relationship with the human race; for nature belongs to
all of us by right of birth—sunrise and sunset; summer and
winter; spring and fall; mountains and plains, etc., but how few
of us really make them our own! Cf. such "nature poets" as Wordsworth, Thoreau; John Burroughs, et al.

> "My heart leaps up when I behold
> A rainbow in the sky."

2. What is true regarding nature is also true regarding God.
He belongs to all of us, but unless we really make him our own,
we will not be blessed of him as he intends that we should be.
Notice the difference between the implications of the following
scriptures: Matt. 5: 45b and Psalm 63: 1-3.

3. Practically all men are religious and very few profess not
to believe in God; but how small is the number of people who are
transformed, upheld, and guided through these trying times by
God personally possessed!

4. When one looks upon the vast expanse of the ocean on a
bright summer day its glorious appearance is a deep blue; but if
he dips up a single glass full of the water, the water in the glass
is not blue. The blueness of the ocean is, in reality, an illusion
of its mass. In the same way, if we look at the church as a whole
—look at congregations at worship with their hymns, prayers, and
communion service—how God-conscious they seem! But take
the members one by one, how God-conscious are they in reality?
How many of us can truly say, "O God, thou art my God"? If
we ever needed a renewal of personal religion, we need it now.
We need to possess our possessions!

5. Few things are more pathetic than the unnecessary loss we
keep bringing upon ourselves through failure to make these possessions our own. Think of the many things we could enjoy, if
we would only make the effort to appropriate the things the Lord
has provided for us.

---

spend the remainder of his days, he discovered the money hidden in the
Bible!

But those who neglect reading the Bible miss a greater treasure than
that, and those who do read it get something which money cannot buy. Do
you own a Bible? If so, do you really possess it? Are you reading it
and searching for the treasure which is called "the hidden treasure"? See
Matt. 13: 44.

THE PRAYER OF JABEZ
1 Chron. 4: 9, 10

Introduction: 1. The verses of the text contain all that which the Bible says about Jabez. They are found in that which is usually regarded as dry genealogical records; but it is certain that no thoughtful person would call these verses dry. Indeed, no one should think of such portions of the Bible as dry and uninteresting; for they tell us of people who once figured in the busy scenes of time, and to whom life was as dear as it is to us. 2. But even if these records do not furnish as interesting reading matter as do other parts of the Bible, still it is evident that they should not be skipped; for in making his way through these uninviting chronicles of births and deaths, the reader does not know what treasure he may light upon. The words of the text are a fine example of this idea. Such an experience is like finding a spring flower in a desert, a treasure hidden in the sand, or a star peeping through the dark storm clouds. But in studying this lesson, let us consider,

I. Jabez, the Man

1. We do not know who Jabez was; but there is much in this brief history which is both interesting and stimulating.

2. It appears that he was born under sorrowful circumstances, but just what they were we are not informed.

(1) His father may have passed away before he was born, leaving his widowed mother lonely and sad as she thought of the new cares and responsibilities which would come upon her as she attempted to rear her fatherless child.

(2) It may have been that the family was in deep poverty, and she saw no way to provide for an additional helpless child.

(3) Or again, it may have been that the mother of Jabez was subjected to unusual suffering and peril in giving him birth. Cf. Rachel, Gen. 35: 16-18. She may have thought that she might have to leave this innocent babe in a cold and stormy world, and for that reason she called him Jabez, "because," said she, "I bear him with sorrow."

3. But whatever the sorrowful circumstances were, the record says that Jabez was more honorable than his brethren.

(1) *It is possible that his poverty may have contributed to this eminence.* Human nature, somehow, needs the vigorous discipline of poverty and adversity to develop the highest manliness.

(2) *The character and scope of his prayer suggest something of the type of man he was.* People who pray such prayers usually excel in character.

II. His Prayer

1. *"Oh that thou wouldest bless me indeed."* Cf. James 1: 17; Acts 17: 28.

(1) *Bless me indeed!* There are many things which seem to be a blessing which are not. Cf., for example, Israel's desire for a king, and Hezekiah's prayer for an extension of life. See 1 Sam. 8: 4-22; Hosea 13: 11; 2 Kings 20: 1-7; 21: 1-18.

(2) Left to ourselves, we are apt to pray for material wealth, success, honor, etc., and they may prove to be curses rather than blessings.

2. *"And enlarge my border."*

(1) The reference here is probably to his inheritance in the land of promise, which had not as yet been entirely redeemed from the enemy.

(2) It is fitting that we, too, ask the Lord to enlarge the field of our activities. For example, we may ask him to make us a blessing,

a. To those in spiritual darkness, Matt. 5: 14-16; Acts 13: 47; 26: 18.

b. To the needy, James 1: 27.

c. To the weak, Gal. 6: 2; 1 Cor. 8: 13.

d. To all men, Gal. 6: 10.

(3) Then, too, there is much of our rightful spiritual heritage still unpossessed. For example,

a. There is much knowledge to be gained, that which God has provided for us. Cf. 2 Pet. 3: 15-18; Hosea 4: 6; John 17: 3; 1 John 2: 3-6.

b. Our faith, hope, and love should be enlarged.

c. The fruit of the kingdom which is available to us should be gathered. Cf. Rom. 14: 17.

3. *"And that thy hand might be with me."*

(1) Although he had asked God to enlarge his border, yet he knew that if his prayer was answered he must himself do his part. Consequently, he expected to go against the enemy; and he reverently asked that God's guiding and protecting hand be with him; for without it he could not hope for the desired victory.

(2) The same principle applies to us, yet how many professed Christians act without calling upon the Lord! Cf. song, "Be with me, Lord." (Chisholm-Sanderson.)

4. *"And that thou wouldest keep me from evil, that it be not my sorrow!"*

(1) He did not pray that no evil might befall him, but that he might be so preserved from its power, as not to be overcome by it.

(2) Much of that which is called evil is a necessary discipline which we need; but we should pray that we be kept from falling under its power. Cf. James 1: 2-4, 12; 1 Pet. 4: 12.

(3) We should not, therefore, be afraid to face evil; but we should always pray for strength to overcome it. See 1 Cor. 10: 13; Rom. 12: 21.

III. THE RESULT

1. "And God granted him that which he requested."

2. The Bible teaches that God always hears the prayers of his children, when they pray in accordance with his will. Cf. 1 John 5: 14, 15; Psalm 84: 11.

3. The course of the Christian, therefore, should be plain when he considers such passages as Rom. 8: 28; Matt. 6: 33; Phil. 4: 6, 7, 19.

◆ ◆ ◆

ASK YOUR PREACHER
1 Cor. 7: 1a

Introduction: 1. The ministry of preaching has been a custom among the followers of Christ since the beginning of his kingdom, nearly two thousand years ago. This kind of work was responsible, probably more than any other, for the rapid growth and development of the early church. Cf. 1 Cor. 1: 21. But it is a truth, not always realized, that no preacher can fulfill his mission, unless the people understand something of how he is fitted to serve them. Cf. the work of a physician. 2. Every one who has any conception of what it means to be loyal to Christ readily understands that all preaching which meets with his approval must be in harmony with the doctrine of the New Testament. See Tit. 2: 1; 2 Tim. 4: 1, 2. 3. Preachers are looked upon as leaders of men, and that is as it should be; but if they are not permitted to offer the benefit of their knowledge and experience, they are to that extent handicapped in the possibilities of their service. 4. Since preachers are constantly dealing with God's word, it is expected, of course, that they should know more about the Bible than any other class of men; and it is but natural when one has a question which troubles him, that he should turn to the preacher for help. Any worthy preacher should be willing to give whatever assistance he can; and he should be able to tell whether or not it is a Bible subject, and if so, what the Bible teaches on the question. But in studying this lesson, let us consider,

I. THE PURPOSE OF PREACHING

1. Preaching is not something which we may or may not have, just to suit our own conveniences and fancies. It was ordained by God himself, and commanded by the Lord Jesus Christ. Cf. 1 Cor. 1: 21; Acts 10: 42; 2 Tim. 4: 1, 2.

2. Gospel preaching proceeds from the basic conviction that life, if acceptable to God, must be lived on his own terms; and that his will regarding man is revealed in Christ Jesus. Cf. Matt. 7: 21; 1 Cor. 2: 1, 2.

3. Every person has a "frame of reference" to which he consciously or subconsciously refers his questions as to what he shall

or shall not do, or what he shall or shall not believe. However, this "frame of reference" is not always dependable, worthy, or intelligent; and the purpose of preaching is to call people's attention to the fact that God's word is the standard to which they must conform, if they would enjoy the blessings he has prepared for them. Cf. Isa. 55: 8, 9; 2 Tim. 4: 1-4.

II. Individual Responsibility

1. One of the clearest lessons taught in the New Testament is that of individual responsibility. No man can please God while blindly following any preacher. It is proper and right that people should listen to preachers, accord them a respectful hearing; but their responsibility does not stop there. Cf. Acts 17: 11; John 7: 17.

2. If the preacher is what he ought to be he will be glad to have people ask him any question which pertains "unto life and godliness," and he will do his best to see that they are told that which the Bible teaches on their question; but if the preacher is not what he ought to be, honest people who have faith in him should not only ask him questions which pertain to their salvation; they should insist that he give them a Bible answer for every question they ask him. Any preacher who asks honest people to listen to him preach is under obligation to do his best to help them see that which the Bible teaches regarding any question of truth and righteousness.

III. Some Questions to Ask Your Preacher

1. *Ask him how many churches of the Lord are revealed in the New Testament.*

(1) The church of the Lord (Acts 20: 28) is that body of people who have been called out of sin in response to the gospel of Christ. Cf. Mark 16: 15, 16; 2 Thess. 2: 13, 14; Col. 3: 15. The term "church" originally meant an assembly (Acts 19: 41, in the original), but it later came to mean an "unassembled" body (Acts 8: 3).

(2) The Lord promised to build only one church, and he is the head of but one. See Matt. 16: 18; Eph. 1: 22, 23; 4: 4; 1 Cor. 12: 12-20.

(3) Every New Testament figure used to describe the church emphasizes its unity. For example,

a. Body, Col. 1: 18, 24.

b. House, 1 Tim. 3: 14, 15.

c. Flock, John 10: 16.

(4) If the Lord has more churches than one revealed in the New Testament, ask your preacher to tell you where you can read about them.

2. *Ask him where you can find the term or name in the New Testament which designates your church.*

(1) It is not enough simply to say that it doesn't make any difference about the name, because one name is as good as another. Nobody either believes or puts into practice in actual life that which is involved in such a theory. Does it make any difference whose name a man's wife wears? Does it make any difference whose name is signed to a check?

(2) Terms of designation which are authorized by the Scriptures:

a. The whole body: The church, Acts 8: 1; his (Christ's) body, Eph. 1: 22, 23; the body of Christ, 1 Cor. 12: 27; Eph. 4: 12 (but the *body* is the *church,* Col. 1: 18, 24: therefore, *the church of Christ!);* the church of God, 1 Cor. 15: 9; the church of the firstborn, Heb. 12: 23. (Note: The original term for "firstborn" is plural and refers to the members of the church, rather than to Christ himself.)

b. In the local sense: Church of God, 1 Cor. 1: 1, 2; churches of Christ, Rom. 16: 16.

c. Individual members: Disciples, Acts 13: 52; believers, Acts 5: 14; brethren, Acts 12: 17; saints, Rom. 15: 25; Christians, Acts 11: 26.

(3) If the term which designates your church, or you as an individual, is different from those found in the New Testament, ask your preacher for the scriptural authority for using it. Cf. 1 Pet. 4: 11a.

3. *Ask your preacher to tell you where the Bible teaches that you can be saved out of the church, as well as you can be saved in it; or that church membership is not essential to salvation.*

(1) The testimony of the Scriptures: 2 Tim. 2: 10; Eph. 5: 23; 1: 22, 23; Acts 4: 12.

(2) Illustrated by Acts 2: 1-41, 47. The people to whom Peter preached on this occasion were guilty of crucifying Christ (vs. 23, 36), did not believe him to be the Son of God, and were, of course, unsaved. They heard the facts concerning Christ, and, believing them to be true, they changed their minds concerning him and came to regard him as both Lord and Christ; and realizing that they were sinners, they asked what to do. Peter told them to repent and be baptized for the remission of their sins, and promised them the gift of the Holy Spirit. They that received his word were baptized and were immediately added to the church, which is the body of the saved. *All the saved were added to the church.* See Acts 2: 47.

(3) Ask your preacher where he gets his authority for saying that a man does not have to be a member of the church in order to be saved.

IV. Voices from the Opposition

1. While the preacher who believes in adhering strictly to that which the New Testament says is trying to get the attention

of the people, so that he may help them realize that God's word must be respected, there are others who would cause them to forget that it is by obedience to God's word that one enters into life. Cf. Rev. 22: 14 (Authorized Version); John 3: 36; 12: 48-50.

2. Any departure from the New Testament order is specifically condemned in the Scriptures. See James 2; 10; 1 Cor. 4: 6; 2 John 9; Gal. 1: 6-10.

3. Jesus Christ is a Sovereign Ruler and the Supreme Head of his church. See Matt. 28: 18; Eph. 1: 22, 23. No one, therefore, has the right to change one *iota* of his will, as revealed in the New Testament. Cf. 2 Tim. 4: 1, 2; Rev. 22: 18, 19.

◆ ◆ ◆

QUESTIONS BEFORE THE HOUSE
Luke 6: 46; 24: 38

Introduction: 1. Any one who is around groups of people, large or small, for very long at a time, will likely hear some very interesting conversations and discussions. The subject matter will likely range from the commonplace and important to the weird and fantastic. In his recent book, *Joyous Adventure,* Dr. David A. Maclennan of Yale tells of a conversation in a Washington cafeteria which had for its subject the decline of the old-fashioned Fourth-of-July celebration, which was climaxed by the bang and whimper of the day's fireworks. 2. During the course of the conversation a woman, described as a "female research assistant in nuclear physics," revealed to her colleagues that she had once smoked a Roman candle. She was asked how she had gone about it, how the smoke tasted, and how long she was unconscious as a result of her experiment; but no one, according to the reporter who related the story, asked her "why" she did it. 3. The word *why* has been spoken of as one of our forgotten words. Despite its usefulness in preserving human rights, including human lives, and perpetuating human knowledge, the word is used less and less by people who ought to know better. Children still use it, and some grown-ups; but the great bulk of humanity does not seem to be aware of its importance. When professing Christians refrain from asking and facing questions which begin with "why," their vitality is approaching a dangerously low ebb. But in studying this lesson, let us begin with

I. The Master Teacher

1. Any one familiar with the teaching of Jesus knows that he frequently used the word "why." "And *why* are ye anxious concerning raiment?" "And *why* beholdest thou the mote that is in thy brother's eye, but considerest not the beam that is in thine own eye?" "And he saith unto them, *Why* are ye fearful,

O ye of little faith?" "And he said unto him, *Why* asketh thou me concerning that which is good?"

2. There are answers to all these questions, and the Lord wanted the people then, and he wants us now, to find them. The Supreme Teacher knew that nothing in true education matters as much as asking the right questions of the right people.

3. New Testament Christianity encourages questions and provides the most complete answers to the questions which deserve to be asked. This, of course, does not imply that every individual Christian has "all the answers;" but it does imply that the Lord's people do receive sufficient light in the mysterious darkness of life to enable them to rise out of confusion and doubt. Cf. John 8: 12; Heb. 5: 14; 1 John 5: 20.

4. There are some questions before the house—your house and mine, the individual Christian and the congregation as a whole—which deserve our consideration today. In this lesson we shall think of two which Jesus asked while he was here on the earth, and which he is still asking today.

II. Reverence and Obedience

The first question is, "And why call ye me, Lord, Lord, and do not the things which I say?" (Luke 6: 46.)

1. This does not suggest that we are not to acknowledge his Lordship, but it does imply that adulation without emulation is not enough. Our divine Leader and Redeemer is to be reverenced and adored, but he is also to be obeyed by all who acknowledge his lordship.

2. His program has been clearly set forth in the New Testament, and his way for us and our time can be discerned. By intelligent study and fervent prayer, we can know that which we should do. So, with this spirit, we ask, "What things, Lord?" His reply is found in such passages as, Matt. 28: 19, 20; 6: 33; John 13: 34, 35; Matt. 18: 21, 22; 16: 24.

III. Faith Is the Victory

The second question is, "And he said unto them, Why are ye troubled? and wherefore do questionings arise in your heart?" (Luke 24: 38.)

1. This question was asked in the evening of the Lord's resurrection day. The inner circle of his disciples had gathered at the old rendezvous. Incredible reports had reached them that their slain Leader had been raised from the dead. They had been amazed by these reports, but they "appeared in their sight as idle talk." It is not strange, therefore, that "they were terrified and affrighted, and supposed that they beheld a spirit," when they saw Jesus in their midst.

2. Why "do questionings arise in your heart?" Why not; for who would remain untroubled by racking doubts as he beheld

his fondest hopes come crashing to the ground around a blood-stained cross? What question would we have asked, had we been there? Perhaps it would have been, "Is the world in which we live the kind in which the good are always at the mercy of the worst?" Or, "What shall it profit to sacrifice for the more excellent way, if the wicked are to have the last word and their way?"

3. But Christ did arise from the dead, and it is through him that we have the promise of the victory. See 1 Cor. 15: 57.

4. In his *Crusade in Europe,* General Eisenhower relates a most interesting and moving incident in connection with the crossing of the Rhine River, in March of the closing year of World War II. The assault on enemy positions was preceded by a violent bombardment in which two thousand guns of all types were used.

> Meanwhile infantry assault troops were marching up to the water's edge to get into the boats. We joined some of them and found the troops remarkably eager to finish the job . . . Nevertheless, as we walked along I fell in with one young soldier who seemed silent and depressed.
> "How are you feeling, son?" I asked.
> "General," he said, "I'm awful nervous. I was wounded two months ago and just got back from the hospital yesterday. I don't feel so good!"
> "Well," I said to him, "you and I are a good pair then, because I'm nervous too. But we've planned this attack for a long time and we've got all the planes, the guns, and airborne troops we can use to smash the Germans. Maybe if we just walk along together to the river we'll be good for each other."
> "Oh," he said, "I meant I was nervous; I'm not any more. I guess it's not so bad around here." And I knew what he meant! (P. 389.)

5. Why are we troubled? and why do questionings arise in our heart? Is it because we have forgotten that he has planned the attack on the enemy for a long time, and that his resources are sufficient to achieve a complete victory? Our divine Commander still speaks this inspiring word to us, "Lo, I am with you always, even unto the end of the world," and, "Let us walk along together." Cf. 1 Cor. 15: 58.

◆ ◆ ◆

A REASON FOR OUR HOPE
1 Pet. 3: 15

Introduction: 1. When Jesus came to the earth to establish his church, the people, on the whole, were in rebellion against God. After living a normal life for about thirty years, he began his active ministry. For a little more than three years he walked and talked among men, and then died on the cross. After his resurrection and ascension, he established his church on the following Pentecost. 2. Opposition to his people was immediately in evidence; and from that day until now there has been a conflict between the truth and error. Cf. context. 3. The early Christians were frequently persecuted for the stand they took; and Peter's purpose in writing the words of the text was to teach Christians how to act under such conditions. But, whether persecuted or not, the lesson is still applicable to all of God's people; and in consideration of it, let us notice,

I. "THE HOPE THAT IS IN YOU"

1. What is this hope, and the foundation of it? Cf. Tit. 3: 7; Heb. 6: 19, 20; Col. 1: 23; Heb. 11: 1.

2. Hope is made up of two elements, namely, desire and expectation. A person may have one and not the other; but there is no *hope* unless both are present.

3. Giving a reason for this hope is equal to giving a reason for believing the Bible.

4. One reason why the church does now grow any faster is that so many of its members cannot give a reason for their hope, or that which they think is their hope.

(1) What would happen if an army of untrained soldiers should go against an army of trained men? Cf. Alexander's 40,000 men *versus* Darius' 1,000,000 men; and see Lev. 26: 8; James 4: 7.

(2) How can this condition be remedied? By making preparation, drilling. Cf. Acts 2: 42.*

II. SOME PERTINENT QUESTIONS

1. Who should be ready to give this reason?

(1) The preacher and all other church leaders. See 2 Tim. 2: 15; Tit. 1: 7-11.

---

*The astonishing spread of Christianity through the length and breadth of the Roman Empire was not merely nor mainly due to the intellectual ability nor the organizing capacity of the early Christian missionaries, nor even to their devotional zeal. These doubtless were contributory factors, but the main factor was the type of life displayed by the Christians themselves. The best men of the time were profoundly dissatisfied with the coarseness and selfishness and ineffective intellectualism with which their social surroundings were charged. They were longing for an atmosphere of thought and feeling, and for modes of life and conduct, to which their nobler nature could respond. And gradually they became aware that what they were seeking for was in their midst—little communities of men and women living together as members of a united family live, tending to their sick, caring for their poor, teaching their ignorant, consigning their dead with reverent hopefulness to the grave, always ready to place their beneficent activities at the disposal of those outside their own fold who were in need of them. And so they were attracted, and the attraction gradually became stronger till at length they found themselves swept into the current of the new movement, and ready to live and die in promoting it.—W. H. Carnegie, *Personal Religion and Politics*, p. 24.

(2) All Christians. Cf. 1 Pet. 3: 15; Col. 4: 6; Heb. 5: 12ff.

2. Why should we be ready?

(1) It is a divine command. See 1 Pet. 3: 15; cf. Matt. 7: 21; James 2: 10.

(2) It is a great means of spreading the gospel. If Christian people would always live and talk more about their relation to the Lord, many questions regarding their profession would be presented to them.**

(3) It furnishes an opportunity for direct teaching on many Bible subjects. For example, *Why belong to this church?* Every member should, in time, be able to give the important facts concerning the church; tell how to become a member of it; and something of its work and worship.

3. When should we be ready?

(1) The question is not, When should the answer be given? but, When should we be *ready* to give it? There is a vast difference in giving an answer and in being ready to give it.

(2) We should be ready *at all times;* but Christians should always try to speak at the *proper* time.

4. To whom should we be ready to give the answer?

(1) *"To every man that asketh you a reason concerning the hope that is in you."*

(2) While Christian people should "walk in wisdom toward them that are without," they should be careful to see that their light is not put "under the bushel." See Col. 4: 5; Matt. 5: 14-16. From the life that we naturally and daily live in Christ, others should be made to wonder at our enthusiasm (Acts 2: 12); our zeal for attending the assemblies at all times, when possible (Heb. 10: 25); our deeds of benevolence, prompted by love (Gal. 6: 10; 1 John 3: 17); and our abstinence from fleshly lusts (1 Pet. 2: 11, 12; 4: 1-5.)

**In the course of the Armenian atrocities a young woman and her brother were pursued down the street by a Turkish soldier, cornered in an angle of the wall, and the brother was slain before his sister's eyes. She dodged down the alley, leaped a wall, and escaped. Later, being a nurse, she was forced by the Turkish authorities to work in a military hospital. Into her ward was brought, one day, the same Turkish soldier who had slain her brother. He was very ill. A slight inattention would insure his death. The young woman, now safe in America, confesses to the bitter struggle that took place in her mind. The old Adam cried, "Vengeance"; the new Christ cried, "Love." And, equally to the man's good and to her own, the better side of her conquered, and she nursed him as carefully as any other patient in the ward. The recognition had been mutual, and one day, unable longer to restrain his curiosity, the Turk asked his nurse why she had not let him die, and when she replied, "I am a follower of him who said, 'Love your enemies and do them good,'" he was silent for a long time. At last he spoke: "I never knew that there was such a religion. If that is your religion tell me more about it, for I want it."—Harry Emerson Fosdick, *Twelve Tests of Character,* p. 166.

III. The Spirit in Which the Answer Should Be Given

1. "With meekness and fear." *Meekness* is gentleness or mildness; *fear* is probably the fear of the Lord. See Thayer *in loco*.

2. The answer, therefore, should not be in the spirit of braggadocio, ridicule, sarcasm, and the like.

IV. Our Hearts and Lives Must Be Back of the Answer

1. The testimony of the Scriptures: Matt. 12: 34; cf. Prov. 4: 23; 23: 7.

2. The meaning of *sanctify:* We should acknowledge Christ as Lord, and act toward him, accordingly. See Thayer; Albert Barnes, *Commentary in loco;* cf. context.

3. A pure heart results in a pure life, and a pure life excites admiration in some and produces shame in others. Cf. Acts 5: 13; Tit. 2: 7, 8; Matt. 5: 14-16.

◆ ◆ ◆

THE RELIGION OF SONG
Col. 3: 16

Introduction: 1. God's people today have few greater heritages than the privilege of singing praises unto him. No great religious movement ever succeeds in the absence of gospel singing. The place and power of song in the Christian's life and program may be learned from such scriptures as the following: 1 Cor. 14: 15; Eph. 5: 19; Col. 3: 16; and James 5: 13. Longfellow wrote,

> God sent his Singers upon earth
> With songs of sadness and of mirth,
> That they might touch the hearts of men,
> And bring them back to heaven again.
> *—The Singers*

2. Christianity is pre-eminently a religion of song; but it is not enough simply to sing. God's people must be careful to sing the right kind of songs. The New Testament not only tells of the place and power of song; it also tells us the kind of songs we are to sing——namely, psalms, hymns, and spiritual songs. All error in singing should be carefully avoided. 3. There are many songs for many occasions, and all scriptural songs have their place; but it is, of course, impossible to call attention to all of them in a single lesson. We shall therefore speak of only a few of the types of songs, and then illustrate each type by some of the well known songs of our day. Let us begin the study, then, by calling attention to the fact that there are,

I. Songs of Salvation

1. Saved people who really appreciate their situation are happy people; and what greater privilege could come to them than the

opportunity to express their feelings toward God in song? Cf. Ex. 15: 1; Psalm 19: 8; Acts 8: 39.

2. Among the many songs suitable for such occasions of praise and thanksgiving, the following may be listed: "Jesus Saves" (Priscilla J. Owens—William J. Kirkpatrick) and "O Thou Fount of Every Blessing" (Robert Robinson—A. Nettleton).

II. SONGS OF PILGRIMAGE

1. The New Testament clearly teaches that Christian people are pilgrims here upon the earth. See Phil. 3: 20; 1 Pet. 2: 11; and cf. Heb. 11; 9, 10, 13-16. The Lord's people are traveling to a better country, and the songs they are permitted to sing always make their journey more pleasant and profitable.

2. Some pilgrim songs which we may sing are, "We're Marching to Zion" (Isaac Watts—Robert Lowry); "He Leadeth Me" (J. H. Gilmore—Wm. B. Bradbury); and "The Unclouded Day" (Words and melody by J. K. Alwood—Arr. by J. F. K).

III. SONGS OF SERVICE

1. Service is one of the essential requirements of Christianity. See Matt. 7: 21; Rom. 12: 1; and cf. Rev. 22: 3. But, aside from this requirement, the happiest people are those who serve best. Cf. Matt. 20: 20-28.

2. Some songs which illustrate this idea are, "Something for Jesus" (S. D. Phelps—Robert Lowry); "Take My Life, and Let It Be" (Frances R. Havergal—Arr. by R. M. McIntosh); and "Must Jesus Bear the Cross Alone?" (Thos. Shepherd—Geo. N. Allen).

IV. SONGS IN THE NIGHT AND IN THE VALLEY

1. Surrounded by sin as they are, God's people, as long as they remain in this world, will be the victims of many heartaches and much suffering? See 2 Tim. 3: 12; Luke 6: 22, 23. Then too, death is inevitable in this wicked world, and the Christian should always endeavor to live so as to be ready when it comes to him. Cf. 2 Tim. 4: 6-8.

2. Songs suitable for such occasions and ideas are, "Lead, Kindly Light" (J. H. Newman—J. B. Dykes); "Be With Me, Lord" (T. O. Chisholm—L. O. Sanderson); "We Are Going Down the Valley" (Jessie Brown Pounds—J. H. Gilmore); "Some Day the Silver Cord Will Break" (Fanny J. Crosby—Geo. C. Stebbins); and "My Latest Sun Is Sinking Fast" (Jefferson Hascall—Wm. B. Bradbury).

V. SONGS OF HOPE AND TRUST

1. As has already been suggested, sin is abroad in the land and there is trouble on every hand, but the Christian has no reason to be afraid of the ultimate outcome. He has God's prom-

ises and he can fully trust in every one of them. Cf. Rom. 8: 28;
Phil. 4: 6, 7; 2 Cor. 1: 20.

2. Among the many songs of this type, the following are suggested: "Nobody Knows But Jesus" (Frances R. Havergal—Jackson Leslie); "O For A Faith!" (W. H. Bathurst—L. O. Sanderson); "Sometime We'll Understand" (Maxwell N. Cornelius—James McGranahan); and "Jesus, Lover of My Soul" (Charles Wesley—S. B. Marsh).

> Lord, may we come before thee with singing,
> Filled with thy Spirit, wisdom, and pow'r;
> May we ascribe thee glory and honor,
> Worthy art thou! Worthy art thou!
>
> Praise God, from whom all blessings flow,
> Praise him, all creatures here below;
> Praise him above, ye heav'nly host;
> Praise Father, Son, and Holy Ghost!

❖ ❖ ❖

THE SCARLET ROBE*
Matt. 27: 27-31

Introduction: 1. The most usual note which runs through the thought and worship of professed Christians is that of gratitude for that which Christ has done for us. Our emphasis is naturally on that. We think of him as the Giver and Benefactor, and ourselves as the recipients. But do we dare face the other side of the question and ask, "What have professed Christians been doing to Jesus?" 2. Those who follow the instructions of a teacher have the advantage of him, especially after he has gone. What is more helpless than a man, however great he may have been, who has lived and taught and died and has passed away from the earth forever. No sooner has he gone than men begin, as it were, to fall upon him, some of the very men who were his friends and followers while he was with them. They use his name for things he never would have used it for, and represent him as thinking that which he never thought. They claim his sponsorship for causes he never would have endorsed, and clothe him in garments of language and ideas which he never would have chosen. But he has gone, and what can he do? His memory and influence are at the mercy of those who are still alive, and when they make claims for him, he cannot deny them. To speak, therefore, about what Christ has done for us is hardly half the story. Think what professed Christians have done and are still doing to him! 3. It will help us in this study if we will consider the process by which men sought to make Christ fit into their ideas and aims while he was still in the flesh; for that is when such an effort had its beginning. His contemporaries endeavored to make of him a Messiah after

*Or, What Professed Christians Have Done to Christ

their own nationalistic expectations; a miracle-worker, instead of a teacher of spiritual life; an earthly king who would serve their own temporal ends. 4. Consider that which was done to Jesus, as set forth in the language of the text! It was bad enough when his enemies put the scarlet robe upon him; but look across the centuries since then and behold what his professed followers have done and are still doing to him! How often have they dressed him in scarlet robes which he never would have chosen! Having decided upon a course of action, or associated themselves with a certain cause, they must defend their position; and what is more satisfactory in this respect than the support of the name of Jesus? This is what psychologists call defense mechanisms. There is hardly a movement in so-called Christian lands but that has been proclaimed in the name of Christ; and that, perhaps, is the most dreadful thing that has ever happened to him. But in studying this lesson, let us ask, "What are some of the scarlet robes which his professed followers have endeavored to put upon him?"

I. They Have Tried to Make Him a Kind of Far-Away Deity—Something He Never Would Have chosen to Be

1. It is true that Christ is now seated at the right hand of God in heaven, but he said that he would always be with his followers here on the earth, not in the flesh, of course, but with them, nevertheless. See Matt. 28: 20; 18: 20; 1 John 1: 6, 7. These passages plainly imply a personal, abiding, and victorious presence.

2. Some one has pertinently asked how professed Christians have managed to get rid of Jesus and his spiritual demands upon their lives. It was not by crucifying him. They would not do that. Nor by denying him. They would not do that. They do it by seeking to honor him with their lips and by pushing him to a safe distance from their lives.**

II. They Have Tried to Make Christ Sponsor Social Causes Which He Never Would Have Sponsored

1. *They have put on him the scarlet robe of carnal warfare in an effort to make him responsible for that horrible system.*

**The story was once told of a missionary in Africa who, while at home on a furlough, bought a sundial so that his people in the African village might have aid in telling the time of day. When he returned to his field of labor he set the dial up in the midst of the village, but his people were so filled with admiration and wonder that they immediately built a roof over it to protect it from the sun and rain! Christ came to help us tell the time of day, to reveal that which the everlasting Sun is doing, so that we might guide our lives thereby; and lo! under the guise of honoring him professed Christians have built a theological roof over him. There are multitudes of his professed followers who could do nothing better than to get that Sundail back into the proper use again.

(1) No honest thinker, who considers all the facts in the case, will say that Jesus is the author of war, or that he is in any way responsible for such a condition. 'Cf. James 4: 1. War is the way to which the world has been condemned because it has rejected God's way. It is the collapse of the divine order which God is striving, with man's cooperation, to establish in the world. It is the terrible punishment which the people in the world have to suffer because they have rejected God's will, which is peace, justice, love, and obedience to his word. *There is a vast difference between the will of God and the judgment of God.*

(2) The early Christians, during the first century or two, stedfastly refused to bear arms in carnal warfare. But when those who professed to follow Christ came into political power through Constantine they became interested in the welfare of the empire. War became advantageous, necessary, they would say, and they did the incredible, though inevitable, thing, viz., they made Jesus the sponsor of their wars; and ever since then they have compelled him to march in his scarlet robe with the armies of so-called Christendom. *That which the Jews and Romans did to him during his trial was nothing compared to this!*

(3) No man can be healthy-minded who does not get back behind his defense mechanisms and face the facts in the case. When he does that in this instance, it will be evident that it is a gross misrepresentation to picture Jesus in the scarlet robe of militarism, as may be seen by reading such passages as Matt. 5: 9, 38-48; John 18: 36; Rom. 12: 18-21; and Heb. 12: 14.

(4) The first message to professed Christians on the war question, then, is, Take that scarlet robe off of Jesus. But, says one, it is sometimes necessary to go to war. Very well; but take that scarlet robe off of *Jesus!* Let those who feel that war is necessary find, if they can, some semblance of an honest argument to support their contention, but don't compel Jesus to sponsor a movement which is the utter denial of everything *he* stood for.

2. *They want him to vouch for that which they think and do, that is, to act as a kind of rubber stamp for them.*

(1) If they are capitalists, they want him to be a capitalist; if they are socialists, they want him to be a socialist; if they want to go to war, they want him to go with them; and if they are satisfied with their way of living, they want him to be satisfied too.

(2) But when they go back behind their defense mechanisms, what do they find? Read John 3: 19-21; Matt. 7: 21; 16: 24; Acts 2: 42. But instead of following the letter and spirit of these passages, how many professed followers of Christ follow their own way of thinking! How many professed Christians make an honest effort to learn the Lord's will regarding the issues of life which confront them before acting upon them?

III. Professed Christians Have Claimed Jesus as Sponsor of Parties Which He Never Would Have Sponsored

1. The Federal Bureau of the Census shows more than two hundred different religious bodies in the United States, the majority of which claim to be followers of Jesus. But if they will only go behind their defense mechanisms and face the facts, what will they find? See John 17: 20, 21; 1 Cor. 1: 10; 12: 12, 13.***

(2) The temptation to twist Jesus into the support of anything we may think or want to do is so strong that few, if any, professed Christians escape it altogether. Accordingly, Dean Sperry of Harvard, in referring to Renan's *Life of Jesus,* said that it "is patently three parts Renan and one part Jesus."

(3) But if we really see this temptation and recognize its ruinous consequence, as recorded in history, we can do something to stop it. The crucifixion of Jesus did him no harm; for he made that the most impressive spiritual force in history. But that which he tried to do with the cross has well-nigh been defeated by that which his professed followers have done to him.

(4) Let every sincere follower of Christ, then, resolve to remove the scarlet robe from him. His enemies removed it in their day; and if his professed friends would do as much, then men would come nearer seeing his quality of spirit, his vision of truth, and his way of life, for the lack of which the world is sick, and to bring which to the men of the earth the church was founded.

◆ ◆ ◆

NO ROOM IN THE INN
Luke 2: 7

Introduction: 1. Every biographer delights to find in the early life of his hero some event which may foreshadow the subject's subsequent career. But did ever a single incident in one's infancy suggest so much as is summed up in the statement of the text? Even as one reads the words now, there is a foreboding in them;

***John Wilkes was a dashing English liberal, and was very popular with a large number of people. It was not long, however, before his followers, calling themselves Wilkites, got out of hand and went wild; and Wilkes himself had to explain, as for example, to George III, that he was not a Wilkite! To think that Jesus has been reduced to that! For if he were here, as he one time was, and looked on the "sectarian Christianity" of our day, he would be compelled to say, If that is Christianity, then I have no connection with it. We may not at once be able to realize our prayer for the oneness of the professed followers of Christ, but there is one thing that we can do, viz., We can take away from Jesus the scarlet robe of sectarianism, and stop trying to identify him with the various sects. For, in truth, he stands outside them all, above them all, alien to them all, lamenting over them all, but praying still that his followers all may be one.

for that was to be the Lord's experience throughout his public ministry—no room for his teaching in the minds of men, or for the quality of his spirit in their lives. And today he meets with the same experience in many pre-occupied lives and bitter human relationships. 2. This is a busy age. Many of the lovely things of life which would enrich us are shut out—great books are not read, great music is not heard, enriching friendships are not cherished, and the beauties of nature are not enjoyed. 3. The major enemy of Christianity is not atheism, but secularism. Cf. Luke 8: 14. 4. But there is a deeper matter behind the crowding out of the higher things of life. If those in the ancient inn in Bethlehem had known what the Christ child would become in the world, some one would have found a place for him. Human beings usually do find a place for the things they really care about. They crowded him out because they had no idea whom he was to become. They, of course, could not know, but we do know and therefore can offer no such excuse. Even our homes and civilization cannot be separated from his influence. Cf. our ideals, books, art, etc. Therefore when we cry, "No room for him!," it is not so much that we are pre-occupied, as it is that our own souls are of such a quality that they desire something else quite different from Christ. 5. It would be a fine experience for us to stand, as it were, before the Bethlehem inn and see how easy it is to shut out the highest things of life by a little inhospitality. If this is done, we will come to understand that to be hospitable is about as important and self-revealing an act as any that we can perform. But in studying this lesson, let us consider,

I. THE SOURCE OF MUCH OF THE RICHNESS OF OUR LIVES

1. If one will only stop to think, he will easily see that the greater part of such blessings comes not from outward strenuousness, but from inward hospitality. Cf. the strenuous vs. hospitable in industry, nature, education, etc.

2. How much, then, of the best in this world belongs to us? Books, friends, music, spiritual blessings, etc. Cf. Phil. 4: 8, 9.

3. Thus, what magical change a little hospitality can make! We should learn to make room for new and ennobling ideas. Cf. the redemption of Silas Marner; Luke 5: 8 (Peter, however, later made room for Jesus); Acts 26: 12-19; Gal. 2: 20. *The incident of Bethlehem is not merely historic; for that ancient scene is being reproduced in many lives today.*

II. THE SIN OF INHOSPITALITY IS SOCIAL AS WELL AS PERSONAL

1. For one to think in terms of personal responsibility is only to see one side of the picture for no one can rightly understand the whole world's troubles unless he views them in terms of inhospitality.

2. What would the result be if mankind in general did not so habitually repeat the scene of Bethlehem! For example, what a difference it would make if, when benefactors come in any realm, we did not meet them with this obdurate, impassive refusal of a welcome! To illustrate:

(1) Thales was the first to predict a solar eclipse, the one which occurred in 585 B. C.; Copernicus was the first to solve the great problem of the movement of the planets; while Galileo distinguished himself by establishing the Copernican theory. But why did these facts have to wait so long before they were generally accepted? Because, as a rule, we write "Welcome" on the doormats of our homes, but not on the doormats of our minds.*

(2) This has practically always been the attitude of the human race toward the teaching of Christ and the apostles. See John 1: 11; Acts 13: 44-46; 17: 10-12.

3. One of the supreme gifts which mankind can enjoy, therefore, is the ability and disposition to recognize and welcome the best in life when it comes.

III. THE MIND AND CHARACTER ARE BOTH INVOLVED

1. That what is true of the mind is also true of the character will become abundantly clear when we consider some of the persons mentioned in the New Testament.

(1) Can any one imagine Pilate as being inwardly hospitable to Jesus? He was a cynical and crafty Roman, habituated to the service of Caesar, sophisticated in his thinking, and hard in his life. Cf. the discomfort of entertaining a guest in a home when the host is alien to him at every point; and what the guest wants forces the suspension or suppression of the host's principal desires.

(2) Caiaphas. What did this shrewd, cagy old ecclesiastic, with a stereotyped religion and a crabbed mind, have in common with this "young Prince of Glory" whose religion was as fresh as the flowers of his native Galilean hills, and whose goodwill was as spontaneous as the affection of the little children whom he loved?

(3) Didn't Judas Iscariot try to be hospitable to him? But there was something else in his heart—the love of money, for example—which crowded the Lord out.

2. It is not always an easy thing to make room for Jesus, but it is a glorious thing; and at the end of the way which will count for the most? Cf. 2 Tim. 4: 10; 4: 6-8.

3. Although the mind and character are both involved, yet

---

*A school board in an American town a hundred years ago, so the story goes, had this to say, "You are welcome to use the schoolhouse to debate a proper question in, but such things as railroads and telegraphs are impossibilities and rank infidelity. There is nothing in the Word of God about them."

one suspects that the real barrier to our making room for Christ in our hearts is an unworthy life. Sin is in the way. If Jesus comes in, many personal and social evils will have to move out. Cf. John 3: 19-21.

4. But if any one is saying that his life seems too soiled for so royal a Guest, then let him be assured that Christ came not at first to a palace, but to an inn; and he has never since despised the humble of earth who will' open the door to him. Cf. Rev. 3: 20.

IV. SOME COMMON CAUSES OF THIS INHOSPITALITY

1. *A tyrant world.* Such a world pre-occupies us and enchains all our perceptions and powers, making it impossible for Christ to have a place in our hearts.

(1) The "world" as used here means the spirit which rules in the majority of men's minds, dominating their interests, and claiming their life power for other purposes than the glory and service of God.

(2) People who are thus controlled cannot make room for Jesus, for Jesus and the world are diametrically opposed to each other. Cf. 1 John 2: 15-17; James 4: 4.

(3) Thus, over how many centers of world life, such as homes, offices, places of employment and pleasure, etc., can one truly write, "No room for Jesus here?"

2. *A dominant passion.*

(1) The word "passion" is used here in its good sense and refers to that governing and coloring influence which controls the whole of our inner being.

(2) In many instances this dominant passion has the effect of crowding Christ out of one's life. For example, a passion for study, business, or pleasure, may absorb all of one's time and energy, and leave none for Christ.

(3) Such things may not be wrong within themselves, but they become wrong when they take first place in one's life. See Matt. 6: 24, 33.

3. *Unshareable secrets.*

(1) These barriers to Christ are often unspoken and even un-formulated, but they are strong enough to exclude him.

(2) Among them we may mention grief, burdens, hopes, and affections; and if we allow them to stand between us and Christ, we deprive ourselves of the friendship and fellowship of the one who is able to interpret them for us and to show us their true meaning, insofar as our own welfare is concerned. See Rom. 8: 28.

ROSES OF BETHANY OR LILIES OF ARIMATHEA
Mark 14: 3-9; John 19: 38-42

Introduction: 1. The lives of most men are characterized by paradoxes. There are joyous surprises and bitter disappointments. Such conditions, of course, have a vital effect upon the lives of people, especially those involved; and a careful study of them will result in an increased knowledge of the formation of character. 2. While paradoxes seem to be the common lot of the average man, and it is to him that the application of this lesson should be made; yet there is, perhaps, no better place for observing their workings than in the life of Jesus, especially during the week immediately preceding his crucifixion. Curious contrasts and vicissitudes strangely unalike rapidly followed each other during that eventful week. 3. However, the main object of this lesson is to emphasize the fact that we should seek to help and encourage others while they need our assistance, rather than wait until it is too late for that which we may say or may do to benefit them. But in studying this lesson, let us consider some

I. Paradoxes in the Last Week in the Life of Jesus

1. *The kiss of Judas and the request of Pilate's wife.* See *Mark 14: 44, 45; Matt. 27: 19.*

(1) One of the disciples of Jesus bargains with his enemies and betrays his Lord with a kiss; while the wife of the Roman governor, an alien to the cause of Christ, and, very likely, a total stranger to him, intercedes in his behalf.

(2) Her deed, in all probability, helped to lighten the blow of the traitor—a blow struck in the dark and under the cover of the sign of friendship.

2. *The defection of the disciples and the confession of the centurion.* See Matt. 26: 56; Mark 15: 39.

(1) The twelve deserted him at a time when he needed them most, but the Roman soldier, accustomed to scenes of bloodshed and human sufferings, was deeply stirred as he surveyed the cross of Jesus. The centurion probably heard Jesus as he made provision for the care of his mother, as he comforted the penitent robber, and prayed for his enemies; and he was, therefore, moved to exclaim: "Truly this man was the Son of God."

3. *The sword of Peter unsheathed against the enemies of Jesus and the Lord's prayer from the cross for those who crucified him.* See John 18: 10; Luke 23: 34.

(1) Here we see a great contrast, both in mind and in emotions. The one sought to kill, while the other prayed that they might live and enjoy the forgiveness of their sins. Think what happens to people who die in their sins!

4. These paradoxes just mentioned are interesting contrasts; but there is another one which has still more interest for us at this

time. It is the one contained in *the episode of roses of Bethany and lilies of Arimathea*. See Mark 14: 3-9; John 19: 38-42. In considering this paradox, let us notice the

II. ROSES OF BETHANY

1. Relate the facts concerning Mary's gracious service.

(1) That which she did may be compared to a cluster of roses which were given to Jesus while he could see their beauty and breathe their fragrance.

(2) This deed has been called "the economy of love's wastefulness," but it must have helped Jesus to bear the thorns of Jerusalem which were soon to pierce his brow.

(3) That which gives such splendor to Mary's ministry is the fact that, seemingly, it had no practical purpose. It seemed wasteful, extravagant, and unnecessary to cold-hearted men, and even to some of the Lord's closest friends. But love can see further than the practical mind; and it is just such an attitude that adds something fine and cultural to life.

(4) This kind of love and its expressions do not need to be justified on the ground that they are useful, for they are ends within themselves. They are not valued for their utility, or even primarily for their beauty, but because of the love they express.

2. Roses of Bethany are flowers for the living—ministries which heal and bless while the struggle of life is on.

GIVE THEM THE FLOWERS NOW!

Closed eyes can't see the white roses,
  Cold hands can't hold them, you know,
Breath that is still cannot gather
  The fragrance that sweet from them blows.

Death, with a peace beyond dreaming,
  The children of earth doth endow;
Life is the time we can help them,
  So give them the flowers now.

Here are the struggles and strivings,
  Here are the cares and the tears;
Now is the time to be smoothing
  The frowns and the furrows and fears.

What to closed eyes are kind sayings?
  What to hushed heart is deep vow?
Naught can avail after parting,
  So give them the flowers now.

Just a kind word or a greeting;
  Just a warm grasp or a smile—
These are the flowers that will lighten
  The burdens for many a mile.

After the journey is over,
  What is the use of them? How
Can they carry them who must be carried?
  O give them the flowers now!

Blooms from the happy heart's garden,
  Plucked in the spirit of love;
Blooms that are earthly reflections
  Of flowers that blossom above.

Words cannot tell what a measure
  Of blessings such gifts will allow
To dwell in the lives of many;—
  So give them the flowers now.
                              —*Leigh M. Hodges*

III. LILIES OF ARIMATHEA

1. Give the facts regarding Joseph and his attitude toward Jesus.

(1) The record says that he was *a good and righteous man,* Luke 23: 50; *a councillor of honorable estate,* Mark 15: 43; *a rich man,* Matt. 27: 57; *a disciple of Jesus, but secretly for fear of the Jews,* John 19: 38.

(2) It is easy to imagine how he must have felt when he saw Jesus being led to the cross. It is true that he had not consented to their counsel and deed; but it is also true that he did not walk by his side, or raise his voice in his behalf.

(3) However, after Jesus had died on the cross, Joseph went in boldly unto Pilate, and asked for the body of Jesus (Mark 15: 43). His request was granted; and then he who hesitated to associate himself with Jesus in life became identified with him in death.

(4) Joseph's ministry, however, should not be lightly regarded, for it has its practical side and is not devoid of sentiment. It cost Joseph something, but his ministry suffers when compared with the fragrant deed of Mary.

2. *White lilies of Arimathea are beautiful, but they are not nearly so lovely as the red roses of Bethany.*

"TO JOSEPH OF ARIMATHEA"

"Strange quiet man, what impulse in your breast
  Invoked your kindness to the Master whom
You had not dared to join? He wanted rest
  Within your heart, but found it in your tomb.

Did you not dare to love him, he who sought
  To give you life, nor asked for recompense?
What pity that in finding him you brought
  Your laggard love in death's cold cerements!"
                          —*From the Christian Century*

3. Dr. Samuel Johnson understood the meaning of lilies of Arimathea. His famous letter to Lord Chesterfield, after the latter had taken a tardy notice of Dr. Johnson's monumental work, *A Dictionary of the English Language,* shows how well he knew the futility of a kindness done too late. The letter follows:

> "Seven years, my lord, have now passed since I waited in your outward rooms, or was repulsed from your door; during which time I have been pushing on my work through difficulties, of which it is useless to complain, and have brought it, at last, to the verge of publication, without one act of assistance, one word of encouragement, or one smile of favor. Such treatment I did not expect, for I have never had a patron before. . . . The notice which you have been pleased to take of my labors, had it been early, had been kind; but it has been delayed till I am indifferent, and cannot enjoy it; till I am known and do not want it. I hope it is no cynical asperity, not to confess obligations when no benefit has been received, or to be unwilling that the public should consider me as owing that to a patron which Providence has enabled me to do for myself."

4. Belated kindnesses and postponed ministries that might have healed and blessed are all too common; and yet it costs so little to be kind, and means so much to be considerate. It is so Christlike to forgive. Why withhold when to share is to save?

5. One of the most revealing and practical sentiments in the writings of Abraham Lincoln is a statement found in one of his letters to his dear friend, Joshua Speed:

> "Speed, die when I may, I want it said of me by those who knew me best that I always plucked a thistle and planted a flower where a flower would grow."

Yes, pluck thistles and plant flowers; plant them wherever they will grow. Plant roses, beautiful red roses of Bethany; and plant them *now!*

◆ ◆ ◆

WHY HAVE A SUNDAY SCHOOL?
Matt. 28: 18-20

Introduction: 1. Christianity, the religion of the New Testament, is preeminently a teaching religion. No one can become a Christian without being taught (Matt. 28: 19; John 6: 44, 45); and no one can live the Christian life without being taught (Matt. 28: 20; Acts 2: 42). It is God's will, therefore, that the church of the New Testament be a teaching institution. Cf. 1 Tim. 3: 15. 2. However, in many instances, it is a well known fact that the period set aside on the Lord's day for Bible study deserves more consideration than is usually given to it. 3. Whether this work should be referred to as the "Sunday school," the "Bible school," the "Lord's day Bible school," or some other similar designation, does not seem to be very important.* The thing that

---

*There are several names by which we designate this Sunday morning program. We commonly speak of it as our Bible school, our church school, or our Sunday school. When we use the term Bible school we refer to the fact that in this school the Bible is taught. The expression

really counts is that the "work" be adequately and clearly described. It seems that this requirement is met by any or all of the designations already referred to; and they shall, therefore, be used interchangeably in this study. 4. The importance of this work is at once seen when it is considered that approximately 80% of the additions to the church come through the Sunday school. Comparatively few of the thousands of criminals. especially among the youth of the land, were members of a Sunday school when their crimes were committed. With these facts in mind, it is easy to see that the important question in this connection is, How may the church best do the teaching which the Lord has authorized it to do? In seeking to answer this question, then, let us consider,

I. The Meaning and Purpose of the Sunday School

1. The true Bible school is the church of Christ engaged in systematic study and teaching of the Word of God, with three great purposes in mind—viz:

(1) To bring into the body of Christ those within the membership of the school who are not yet members of the church.

(2) To train those who are in Christ into full-grown knowledge and appropriation of the riches which are theirs, because they belong to Christ.

(3) To send out into the world fully equipped, victorious soul-winners, who shall be Christ's living epistles to those who do not yet know him.

2. *The whole work of the Bible school centers about its text-book, the Word of God.* Bible study in this capacity is made the means of the threefold purpose of the Bible school, which has for its end *salvation, character building,* and *equipment for evangelism;* or, to express the same thing in other words, *justification, sanctification,* and *service.*

3. The Lord's day Bible school, therefore, is a place to get a Bible education. It is an effort, on the part of the church, to

church school is indicative of the fact that the school is conducted by the church. The name Sunday school suggests that the school is conducted on Sunday and distinguishes it from the regular day schools of the public school system. So far as these terms are concerned one is as scriptural as the other. Not one of them is to be found in the Bible. Neither are such expressions at "Lord's Day Worship Service," "Prayer Meeting Program," "Protracted Meeting," "Lectureships," "Radio Programs," and dozens of other expressions in common use today. But the idea of the work described by these expressions is found in the Bible. If modern methods are to be used in carrying the gospel of Christ to the world we will have to use modern terminology in describing the activity. Jesus Christ rode into Jerusalem on an ass, but it is not necessary for us to make the approach to Jerusalem that way, nor is it necessary for us to say, when we entered by automobile or airplane, that we rode on an ass just because it was said of Jesus. Since the name Sunday school is descriptive of the time of the school it appears to be just as appropriate as any other name and I do not think any well-founded objection can be lodged against its use. — Robert M. Alexander.

carry out the requirements of the great commission. Cf. the purpose of a series of evangelistic meetings. The school gets its name from its principal study and the day on which it is conducted.

II. Is the Sunday School a Necessity?

1. Regardless of that which may be said about the school itself, it is absolutely essential that the work which the school proposes to do be done.

2. As has already been observed, the Sunday school is only a method of doing the things which God requires; and since that work must be done in some way, we should either employ this method, or devise or select a better one.

3. It should be kept in mind that the *true* Lord's day Bible school is not an extra organization, functioning within the church. It is, rather, the *entire* church at work, doing the things which the Lord has authorized it to do.

III. The Importance of Knowing God

1. The testimony of the Scriptures: John 17: 3; 2 Thess. 1: 7-9; 1 John 2: 3, 4.

2. Man, left to himself, is not able to direct his own steps. See Jer. 10: 23. Without some knowledge of the Bible, no one can know his origin, mission, or destiny.

3. But the only way that man can acquire a knowledge of God, and subsequently, a knowledge of his will regarding man, is through his Word, the Bible. Cf. Acts 17: 22, 23; 1 Cor. 1: 21.

IV. The Church's Obligation

1. In the light of that which has already been said, it is unnecessary to argue the need for a Sunday school, or its equivalent.

2. The testimony of the Scriptures: Matt. 28: 19, 20; John 6: 44, 45; 1 Tim. 3: 14, 15.

3. The study and teaching of the Bible are not matters of indifference. Every individual Christian, to the extent of his ability and opportunity, is obligated to do that which he can to make the work which the Lord's day Bible school proposes to do such as God would have it. The teacher's diligent preparation, and the enthusiastic interest on the part of both teacher and student will count for much.

V. Some Objections Considered

1. *Why not teach the whole congregation at one time?* That would be a class, but the basic laws of learning would either be violated or ignored. The mere division into different groups does not make the several classes; God has already made them, and the division into the different groups is simply the recognition of the classes. Cf. Tit. 2: 1ff; Heb. 5: 11-14.

2. *Are not the elders the divinely appointed teachers?* The

elders are the overseers of the congregation, and all the teaching done in the public capacity of the church should be under their oversight; but the New Testament nowhere intimates that all such work is to be done by them personally. See Heb. 5: 12; 2 Tim. 2: 2.

3. *Why not do the teaching at home and thereby eliminate any kind of public Bible school?*

(1) Teaching should be done in the home, and that which is done in the Bible school should not supersede it; but it remains true that not every family is capable of such work. Why not apply the same principle to secular learning? Every family should endeavor to keep the members of its household well; but it is sometimes necessary to call in a physician, one who is more skilled in such work.

(2) The average Sunday school should enroll in its membership many whose parents are not religious, or who are not members of the church. Such parents, of course, would not be expected to teach their children the Bible.

4. It is the duty of every congregation, therefore, to provide adequate teachers and facilities for this work.

❧ ❧ ❧

SALVATION IN TYPE
1 Cor. 10: 1-13

Introduction: 1. One of the fundamental and remarkable facts concerning the Bible is the typical system which characterizes it. There may have been many reasons for this arrangement, but there are two which seem to be among the most important—viz: (1) To illustrate and make plain the scheme of human redemption; and (2) to secure future generations against the many impostures which have obscured the Lord's will as age after age has rolled by. We may be sure, therefore, that any system of religion which lays claim to our faith is not of divine origin, unless it bears the stamp of God's omniscience as seen in its typical co-relation. 2. The deliverance of the children of Israel from Egyptian bondage, their history during the wilderness wandering, and their entrance into the land of Canaan is a type of the salvation wrought by Christ; and since Christianity, as revealed in the New Testament, is the very complement of its typology, we know that it must be the religion for this age which is pleasing to God. 3. It was no accident, therefore, that the Israelites were placed in the land of Egypt, where they were enslaved, oppressed, and corrupted; for their deliverance and subsequent history furnish one of the clearest types of the salvation made possible by Christ to be found in all the Bible. But in studying this lesson, let us begin by considering,

I. THE BONDAGE IN EGYPT AND THE BONDAGE TO SIN

1. The bondage of the Israelites in Egypt and their subsequent deliverance were foretold by Jehovah hundreds of years before they took place. Cf. Gen. 15: 13, 14; Ex. 1: 13, 14.

2. Egypt was a type of the world and all people today who commit sin are the bondservants of sin. See John 8: 34; Rom. 6: 16.

II. MOSES WAS SENT TO DELIVER ISRAEL, WHILE CHRIST WAS SENT TO SAVE FROM SIN

1. Ex. 2: 23-25; 3: 7-10.

2. John 3: 16; Matt. 1: 21; Luke 19: 10; Acts 3: 22, 23.

III. THE DELIVERANCES WROUGHT BY MOSES AND CHRIST

1. God never calls on any one to act in the absence of confirmed testimony. Consequently, his message through Moses was delivered, signs were wrought, and the people believed. See Ex. 4: 29-31. Following that, the Israelites turned their backs upon Egypt. But when were they saved? Cf. Ex. 14: 13; 1 Cor. 10: 1, 2; Ex. 14: 30.

2. In like manner, the message through Christ was delivered, signs of confirmation were wrought, and the people believed. Cf. John 20: 30, 31; Mark 16: 14-20. When once the message was confirmed, there was no further need for miracles. Cf. 1 Cor. 13: 8; Eph. 4: 7-13.

IV. THE WILDERNESS JOURNEY AND THE CHURCH

1. After the Israelites entered the wilderness they received the law which was to govern them as God's chosen people, and the food and drink necessary to sustain them on their journey. Cf. 1 Cor. 10: 3, 4.

2. Likewise, the law for the Christian is to be taught him after he has been inducted into the body of Christ. See Matt. 28: 19, 20; cf. Heb. 3: 7-4: 2.

V. THE ENTRANCE INTO CANAAN AND HEAVEN

1. The passage through the Jordan.

2. The Jordan of death.

"On Jordan's Stormy Banks."

◆ ◆ ◆

THE FOLLY OF EASY SATISFACTION
Phil. 3: 14

Introduction: 1. The religion of Christ presents the highest ideals that are known to men; and every one who would really benefit by Christianity must constantly make the effort to reach and remain with those ideals. To do less is to be guilty of the folly of easy satisfaction. 2. Some one has said that the expression, "That will do," has done more harm than any other expression in the English language. It indicates an acceptance of a standard below the highest; and the one who thus accepts it knows that he could do better. He simply decides to let it pass. 3. All the standards of life are affected by this attitude, and conduct, accordingly, is not what it should be. This spirit affects a man's work or business, and he is therefore contented with small achievements and low attainments. But in studying this lesson, let us observe that

I. IT IS A GREAT THING TO HAVE A LOFTY IDEAL AND TO LIVE UP TO IT

1. Michael Angelo said, "Nothing makes the soul so pure, so religious, as the endeavor to create something perfect; for God is perfect, and whoever strives for perfection strives for something Godlike."

2. The text plainly indicates that Paul would not be content with anything short of the goal which the Lord had set for him. Cf. Phil. 3: 12-16.

3. This is the spirit of the entire New Testament. Cf. Matt. 5: 48; 2 Cor. 5: 9; 1 Thess. 4: 1-3a.

II. ALTHOUGH WE ARE NOT ALWAYS ABLE TO REACH OUR IDEAL, THE EFFORT WE MAKE TO REACH IT NEVER FAILS TO DO US GOOD

1. The New Testament takes into account the weakness of humanity, but it does not excuse one's unwillingness to do the best he can. See Luke 17: 10; James 2: 10; 4: 17; 2 Pet. 1: 9.

2. Consider the effect that the doing or not doing one's best has on those who manifest such an attitude. See Matt. 25: 14ff. The expression "Thou hast been faithful over a few things" indicates something less than perfection, yet the context shows that the master was pleased with the ones who had made an effort. The one-talent man just didn't try.

III. STRIVING AFTER THE PERFECT IDEAL ALSO LIFTS US STEP BY STEP TOWARD THE EVER-UNATTAINED EXCELLENCE

1. The meaning of this is that we grow better by every effort we make to be better. The nature of perfection, so far as we are concerned, is such that it can only be attained by a constant effort to reach it. Cf. 2 Pet. 3: 18; 2 Cor. 3: 18; James 1: 23-25.

2. Character is the only thing that we can carry out of this world, and character can only be built by having an ideal before us. Ideal, conduct, character, and destiny is the pathway along which we must travel to God. Edward Ward Carmack said, "An act often repeated hardens into a habit, and a habit long continued petrifies into character."

IV. THE SUBTLE EFFECT OF INDOLENCE ON THE CHARACTER
    WE ARE BUILDING
    1. When one does anything indolently, that is, slovenly and
less skillfully than he could have done it, he not only leaves a
piece of work in the world which will bring shame to him some-
day, he also does harm to his own soul. Cf. Matt. 7: 26, 27;
25: 3.
    2. Ignorance of that which one should do does not lessen the
serious effect which such conduct has on his character; and if
something cannot be done to correct it, the result will prove fatal.
The Apostle Paul is a living illustration of this principle. See
1 Tim. 1: 13.

V. A REASON WHY A LESSON OF THIS KIND IS SO BADLY
    NEEDED
    1. We are not accustomed to consider the close relation be-
tween our common tasks and our own spiritual growth and development. Too much emphasis cannot be placed on the fact
that carelessness in our daily duties hinders our growth in grace
and character. Cf. James 4: 17; 1: 23, 25.
    2. Many catastrophes come in later years from doing imper-
fect or careless work in youth. It sometimes happens that when
digging for the foundation of a great building, the workmen come
upon a piece of old wall. "That will do," they say; and they
leave it in the new wall, and build around it. The great structure
goes up, and is later filled with business. One day there is a
great crash. The fragment of the old wall has given away.
and the whole building falls in ruins.
    People are continually leaving in the foundation walls of
their character a fault, a wrong habit, a weakness, a flaw. It
is much easier to build over and around, and so they let it stay.
"That will do," they say apologetically. Then years later, in
some great stress or strain, the character fails and falls in ruins.
It is then seen that the careless piece of foundation-building was
the cause of it all.

◆ ◆ ◆

THE SOLDIER OF THE CROSS*
Eph. 6: 10-20

Introduction: 1. As life moves forward there comes to most
of us a clearer view of its meaning, and of its intense importance.
We are led to realize more and more that we are surrounded by
many strange and hidden alien forces, and are harassed by num-
berless unseen foes. And it becomes increasingly apparent that
the greater our effort to live a life which is pleasing to God (2
Cor. 5: 9), the greater is our danger of being assaulted by the

――――――――
*Or, The Christian Warfare

evil one. Cf. 2 Tim. 3: 12; 1 Pet. 4: 21-19. 2. All of this is
true because Christ and the sinful world are diametrically opposed
to each other. There is a life and death struggle in progress between them, with issues involved so far-reaching and the conflict
so universal as to make impossible the exemption of any responsible human being from the contest. Every one, therefore, must
take a stand, either for or against the Lord. Cf. Matt. 12: 30.
3. Our study today has to do with the Christian's side of the
conflict; and we shall consider it from the standpoint of Paul's
well known and favorite figure—namely, the soldier of the cross,
or the Christian warfare. It is interesting to go through the letters which Paul wrote to the Lord's people and observe the number of times he refers to the Christian soldier or the Christian
warfare. 4. The principal phase of army life is the conflict itself,
but closely related to that are the equipment, training, and attitude
of the individual soldiers which are so essential to a successful
warfare. It is to these last named phases of the question that
we are to direct our attention today; and in doing so, let us consider,

I. THE PREREQUISITES OF A GOOD SOLDIER

1. He must love the cause for which he is fighting.
2. He must have faith in his leader.
3. He must have faith in his comrades.
4. He must have hope of victory.

II. THINGS ESSENTIAL TO A SUCCESSFUL STAND

1. "Having girded your loins with truth."

(1) The girdle was not a mere ornament, but was an essential
part of the soldier's equipment. Placed around his loins, it supported his sword and was useful in keeping his armor and clothing in place. Paul's figure, of course, was based on the Roman
soldier of his day.

(2) The application to the Christian soldier was with reference to the state of his heart as it respects the truth of God—
the practical acknowledgement of the truth as it is in Christ, or
the agreement of our convictions with his revelation. Cf. John
8: 31, 32.

2. "Having put on the breastplate of righteousness."

(1) As its name indicates, this part of the soldier's armor
was worn over his breast and served to protect his vital organs.

(2) Righteousness here is used in the sense of moral rectitude, or correctness in thinking and feeling and acting. Cf.
Prov. 4: 23; 1 Thess. 5: 8; 1 John 3: 7, 10.

3. "Having shod your feet with the preparation of the gospel
of peace."

(1) The soldier who makes a determined stand against the

enemy must have his feet protected. This would make it possible for him to move with quick and certain step. Cf. Isa. 52: 7.

(2) To be shod with the preparation of the gospel of peace is to have a cheerful and willing attitude of mind which gives a spirit of courageous readiness for the battle with evil. This state of mind is produced by the gospel, which is the gospel of peace. Cf. Rom. 5: 1ff.

4. "Taking up the shield of faith."

(1) In addition to (withal) those parts of the armor which were to be worn on the body, an essential part of the soldier's equipment was the shield. This shield was oblong in shape and was large enough to afford protection for the whole body. It was carried on the left arm and held in place by means of a handle. An ordinary shield was about four feet long and two and one half feet wide.

(2) The shield of the Christian soldier is faith, or a conviction which makes him sensitive to holy influences which neutralize the power of temptations and evil influences. Such faith enlists the direct help of God in overcoming these evil things. Cf. 1 Cor. 10: 13; 2 Pet. 2: 9; James 1: 2-8.

5. "Take the helmet of salvation, and the sword of the Spirit."

(1) A different word is here introduced, as well as a difference in grammatical construction. (The word for "take" in verse 17 is a different word *(dechomai)* from the word used in verses 13 and 16 (analambano). Verse 16 has the participial form, while verse 17 has the direct imperative.) In the latter instance the idea is *to take up* or *receive* something. The Christian soldier was to gird his loins, put on the breastplate, shoe his feet, and take up the shield; but now he is to *receive* something from the divine side—namely,

a. "The helmet of salvation." Cf. 1 Thess. 5: 8. This knowledge of salvation enables the Christian soldier to hold up his head with joy and confidence, and it comes to him as a result of the assurance of the Scriptures. Cf. Eph. 2: 8.

b. "The sword of the Spirit." This sword is described as the word of God, and it is the weapon which the Spirit himself puts into the hand of the Christian soldier. Cf. 2 Tim. 3: 16, 17.

(2) Prayer, supplication, and watchfulness enjoined.

III. THE DIVINE ORDER IS TO STAND

1. It should be observed that no provisions have been made for retreat on the part of the Christian soldier. He is commanded to fight the good fight of faith and lay hold on the life eternal (1 Tim. 6: 12). Cf. 2 Tim. 4: 6-8.

2. Not only have no provisions been made for turning back, but the Lord has revealed his mind regarding those who do turn back. Cf. Luke 9: 62; 2 Pet. 2: 20-22.

3. Although commanded to stand and forbidden to turn back,

the Christian soldier is sometimes made the target of attack from the rear.** This, of course, is sad, but if the Christian soldier remains faithful to the Lord, continues his good fight of faith, and does not retaliate, his reward will be great. Cf. Luke 6: 22, 23.

◆ ◆ ◆

SOME THINGS WE BELIEVE AND PRACTICE, NO. 1
2 Cor. 4: 13

Introduction: 1. The church of the New Testament is an evangelistic institution, and every member of it should, in due course of time, be both able and willing to give a scriptural reason for his faith and practice. Cf. Heb. 5: 12; 1 Pet. 3: 15. This course, if zealously followed, will have a powerful effect in turning the attention of many to those things which are set forth in the Word of God. 2. The "we" of the subject now under consideration refers, of course, to those people who are members of the New Testament organization known as the Lord's church. 3. It is not possible, of course, in a short study like this to call attention to everything we believe and practice, but the things which we shall mention should suffice to illustrate the principle involved. 4. The particular points to be considered in this lesson will have to do with the church and how to become a member of it. Let us begin, then, by observing that

---

**Word was received in heaven once, so the story goes, that a faithful and courageous soldier of the cross was about to arrive there. Many a good fight had this man fought on earth against the forces of evil, and many an ugly wound he was said to have received. At last he had fallen, mortally wounded, at the head of his company of Christian soldiers. All heaven turned out to meet him and to do him honor. But as the spirit of this supposedly battle-scarred veteran of the cross approached, as naked a soul as when he had his beginning on earth, he seemed unharmed and perfect, so that great was the amazement felt by those who had gone out to meet him.

After a little exclamation it was noticed that he had been fatally shot in the back!

"What does this mean!" exclaimed one in great surprise. "Have you always turned your back upon the enemies of the Lord with the result that you have been shot in the back?"

"No, no," replied the spirit of many scars; "that is not the way of it at all. On the contrary, as the church of God moved forward like a mighty army, I received all these wounds in my back from the troops I was leading.

"The shield of faith enabled me to guard myself against the fiery darts of the evil one, but I have suffered grievously from the arrows of the Lord's own people—those who make it a practice to shoot their leaders and comrades from the rear.

"Indeed, they often make a pastime of it, and few are they whom the Lord has charged with leading his people whose backs have escaped their cruel shafts, while many like myself have come down to their death from such treacherous wounds."

I. We Believe That There Is One and Only One True Church

1. This should not be regarded as a conceited attitude; for practically all denominational people unite in saying the same thing. The difference between denominational people and us is this: We believe in the unity of the church and that division among the professed followers of Christ is wrong; they, on the other hand, hold that denominationalism, which in its very nature is division, is acceptable to the Lord. These views are diametrically opposed to each other, and one or the other must be wrong. Cf. John 17: 20, 21; 1 Cor. 1: 10; John 15: 1-6. Note: Men (individuals) and not denominations are the branches. See verse 6.

2. The Lord only promised to build one church, and he is the head of but one. See Matt. 16: 18; Eph. 1: 22, 23; 4: 4; 1 Cor. 12: 12-20.

3. Every New Testament figure used to describe the church emphasizes its unity. For example:

(1) Body, Col. 1: 18, 24.

(2) House, 1 Tim. 3: 14, 15.

(3) Flock, John 10: 16.

4. The church is that body of people which has been called out of sin in response to the gospel of Christ. Cf. Mark 16: 15, 16; 2 Thess. 2: 13, 14; Col. 3: 15. The word "church" originally meant an assembly (cf. Acts 19: 41), but it later came to mean an unassembled body. See Acts 8: 3.

II. We Believe That This Church Should Be Designated by Terms Which Are Set Forth in the New Testament

1. Terms of designation which are authorized by the Scriptures:

(1) *The whole body:* The church, Acts 8: 1; his (Christ's) body, Eph. 1: 22, 23; the body of Christ, 1 Cor. 12: 27; Eph. 4: 12 (but the *body* is the *church,* Col. 1: 18, 24: therefore, *the church of Christ!);* the church of God, 1 Cor. 15: 9; the church of the firstborn, Heb. 12: 23. (Note: The original term for "firstborn" is plural and refers to the members of the church, rather than to Christ himself.)

(2) *In the local sense:* Church of God, 1 Cor. 1: 1, 2; churches of Christ, Rom. 16: 16.

(3) *Individual members:* Disciples, Acts 13: 52; believers, Acts 5: 14; brethren, Acts 12: 17; saints, Rom. 15: 25; Christians. Acts 11: 26.

2. Denominationalism only emphasizes certain features of the church or Bible teaching.

(1) *Methodist:* This term was first applied derisively because

of the methodical habits of study and religious observance of those who originated the movement.

(2) *Baptist:* This term, as a denominational name, was first applied to people who advocated and practiced the immersion of believers only, in opposition to infant baptism and the substitution of sprinkling and pouring for immersion. Its purpose, therefore, was to emphasize baptism. "The use of the term 'Baptist' as a denominational designation is of comparatively recent origin, first appearing about the year 1644." *(The New Schaff-Herzog Encyclopedia of Religious Knowledge, Vol. I, p. 465.)*

(3) *Presbyterian:* This term emphasizes a peculiar form of church government, i. e., government by presbyters or elders.

III. We Believe That One Must Be a Member of This New Testament Church in Order to be Saved

1. The testimony of the Scriptures: 2 Tim. 2: 10; Eph. 5: 23; 1: 22, 23; Acts 4: 12.

2. Illustrated by Acts 2: 1-41, 47.

IV. We Believe That Faith, Repentance, and Baptism Are Necessary Conditions to Membership in the New Testament Church

1. What say the Scriptures? Matt. 28: 18-20; Mark 16: 15, 16; Luke 24: 46, 47; Acts 2: 36-39.

2. These three steps involve a threefold change—viz:

(1) Faith: a change of mind regarding Christ.

(2) Repentance: a change of mind regarding sin, involving a turning away from sin, a renunciation of it and a determination to think and act differently regarding it.

(3) Baptism: a change of state—from without to within Christ. See Gal. 3: 26, 27.

◆ ◆ ◆

SOME THINGS WE BELIEVE AND PRACTICE, NO. 2
James 2: 14-26

Introduction: 1. The religion of Christ appeals to the reason of man, as well as to his feelings; and the Lord has taught his people to exercise care in being able to speak convincingly of those things which pertain to life and godliness. 2. No one is required to believe anything without sufficient evidence to convince any reasonable person that it came from God. Every faithful Christian, therefore, is always glad to tell others that which he believes the Lord teaches, and to give a reason for any practice which he considers authorized by the word of God. 3. The previous lesson on this subject had to do with the church and how to become a member of it. This study will be concerned with the church in fulfilling its God-given mission. As a beginning point, then, let us consider,

I. THE SUFFICIENCY OF THE CHURCH FOR ITS WORK

1. The work which the Lord authorized the church to do may be divided into three classes—viz:

(1) Self-edification, or building up the church itself. Cf. Eph. 4: 16.

(2) Evangelization, or preaching the gospel to the unsaved. See Mark 16: 15; cf. 1 Tim. 3: 14, 15; 1 Thess. 1: 8.

(3) Benevolence, or helping those who need material assistance. Cf. Gal. 6: 10. (Note: *Working that which is good* probably includes any type of service which the Lord's people may render to others. The context, however, seems to indicate that the reference is primarily to material aid.)

2. Those who call themselves Christians only believe that the church is sufficiently able, being the God-appointed agency for that purpose, to accomplish this work without the aid of human societies, conventions, or any other method devised and authorized by man. Cf. 2 Tim. 3: 16, 17; 2 Pet. 1: 3; Col. 3: 17.

II. THE PERFECT RULE OF WORSHIP

1. Man has been described as incurably religious, and his very nature requires that he offer worship to some object. It is as natural for man to worship as it is for him to breathe. He may not always worship the right object, or in the right way; but he will worship, nevertheless.

2. It is also true that the nature of worship is such as to cause the worshiper to become like the object of his worship.

3. In keeping with these natural conditions, God has provided a plan of worship which is exactly fitted to man's need in his effort to grow into the likeness of his Maker.

4. The New Testament plan of worship provides for the five following features—viz:

(1) Singing, Eph. 5: 19.

(2) Praying, 1 Cor. 14: 15.

(3) Teaching, 1 Tim. 4: 13.

(4) The Lord's supper, Acts 20: 7.

(5) Benevolent contribution, 1 Cor. 16: 1, 2.

5. We believe that this plan of worship, if followed as the Lord intended, will supply every need which man has with respect to worship. Anything else is superfluous and will meet with God's disapproval. Cf. Matt. 15: 9; 1 Cor. 4: 6; 2 John 9.

III. THE LORD'S DAY WORSHIP

1. Worship as such is not limited to any time or place. Cf. John 4: 21-24; Eph. 6: 18; 1 Tim. 2: 8. Thus, men may worship the Father whenever and wherever they can meet the conditions of acceptable worship.

2. This does not mean, however, that no provisions have been made by the Lord for a public period of worship on the Lord's day. That is exactly what has been done. Cf. 1 Cor. 16: 2. The

expression *kata mian sabbatou* means, according to Thayer, "on the first day of *every* week." See also Acts 20: 7; Heb. 10: 25. (There is no indication that this last passage is limited to the Lord's day assembly; but there is sufficient reason for saying that it includes that assembly.)

3. We believe, therefore, that the Lord expects his people to meet for public worship upon the first day of every week; and that is the general practice of the churches of Christ throughout the country, or wherever they are found.

◆ ◆ ◆

THE PRODIGAL SON
Luke 15: 11-24

Introduction: 1. The parable of the prodical son has, by common consent, come to be regarded as the pearl of all the parables of Jesus—the heart of the gospel of Christ. It is one of a series of four parables, found in Luke 15, the design of which was to rebuke the "cold-hearted and self-righteous exclusiveness of the scribes and Pharisees; and to show them, that, in despising Jesus for receiving sinners and eating with them, they were altogether out of harmony with him in whose presence there is joy over one sinner that repenteth." 2. But this parable differs from the first two in that, while they illustrate the earnestness with which God seeks the lost sinner, this one describes the result of that search in the voluntary return of the sinner himself. The first two view the matter from the divine side and permit us to see the efforts which God has put forth through his Son to recover the lost, while this one presents the human side and shows us the sinner's part in returning to the Father. 3. The whole picture has been admirably described by Arnot in these words: "It is not that some fallen human kind are saved after the manner of the strayed sheep, and others after the manner of the prodigal son; not that the Saviour bears one wanderer home by his power, and that another, of his own accord, arises and returns to his Father. Both these processes are accomplished in every conversion. The man comes, yet Christ brings him; Christ brings him, yet he comes." *(Arnot on the Parables,* p. 428.) 4. Again, in the two preceding parables, little or nothing is said of the sinner's departure from God, and his misery and degradation in his estrangement from him. The loss which the first two parables emphasize is that which is sustained by God; and scarcely any hint is given, in either of them, of the loss which is incurred by the sinner himself. In this one, however, the deplorable condition of the man away from God, in the far away land of sin, is set in the forefront; and nowhere in the whole range of literature, either sacred or secular, do we have a more vivid picture of the awful truth that "the way of the transgressor is hard" than that which is presented to us in this matchless story. 5. "The salient message of the parable is unmistakable, namely, the hunger of the heart of God for the return of the prodigal and the hunger at the heart of the prodigal for God and home." But in studying this lesson, let us begin by considering,

I. The Request of the Prodigal Son

1. *Verses 11, 12.* Having become weary of the wholesome restraints of the parental household, he wanted to be his own master, and thereby be independent of all authority and interference.

2. This story was not told primarily for its literal truth and pathos, exquisite as they are; it has a spiritual significance underlying its external incidents, and every man may see himself in this prodigal son.

3. Sin is but a departure from God, a desire to be independent of God, a casting off of our allegiance to him, a taking of things into our own hands, and a determination to do as we please.

4. All the good things we have come from God (James 1: 17), and instead of being content to use them in his service, many want all the blessings of God, such as life, talents, favorable surroundings, etc., for selfish purposes. Cf. Acts 14: 16.

II. His Season of Indulgence and Misery

1. *Verses 13-16.* The experiences of this young man present a vivid picture of the three stages of the sinner's progress in the ways of sin—viz:

(1) *His riotous joy.* There is a sort of pleasure in wrongdoing. If that were not so, men would not be so freely engaging in it. See 2 Pet. 2: 12-15 and cf. 1 Pet. 4: 1-4.

(2) *Wasted substance.* A sinful life is the most expensive thing possible. It results in the waste of one's material resources, wears out the body, blights the intellect, withers the moral nature, weakens the will, blunts the conscience, and hardens the heart. Cf. Heb. 3: 13; Eph. 4: 17-19; Rom. 1: 28. *One's influence might be used to save a soul, but as it is, he is in danger of losing his own soul!*

(3) *Enslaved degradation.* Inasmuch as the world cannot satisfy the soul, sinful practices will, sooner or later, lose their charm. But worse still, the sinner will eventually find himself firmly caught in the clutches of sin. Cf. John 8: 34; 2 Pet. 2: 18, 19.*

2. The word "joined" means to "glue" or "cement," implying that he forced himself upon the citizen, who was unwilling to en-

---

*That which was at first a joy becomes in the end a bondage. That which was at first a pleasant companion becomes at length a cruel taskmaster, who compels him to make brick without straw, and sometimes even without clay. I have read in the memoirs of a detective, how once, having discovered his man, he joined himself to him as a boon companion, went with him to his haunts, secured his confidence by long fellowship, until at length, when all suspicion had been allayed, he got him, as a

gage him, and who only because of his persistent entreaty took him into his service.

3. He has now rached the lowest depths of degradation, and he must have realized how unstable are the friends and principles that money can buy.

III. HIS REFLECTION AND REPENTANCE

1. *Verses 17-20a.* When once the blinded eyes of the soul are opened, no one is content to abide in sin.

2. "But when he came to himself." This young man had not been himself while engaged in sin. He had been under the influence of another, even Satan; but now he has regained his senses. *So it is with every sinner*

3. One of the first evidences the sinner gives that his eyes are opened is in the perception of his misery. This, of course, will lead to reflection. There is hope for the worst of men, if only they can be induced to reflect on their condition.

4. On what did the prodigal son reflect?

(1) He reflected on his present condition. *Let the sinner do the same!*

(2) He reflected on his past errors, follies, and sins.

(3) He recalled the privileges and blessings of the home on which he had so lightly turned his back. *Cf. the church and its blessings.*

5. Repentance is a change of mind regarding sin, or, in keeping with the idea of the text, repentance is to have another mind regarding sin.**

6. Repentance is here pictured as a journey, and the prodigal son struck while the iron was hot.

IV. HIS FORGIVENESS AND RESTORATION

1. *Verses 20b-24.* The meaning of this part of the parable is that the heavenly Father will receive the penitent with gladness, and, instead of taunting him with his guilt, he will honor him by giving him the richest blessings he has to bestow.***

---

mere jest, to try on a pair of handcuffs, and then, snapping the spring that locked them, he took him, all helpless as he was, an easy prey. So sin does with its victim. It first ministers to his enjoyment, then drowns his vigilance, and then leads him away in helpless bondage to utter ruin. —William M. Taylor, *The Parables of Our Saviour*, p. 344f.

**Repentance is not forsaking sin; that is the result of repentance. It is to have another mind regarding sin. It implies a true knowledge of sin, a conviction of sin, with its folly, guilt, condemnation, and terrible consequences. It means that the sinner changes his thoughts and attitudes, insofar as they are wrong, toward God, Christ, his fellow man, and himself. Cf. Matt. 21: 28, 29. This will inevitably lead to a change in conduct.

***In this wonderful picture Jesus has given us the most attractive and most perfect image of God that came from his lips. That longing and looking for his lost one's return; the going out to meet him; the kiss of welcome and the fond embrace; the prompt, frank, and complete for-

2. Although the prodigal son sinned, as the parable shows, the father's heart never changed. The responsibility, therefore, for the separation between God and man has always been on the side of man. Cf. Isa. 59: 1, 2; 2 Cor. 5: 18-20. The text, however, makes it plain that God can save man at his worst, and always rejoices at his return.

3. The father's welcome always exceeds the wanderer's fondest dream, and the new life always begins with a feast, a feast of love.**** Cf. Acts 8: 8, 39; 1 Pet. 1: 8.

◆ ◆ ◆

HE WOULD NOT GO IN
Luke 15: 28

Introduction: 1. Many sermons have been preached on the parable of the prodigal son, but relatively few on the elder brother. The Lord, of course, intended that the facts surrounding each son should teach a lesson; and it will be beneficial to us to consider them. 2. It is obvious from that which is said in the first part of the chapter (Luke 15) that the primary lesson had to do with the self-righteous scribes and Pharisees, on the one hand, and the self-condemned publicans and sinners, on the other. It was easy for the scribes and Pharisees to see that the publicans and sinners were lost, but it seems that it never occurred to them that they

---

giveness; the utter silence and forgetfulness concerning the evil and shameful past, as if it had never been; the festal robes and the rejoicing guests; the infinite tenderness, delicacy, and sweetness of it all, making up an appealing and affecting portrait which chains our admiration, stirs our deepest hearts, and goes beyond all thought. We feel that there is something far more than human in this. It is the beauty of God; it is the unspeakable grace of the Divine Fatherhood; and it is the great, pitiful, forgiving heart of God that the story brings to view, and that stands forever prominent in our thoughts of it.—James Hastings, *Great Texts of the Bible—Luke,* p. 229.

****There are no degrees of forgiveness. There are degrees in the holiness that follows forgiveness; but pardon must be perfect at its birth. Forgiveness restores each man to the place he had before he fell. If the prodigal had been a hired servant previous to his fall, he would have been made a hired servant again. There would have been no sting in that; it would have involved no stigma. But to make him a servant after he had been a son would have perpetuated the pain of memory. Nothing impedes my progress like the remembrance of a dark yesterday. When the page is already blotted, I am apt to blot it more. I lose heart; I say, "It is already tarnished; what does it matter now?" If I am to get a fair start, it must be a bright start—a start with the ring and the robe. It will not help me that you lift me from the far country if you give me a place second to my former self. The second place is my yesterday, and I should walk by its darkness. It would dog my footsteps; it would never let me go. I should not feel that sin was unworthy of me—below me. I should always be fingering my ticket of leaves. I should never be able to soar for the remembrance of the irons; memory would clip the wings of hope.—G. Matheson, *Leaves for Quiet Hours,* p. 126.

were lost, too. The fact is, they were in a worse condition than
the self-condemned sinners. 3. But the principle which underlay
the Lord's teaching was not limited to that occasion; it is equally
applicable to people today. There are many people now who consider themselves righteous, but who are completely out of harmony with the will of the Father. This fact will become more
apparent as we proceed with our study. Our first consideration
has to do with the question,

I. WHY DID HE REFUSE TO GO IN?

1. *He did not have the right attitude toward his brother.*

(1) It is altogether possible that he never thought very much
of him in the first place, since it seems that their natures were
quite unlike. It appears that the younger son was generous to a
fault, and was always getting into trouble somewhere; whereas,
the older son was a pattern of sobriety, and was as cautious as he
was laborious.

(2) Not only did the elder brother not love the prodigal; it
seems that he could not understand why any one else should love
him either. *Isn't that like life?*

2. *He did not understand his father's ways.*

(1) The elder brother no doubt thought that he loved his
father, and had always honored him. He probably felt that his
father was very wise, but now, in the light of that which was being
done in honor of the wanderer's return, it seemed to him that his
father's justice was being dissipated.

(2) Was *this* the way to receive a prodigal back home? Didn't
his father's attitude toward him put a premium on sin? And was
he fair to the one who had stayed at home and faithfully served
him?

3. *He got his information and impressions from the wrong
source.*

(1) He should have gone into the house and seen for himself.
One look at his brother might have softened him and changed
his whole outlook. But instead of going in himself, he called to
him one of the servants, and inquired what these things might be.

(2) It is true that the servant told him the truth about the
matter, but it sometimes happens that even the truth can be told
in such a way as to irritate and cause suspicions to arise in one's
mind. *Didn't the elder brother feel that he was being discrimi-
nated against?* But if he had had the right attitude toward his
brother, and had gone in and seen for himself, it is altogether
possible that he would have rejoiced with his father at the prodigal's return.

II. SOME THINGS HE MISSED BY NOT GOING IN

1. *Refreshments and a change of raiment.* Cf. Matt. 11: 28-
30.

2. *He missed the merriment and gladness.* Cf. Prov. 17: 22. As it was, he was out of touch with everybody, and was filled with jealousy, offended, and miserable. Cf. Prov. 23: 7. The wrong spirit was in Judas Iscariot, and one needs only to examine the record to be able to see that which wrong attitudes and feelings will drive one to do. See Mark 14: 10, 11.

3. *He missed his chance of making others happy.* He may not have realized it, but his absence was the one shadow which lay across the feast. *There are many people today with the same opportunity of making others happy. Will they go in?*

III. His True Status

1. One of the best ways to see the true character of a person is by means of contrast. *The darker the night, the brighter the stars will shine.* Cf. 2 Sam. 12: 1-6.

2. The prodigal son had deliberately left home and had engaged in the sins of the world; and every one, including himself, knew that he was a lost sinner. But the elder brother had remained at home amid an environment which was clean and wholesome; and neither he nor others felt that he was lost. But if one will only stop to think, it will be easy for him to see that he *was* lost because he was completely out of sympathy with both his father and his brother. It should be observed that while the prodigal came home and was restored to his place, the elder brother apparently remained unresponsive to the final appeal of his father's love.

3. One of the great lessons illustrated by the parables involving these two sons is that of repentance. The conduct of the younger son shows what repentance is, while that of the elder shows what it is not.

◆ ◆ ◆

GROWING A SOUL
2 Pet. 3: 18

Introduction: 1. The soul of man is the most important truth about him; for it has a direct connection with God. Jesus has made it plain that there is nothing that can compensate for its destruction. See Matt. 16: 26. Notwithstanding its immortality, the soul must grow if the blessings which it is capable of enjoying and which the Lord has provided for it are to be received; and like all other growth, it must be according to the fundamental laws of God which govern all growth and development. 2. At the beginning the soul of man enjoyed direct and intimate fellowship with its Maker, but because of sin that relationship was broken; and, being cut off from God, it became necessary for the soul of man to be redeemed, if it would live with God eternally. This redemption was made possible through the sacrifice of Christ. But in studying this lesson, let us ask,

I. How Is the Soul of Man Redeemed?

1. The testimony of the Scriptures: 1 Pet. 1: 22-25; Eph. 1: 13; Mark 16: 15, 16.

2. Having complied with the Lord's terms of forgiveness, the soul is again made pure and clean in his sight. Cf. Isa. 1: 18; Eph. 5: 25-27.

3. However, if the soul is to remain pure, it must grow; for there is no such thing as standing still and pleasing God at the same time. See 2 Pet. 3: 18; 1 John 1: 6, 7. This leads us to consider,

II. The Fundamental Laws of Growth

1. *Vital force.* A plant cannot grow unless it is rooted in its native soil and surrounded by a wholesome atmosphere. Cf. Luke 8: 14. No soul can grow as it should if it is where it ought not to be, and surrounded by conditions which are contrary to its best interests.

2. *Wholesome food which meets all the requirements of the body.* In addition to the needs for growth and development, there is a constant process of wasting and wearing which must be continually repaired. Just so with the soul. See 1 Pet. 2: 1, 2; Heb. 5: 11-14; Eph. 4: 11-16.

3. *Active use of all of our powers.* Cf. Matt. 25: 14-30.

(1) The duties which have been ordained for us were not arbitrarily chosen. Each one is designed to exercise and strengthen one or more of our spiritual members. Cf. Eph. 4: 16.

(2) The neglect of any one of these duties can never be compensated by any additional activity in the performance of any other. Cf. James 2: 10, 11; 4: 17.

(3) We can never, therefore, omit any one of them without injuring and weakening some corresponding grace—without making our Christian character one-sided and distorted, and, consequently, weak and sickly. *Every talent must be accounted for.*

4. *Periods of rest.* All living things need sleep, and God has provided rest periods for our spirits. Cf. Isa. 26: 3. *The Christian life is both active and meditative.* The active, energetic follower of Christ is in danger of becoming irritated and irritating. The remedy for this condition is trust in God. Cf. Psalm 23: 2. The lying down is intended to fit one for better service. Cf. songs, "Take Time to Be Holy" and "I Came to the Garden Alone."

III. The Direction of Growth

1. *Upward.* See Eph. 4: 15; Col. 3: 1-4; 1 John 2: 1-3; Psalm 17: 15.

2. *Downward.* That is, growth in the knowledge of our own

hearts. One must study himself if he would educate and develop his soul. Cf. 1 Tim. 4: 16.*

3. *Outward.* Cf. Gal. 6: 1, 2, 10. The man who does something for others, likewise does something for himself.

IV. THE TESTS OF GROWTH

1. *A warmer and more unselfish love.* As our knowledge of Christ and his cause grows more intimate, we love him for what he *is*, rather than for what he *did*. Cf. 1 John 5: 1-3.

2. *What we outgrow.* A child outgrows his clothes, works, and pleasures; and, in like manner, the soul outgrows many of the things which once seemed to be the height of spiritual development. Cf. 1 Cor. 13: 11, 12; Heb. 6: 1-3.

3. *The power to resist temptation.* A *boy* can uproot a young tree, but a *man* can't pull one up which has been growing for fifty years! "Growth so roots us and grounds us that storms which would once have caused us terror come only as music." Cf. 2 Cor. 4: 16-18.

4. *Beauty of character.* .This is a test which we ourselves may not be able to apply; for its very existence is dependent upon our unconsciousness of its presence. However, it is the most effective test which others apply to us. Cf. John 13: 34, 35.**

THE LILY

"O star on the breast of the river,
  O blossom of marvel and grace!
Did you fall right down from heaven,
  Out of the sweetest place?
"You're as fair as the thoughts of an angel,
  Your heart is steeped in the sun;
Did you grow in the radiant city,
  My pure and holy one?"
"Nay, nay," said the lily, "I fell not from heaven,
  None gave me my saintly white;
I slowly grew in the darkness,
  Down in the dreary night.
"From the ooze and the slime of the river
  I won my glory and grace;
White souls fall not, O my poet,
  They rise to the highest place."
—*Anon*

---

*A man once bought a barometer under a mistaken idea of its purpose, so the story goes, and then complained that he could not see that it had made any improvement in the weather! The spiritual barometer of self-examination may not directly improve the weather, but it will show what the spiritual weather is; and it will help us to know ourselves.

**G. Campbell Morgan once told of a member of one of the congregations where he formerly preached, a woman of refinement and of great consecration, who went to stay in the home of her sister in the country, where she had not stayed for many years. Her sister was a woman of the world, engrossed in worldly pleasures and interests. When Dr. Morgan's friend was leaving the home, after a stay of two weeks, her sister, taking her by the hand, and looking into her face, said, "I do not understand your religion, but I will tell you one thing; it has made you far easier to live with."

THE UNRIGHTEOUS STEWARD
Luke 16: 1-13

Introduction: 1. It seems, from Luke's record of the gospel, that the parable of the text was spoken immediately after those in the preceding chapter. The opening words of this parable seem to indicate that Jesus was speaking directly to his disciples; but from verse 14 we get the idea that the Pharisees regarded the Lord's words as meant for them too. Cf. Matt. 5: 1, 2; 7: 28, 29. 2. Two of the outstanding characteristics of the Pharisees were self-righteousness and coveteousness. The first of these was severely condemned by the Lord in the series of parables in chapter 15, and now it seems that the second characteristic is just as soundly condemned in the two parables of chapter 16. 3. It should be easy for even the most cursory reader to see that there is a point of contact between the parable of the text and that of the prodigal son which precedes it. The prodigal was guilty of "wasting his substance," while in the case now before us the steward was charged with "wasting his Lord's goods." It was evidently the Lord's purpose to teach those who held to the idea of self-righteous respectability that there are other ways of misusing that which had been entrusted to them, than by riotous living. Thus, according to Jesus, when one appropriates to himself that which should be used in the Lord's service, he is in reality just as unfaithful to God as is the abandoned sinner who spends his substance in riotous living. This parable, therefore, is an exposure of the sin of coveteousness, with a special application to the children of God. Let us begin our study, then, by considering,

I. THE SETTING OF THE LESSON, Vs. 1-7

1. The principal figure in the story is that of a steward who had been entrusted by a certain rich man with the entire control of his affairs. Cf. Gen. 24: 2; 39: 8.

2. The rich man, of course, had perfect confidence in his steward, but after a time evidence was laid before him which proved conclusively that his confidence had been misplaced.

3. Thus, instead of being benefited, he was being systematically robbed by the very man whom he had so greatly trusted.

4. The householder called the steward before him, demanded a reckoning, and announced that he could no longer continue in his service.

5. Being unable to establish his innocence, the unfaithful steward was put to the necessity of finding some other way of making a living.

6. After surveying the possibilities before him, he finally decided to continue his dishonest practices, with this addition: he intended to make others share with him in his unrighteous dealings, so that they would be obligated to him and would, therefore,

be compelled to contribute to his upkeep, or have their dishonesty exposed.

II. THE HEART OF THE PARABLE, V. 8

1. It seems that the Lord's main purpose, in exposing the spirit of coveteousness, was to stimulate his disciples to prudence and energy in the prosecution of their high calling. He, accordingly, selected for this purpose a son of this world who manifested the very trait which he wanted his disciples to possess.

2. It should be kept in mind, however, that it was the steward's master, and not Jesus, who commended him for the wisdom which he displayed; but it was Jesus himself who pointed out the difference between the sons of this world and the sons of light.

3. In what way did the unrighteous steward manifest superior wisdom?

(1) He had a clear view of his aim in life, and he, accordingly, subordinated all other considerations to the attainment of his goal. Cf. his present comfort vs. the Christian's aim at the formation of a holy character.

(2) The promptness with which he set about his work. Contrast his action with the procrastination which is so often manifested by professed Christians.

(3) He selected means which were well adapted to his needs. They were dishonest, but they placed his lord's debtors under obligation to him. Many professed followers of Christ often manifest a total lack of practical sagacity in the selection of the means so necessary to the accomplishment of their high aims in this life. For example,

a. The blessings which come to those who regularly attend all the meetings of the church. Cf. Heb. 10: 24, 25. But how many professed followers of Christ deliberately choose other things instead of attending these meetings!

b. The choice of friends, and especially one's life companion. Would a worldly-wise man select a business associate who was not vitally interested in the success of their undertaking. Cf. 2 Cor. 6: 14—7: 1.

III. THE LORD'S SPECIAL APPLICATION, Vs. 9-13

1. The proper way to use the material possessions which have been entrusted to us, v. 9. Cf. 2 Cor. 9: 6-10.

2. The principle which will determine God's attitude toward his people, v. 10. Cf. Matt. 13: 12.

3. The lesson illustrated, vs. 11, 12. These verses plainly show that whatever material blessings we may have in our possession are ours only in trust. They in reality belong to God.

4. The impossibility of divided allegiance, v. 13. If we repudi-

ate our responsibility to God for money, we thereby become the servants of mammon; and we shall be dealt with as such in the last day.

◆ ◆ ◆

"TAKE YE AWAY THE STONE"
John 11: 39

Introduction: 1. As a worker, the Lord Jesus Christ stands alone. No one among men can unite his voice with his power as Jesus did; and yet he is pleased to associate his disciples with himself in his work of saving the souls of men. 2. This principle is forcefully illustrated by the words of the text. Jesus could have done everything by himself; but he chose to give those who were also concerned with the matter something to do. 3. A careful reading of the Bible will reveal that the Lord always gives men something to do when his work concerns them. Cf. John 11: 34, 39, 44; Rom. 1: 16; 2 Cor. 4: 7; Mark 16: 15, 16. But in studying this lesson, let us ask,

I. WHY DID JESUS REQUIRE THEM TO REMOVE THE STONE?

1. He could have removed it himself, or he could have raised Lazarus without its being taken away.

2. His action was in keeping with the well known Bible principle that God does not do for man that which he can do for himself; and neither does he seek to bless man without man's cooperation.

3. The Scriptures teach that there is a human as well as a divine side in the matter of our salvation. See Heb. 11: 6; John 3: 36; Heb. 2: 3; Acts 2: 40; Phil. 2: 12.

II. THE SIGNIFICANCE ATTACHED TO THE STONE'S REMOVAL

1. The stone had to be removed before Christ would do his work; and the same is true, in principle, with people today.

2, There are many things which stand between alien sinners and their salvation, and in the way of the progress of Christians, which must be removed before they can rightfully expect the Lord's blessings. This leads us to consider,

III. SOME OBSTACLES WHICH THE ALIEN SINNER MUST REMOVE

1. In many cases ignorance must be removed. Cf. John 6: 44, 45; Heb. 8: 11; Rom. 1: 16, 17; 10: 1-3.

2. Then, too, prejudice frequently keeps people from accepting the pure word of God. See Acts 17: 1-12; John 1: 43-51.

3. Self-esteem is a formidable barrier in the way of salvation. Cf. Matt. 18: 3; 5: 3.

4. All things which are not in harmony with the revealed will of God must be removed. See Matt. 7: 21-23.

IV. SOME HINDRANCES TO THE PROGRESS OF CHRISTIANS

1. Anything which keeps them from seeing and accepting the truth. Cf. John 8: 31, 32; 1 Pet. 1: 22; 2 Thess. 2: 8-12.

2. All bad feelings must be removed. See 1 Pet. 2: 1; James 4: 11, 12; 2: 12, 13.

3. All indifferences must be removed. Cf. Matt. 12: 30; Rev. 3: 14-20.

4. All sectarianism must be removed. See 1 Cor. 1: 10-13; 3: 1-5.

V. THE DIVINE AND HUMAN PARTS IN THE PLAN OF SALVATION

1. There are some things which God has done for man which man could not have done for himself. Cf. Rom. 5: 6-8.

(1) God gave his Son to die for the sins of mankind; made possible a plan of salvation; and then revealed to man how he could make this salvation his.

(2) Or, to express the matter in another way, God gave the gospel— facts, commands, and promises—but man must hear, that is, learn the gospel, believe the facts, and obey the commands, if he is to enjoy the promises.

2. God will never do man's part for him; because if he should do that, then man's freedom of will would be destroyed and he would no longer be a free moral agent, or, which is the same thing, a responsible being.

3. Christ raised Lazarus from the dead; but he required others to roll away the stone from the door of the tomb, and then remove the grave-clothes.

4. He has likewise done for us that which we could not do for ourselves; but he demands that we remove every obstacle, lay aside every hindrance, and obey his commands, if we are to enjoy his salvation. What are we going to do about it?

❖ ❖ ❖

A STREETWALKER WHO CRASHED A DINNER PARTY
Luke 7: 36-50

Introduction: 1. Some of the most exquisite stories of the Gospels are told only by Luke. Among them is the one about the sinful woman who came uninvited to Simon's house when Jesus was eating with him. 2. This story is unsurpassed in tenderness and beauty. It has been called "one of the most touching which even the Word of God contains," and one which reveals "the heart of Christ." The loveliness of this story is apparent to all who will take the time to read it. 3. Our purpose in this study is to call attention to some of the lessons which are suggested by it. Let us begin, then, with a consideration of

I. THE SETTING OF THE STORY

1. Jesus had been invited by a Pharisee named Simon to eat

with him, and had accepted the invitation. After reading the entire narrative, one naturally wonders just why Simon invited Jesus into his home. It is very evident that it was not purely a social gesture; for, as Jesus himself points out, Simon dispensed with the usual courtesies offered by a host to his guest. Judging from the thoughts which passed through Simon's mind, it is very likely that one of his prime purposes in inviting Jesus was to have the opportunity of scrutinizing him more closely than he could have done out in the open.

2. Another question which arises is, Why did Jesus accept the invitation, since it is evident that he knew what was in the heart of Simon? The answer to this question is found in the fact that Jesus never held himself aloof from any class of men, and he desired to use the opportunity to further his great work of seeking and saving the lost.

3. As the scene opens in Simon's house, we can see the guests around the table in Oriental fashion which means they were reclining on couches instead of sitting in chairs as we do. The body usually rested on the left elbow, thus leaving the right hand free to use while eating, and the feet, with sandals removed, lay on the couch away from the table. In addition to the couches provided for the guests, there were divans, or other suitable items of furniture on which to sit, arranged around the walls of the room which uninvited guests, who would come in to see the banquet or to talk with the guests at the table, might occupy.

II. ONLY LOVE CAN INTERPRET LOVE

1. It is not hard to imagine the feelings of those at the table, judging from the reaction of Simon, when the sinful woman came in and gave her attention to Jesus. It appears that Jesus alone understood her motive. As we view the scene from our vantage-point, it is clear to us that she was acting from a deep sense of gratitude; and with this in mind, we can think of two basic reasons why Jesus alone understood her. (1) Only love can interpret love, and (2) no one but Jesus was acquainted with the unrecorded history which lay between her sinful past and her unusual behavior at this banquet.

2. Since only love can interpret love, that which seems extravagent and wasteful to on-lookers is, between the lovers themselves, the ordinary language of affection. That was true on the occasion of the episode at Bethany, recorded in Mark 14: 3-9.

3. As already indicated, it is very likely that Jesus alone was familiar with the unrecorded history which prompted this singular action on the part of the sinful woman. She had evidently been under the influence of Jesus in some way before she came to the house of Simon; and this contact with the Saviour of men had caused her to forsake the primrose path and resolve upon a better life. She may have been attracted to him by his friendly attitude

toward sinners, or she may have been in the crowd when he uttered his tender invitation to the weary and heavy laden. See Matt. 11: 28-30.

III. "I Have Somewhat to Say unto Thee"

1. Simon did not in the least comprehend the woman. He looked upon the scene in amazement, mingled with disgust. That, of course, was because he knew nothing of her change in attitude and life. Simon had, it seems, a high regard for morality: he would not go near such a woman if he should see her on the street or in the house; but he made the mistake of judging by appearance only. This is why the thoughts referred to in the text came into Simon's mind.

2. But Jesus showed that he was a discerner of spirits by replying to that which Simon himself had not ventured to utter. "And Jesus answering said unto him, Simon, I have somewhat to say unto thee. And he saith, Teacher, say on." The words of the parable of the two debtors then followed.

3. Jesus himself gave the interpretation of the parable, making God the creditor and Simon and the woman the debtors. And in giving the reason for the woman's demonstration of her great love for Jesus, he explained that the measure of one's gratitude for forgiveness is in direct ratio to his conception of what it means to be a sinner in God's sight.

IV. Jesus Also Has Some Things to Say to Us

1. The teaching of Jesus is still just as applicable to us today, as it was to the people in his own time. It is just as necessary for us to try to lift up fallen humanity, as it was for John, or Paul, or any other New Testament Christian. The Lord's message to us, therefore, is found in such passages as Luke 17: 3; James 5: 19, 20. We have a responsibility when others do wrong, and in many instances we can do something about it, if we will follow the Lord's instruction.*

2. But we can never have a part in making men better as long as we are cold and indifferent toward them, and remain aloof from them. We must come into warm, loving, personal contact with them, if we expect to influence them in the right direction. How can we expect people to come to us and try to correct mis-

---

*John Ruskin, so the story goes, called on a literary collaborator and found her in mental distress. She owned a costly handkerchief which had been ruined by a blot of ink.

"Nothing can be done with it," she cried. "It is absolutely worthless!"

"Are you sure?" said Ruskin. "Let me have it awhile."

A little later the handkerchief came back by mail, and his friend could scarcely recognize it. Ruskin, with the skill of an artist, had used the blot as a basis, and had made a design in India ink of surpassing beauty. It was then many times more valuable than in its original loveliness.

What we think are fatal blots of life can often be made the foundation stones, the decisive markers, of a life of unusual usefulness.

takes which have been made in the past, if we make it plain to them that we do not want anything to do with them? What we need to remember is that the Lord has a message for us on this subject. See Matt. 18: 21-35.

❖ ❖ ❖

"TALK IS CHEAP"
Matt. 12: 36, 37

Introduction: 1. One can well imagine what a difference it would make in our conversation, if we were compelled to go to the market each morning and buy the words we expect to use during the day. For example, we would have to buy so many nouns, so many verbs, adjectives, adverbs, prepositions, conjunctions, etc. If such a practice were mandatory, how much profanity, idle gossip, self-pity, and complaint about the weather would disappear from our conversation! Unclean stories and idle gossip would die the natural death they deserve to die. 2. On the other hand, if words of praise, expressions of love, appreciation, and friendship cost us money, we would always buy them, rather than the kind mentioned above. But because "talk is cheap," as many say, gossip, profanity, and the like, are freely used; while those expressions which make life easier—thanksgiving, praise, and words of appreciation—are so often neglected. 3. But talk is not cheap. See the text. It is true that our words do not always have to be paid for in dollars and cents, but they sometimes do! Their cost is usually in terms of reputation, character, heartache, home happiness, and the like. What a price we sometimes have to pay when we insist upon being plain spoken, that is, saying that which we think. It is often that a sentence hastily spoken costs us a friendship which has taken years to build. Just a few unkind words may break up a home and mar the happiness of several lives. A small bit of gossip has ruined many reputations. Idle criticism has destroyed the usefulness of many Christian institutions. But in studying this lesson, let us observe that

I. THE BIBLE IS VERY CLEAR ON THIS SUBJECT

1. The testimony of the Scriptures: Prov. 12: 23; 15: 1; 25: 11; Eph. 4: 29.

2. What of those who boast that "we speak that which we think?" Cf. James 1: 26; Psalm 39: 1.

3. The personal effect of one's speech, that is, the effect it will have upon himself. Cf. Matt. 12: 37; 26: 73.

> O that my tongue might so possess
> The accents of his tenderness;
> That every word I breathe might bless.
>
> For those who mourn, a word of cheer;
> A word of hope for those who fear;

And love for all men far and near.

O that it might be said of me:
Surely, thy speech betrayeth thee,
As friend of Christ of Galilee.

—Anon

II. THE POWER OF SPEECH IS DISTINCTLY HUMAN

1. Insofar as it is known, man is the only earthly creature which has a highly developed system of communication. *The power of speech is a fundamental mark of the superiority of man over the lower animal world.*

2. The quality of one's speech, therefore, indicates the width of the chasm which separates him from the brute creation.

3. There are two outstanding tragedies in this connection, which have caused untold sorrows and heartaches—viz:

(1) *The tragedy of the open mouth.*

a. Its owner protests that talk is cheap; and, indeed, it is about the only kind he usually produces.

b. When one listens at length to a siege of idle gossip, profanity, or unclean jokes, he is reminded of nothing quite so much as a leaky faucet or a running sore. Cf. Matt. 12: 33-37.

c. The intellectual and spiritual gulf which separates such a man from his dog is not very great.

(2) *The tragedy of the closed lips.*

a. No words of praise or thanksgiving, and no expressions of sympathy or appreciation ever escape.

b. It is a pitiful sight, indeed, to see a man who has lived three score years and ten, being blessed by a heavenly Father, but whose eyes have never been lifted in gratitude and whose lips have never learned to pray.

c. Parents neglect to counsel and encourage their children; friends let the hour of sorrow pass without a word of comfort; and Christians allow the years to go by without any attempt to win a soul to Christ, by speaking the word of the Lord to him. Cf. James 4: 17.

III. SPEECH IS THE TEST OF CHARACTER

1. We have a barometer to measure atmospheric pressure, a thermometer to measure temperature, a speedometer to measure velocity, etc., but the oldest instrument of this kind is the tongue. It reveals the depths of one's soul and measures his character.

2. If one listens to a man talk for an hour, he can then read his ideals and character, just like he can tell the temperature by looking at a thermometer. Cf. Luke 6: 45.

3. When Peter denied Christ, he did it with words; but later on, with words again, he defied the Sanhedrin; and each time his words clearly showed the kind of man he was. See Matt. 26: 73; Acts 4: 13-20; 5: 27-29.

4. That which has been said is not inconsistent with the practice of endeavoring to show one the need of exercising care in his relations with some people (cf. 2 Tim. 4: 14, 15); but to tell some one that which another said about him when it is almost certain to cause hard feelings is clearly out of harmony with the teaching of Christ, unless, indeed, good can be accomplished by telling it. Cf. 1 Sam. 25: 2ff.

IV. Speech Is Our Means of Progress

1. Each animal starts where other animals of his kind started, but men start where the last man left off. If a dog which died in 1776 could be brought back to life, he would be the equal of the dogs today. He would know as much and would be just as capable as his more modern descendants. But if a man who died in 1776 could be brought back to life today, he would be lost. Radios, automobiles, steam, electricity, telephones, airplanes, television, and the like, would all be new to him. The next generation will not need to discover any of these conveniences. We shall pass them on to them, and they will begin where we leave off. How, you say? By the use of words; for speech makes progress possible.

2. Our whole educational system is dependent on the twenty-six letters of the alphabet; and every professional ánd trades-man must learn by means of words. Without speech business would be at a standstill.

3. Who said, Talk is cheap? It would be hard to find a more important link in the whole chain of our civilization.

4. Talk is never cheap, but it may be cheapened; and when it is it brings crime, war, exploitation, injustice, suffering, and death.

V. Words Are the Means by Which the Kingdom of God Is Advanced

1. Some one has said that preaching is using words to the glory of God and the salvation of men.

2. The Lord expects every follower of his to use just those words which will have a tendency to lead men to accept the gospel of Christ and live for him. Cf. Col. 4: 6; Matt. 12: 36; Psalm 19: 14.

✦ ✦ ✦

THE CALL OF THE UNATTAINABLE
Deut. 3: 23-29

Introduction: 1. Moses, like many other great men, was born of lowly parents and in the midst of humble circumstances; but through the providence of God he reached a greatness which few men of earth have ever attained. Cf. Deut. 34: 10-12. The secret of his great success may be learned from the inspired record concerning him, especially Heb. 11: 24-27. No one can read these words regarding Moses without realizing something of the goal which he was able to see in the distance. 2. There are many great lessons to learn from the life of Moses, but the one we are interested in today is the call of the unattainable. We shall begin our study at the waters of Meribah (Ex. 17: 1-7; Num. 20: 2-13; 27: 12-23; Psalm 106: 32-33), and then briefly follow the experiences of Moses until we see him as he is revealed in the text now before us. In studying this lesson, then, let us ask,

I. WHAT IS THE CALL OF THE UNATTAINABLE?

1. It is the call of an ideal which never can be realized. Cf. Deut. 34: 4. Such an experience is always accompanied with sadness. This was especially true in the case of Moses, as the inspired text plainly indicates.

2. This unattainable goal had long been the cherished ideal of Moses, as one would gather from Heb. 11: 24-27 and other passages which give the record of his life. He had sacrificed all that Egypt offered him and had endured all the trials and hardships of the wilderness in order to reach his goal

3. When God told him that he could never enter the land of Canaan, he passionately pleaded with him to revoke the decree, but the divine response was clear and decisive: "And Jehovah said unto me, Let it suffice thee; speak no more unto me of this matter."

II. THE CALL OF THE UNATTAINABLE WAS NOT A UNIQUE EXPERIENCE OF MOSES

1. It is a mistake to think that what happened in the case of Moses was peculiar to him. It is true that the call of the unattainable finds a picturesque embodiment in his life, but the call itself is one of the common experiences of civilized man.

2. What life is there that does not at its close lay down many unfinished tasks which have been dear to the heart?

> Not now, but in the coming years,
> It may be in the better land,
> We'll read the meaning of our tears,
> And there, sometime, we'll understand.
>
> We'll catch the broken thread again,
> And finish what we here began;
> Heav'n will the mysteries explain,
> And then, ah then, we'll understand.
>
> We'll know why clouds instead of sun
> Were over many a cherished plan;
> Why song has ceased when scarce begun;
> 'Tis there, sometime, we'll understand.
>
> God knows the way, he holds the key,
> He guides us with unerring hand;
> Sometime with tearless eyes we'll see;
> Yes, there, up there, we'll understand.

> Then trust in God thro' all the days;
> Fear not, for he doth hold thy hand;
> Though dark thy way, still sing and praise,
> Sometime, sometime, we'll understand.
> —*Maxwell N. Cornelius*

3. Furthermore, one does not have to wait until life's close to see this principle in operation. Many people are forced by the hard pressure of circumstances into situations which are perpetual drudgery to them. For them the door of opportunity has long been closed, and they are compelled by the unyielding demands of life into limited activities. They have seen their cherished desire, but are not permitted to reach it, e. g., some profession, special work, travel, etc.

III. WHAT SHOULD BE OUR ATTITUDE TOWARD THE CALL OF THE UNATTAINABLE?

1. We should not look upon the unattainable longings of life as a hindrance or a void, but as a stirring inspiration to do our best in that which is possible for us. This is a great test of character. Moses did not allow the longing for the unattainable to prevent him from achieving the attainable; and in this is revealed his greatness. See Num. 27; 15ff.

2. R. C. Foster has observed that the fact of an ideal being unattained is the very thing that makes it an ideal. When it is attained, it ceases to be an ideal and passes into the realm of the actual. Even though it is unattainable, it does not lose its compelling force. As Browning would say,

> A man's grasp should exceed his reach,
> Or what is a heaven for?

3. If a man is unable to realize his ambition to do some great work in this life, he can so live that this great ideal will draw him into doing the best he can. The ideal state remains our goal, even though unattainable, and keeps us trying to come as close as possible to its realization. Cf. the one-talent man and the widow who gave two mites.

IV. THE ASSURANCE WHICH COMES WITH THE RIGHT ANSWER

1. When one answers the call of the unattainable he is filled with the intense satisfaction of having done his best. The sharpness of disappointment is always mitigated for him who does his best, even though he is unable to reach his goal. This was the attitude of Moses, and it must have softened the tragedy of his life as he turned his back upon Israel and Canaan and climbed the heights of Nebo.

2. And, too, the answer to this call furnishes a powerful example to others. Suppose Moses had given up when he was first told that he could not lead the host of Israel into Canaan? (Num.

20: 10-13.)   What would have been the effect upon his contemporaries and upon succeeding generations?

3. And, finally, the answer to this call gives one the assurance that his noble ideals which are unattainable in this life will be attained in eternity.   Moses was not permitted to enter the earthly land of Canaan, but by answering the call of his unattainable ideal he was assured a home in that heavenly Canaan where sin, sorrow, and disappointment are no more.

◆ ◆ ◆

THE THINGS WE LEAVE UNDONE
James 4: 17

Introduction: 1. We are nearing the end of another year, this being the last public service we have scheduled before the coming of a new year.   The occasion, therefore, furnishes us with a good opportunity for reviewing our lives in the light of that which God expects of his people; and it will be a fine thing if every one present will do that at this time.   2. No Christian should be satisfied unless he has tried to obey God.   But no one is likely to be very zealous in that direction who does not frequently inspect himself in the light of the Lord's teaching.   Therefore, in discussing this lesson, let us consider that

I. THERE IS SIN IN OMISSION

1. In the year 1744 Louis XV of France was smitten with a malady which threatened to end his life.   The people of Paris and the entire nation of France prayed earnestly for his recovery. Their fervent prayers were interrupted by sobs.   This wide-spread interest in and deep affection for the king earned for him the surname of "Louis the Well-Beloved."   This love for him was not inspired by that which he had done, but by that which the people had hoped he would do.   They had long been crushed under the heel of a cruel tyrant, and they regarded the accession of this new king as the dawn of brighter and happier days.   He recovered from this illness, but was stricken again thirty years later.   This time there were no prayers offered for him, and no tears were shed for him.   Instead, he was perhaps the object of more hate than any other man in France.   In 1744 when the people were praying for him, he asked, "What have I done to be so loved?"   Thirty years later he might have asked, "What have I done to be so hated?" and the answer would have been, "He had done nothing!"

2. One of the most impressive facts in the moral and religious teaching of Jesus is the stress which he laid on positive and active goodness.

(1) Matt. 7: 12, 24-27.

(2) Luke 10: 25ff.   The priest and the Levite were not guilty of any positive act of wrong doing.   If the wounded man had

died, the law could not have touched them for turning a deaf ear
to the call of humanity. Yet in the eyes of Divine Justice, and
of higher human justice, they would have been guilty of murder.
Their omission of duty was as wicked as the crime of the robbers;
and little did they think when they passed by on the other side,
that they would be for all time to come an outstanding example of
the baseness of doing nothing, and of the wickedness of negative
failure.

(3) Luke 16: 19ff. The rich man was not sent to torment
for that which he did, but for that which he might have done.
He was not accused of any positive transgression, nor called a bad
man. He was, in all probability, a highly respected citizen in
the eyes of his contemporaries; but in the eyes of God he was a
sinner. The original word from which we have our word "sin"
literally means to "miss the mark," or failure to hit the mark—a
failure to do which is required, whether by omission or commission. The rich man had sinned in that he had missed the true end
and scope of his life—he had failed to regard his wealth as an obligation and an opportunity.

(4) Matt. 25: 14ff. The one-talent man was not accused of
spending his lord's money. Indeed, in a negative way he had
acted with the most scrupulous honesty and care. He was exact;
for when his master returned he gave back to him all that had
been put into his hands. Yet he was condemned—condemned because he had not done anything with the one talent which was in
his possession.

(5) Matt. 25: 31ff. The ones on the left hand were send into
eternal punishment simply because they had failed to administer
to the needs of the Lord's people.*

II. CONSEQUENCES OF SINS OF OMISSION

1. The injury these sins do to ourselves.

(1) Consider the failure of one during young manhood to prepare himself for work and service in later years. There are few
who realize the loss at the time; but their eyes are usually opened
when the demands and needs of future years press upon them.

(2) The soul of many a person has been destroyed by a failure

---

*Does the sentence of doom seem harsh? It is the Lord's righteous
and reasonable condemnation of people who knew what they should have
done, but did not do it. The story is told of an ill-clad, barefooted boy who
was met by a man as the boy was returning from Sunday school. The
man asked him, "Where have you been?" "To Sunday school," was the
boy's reply. "And what did you learn there?" continued the man with a
sneering look upon his face. "I learned that God is Love," was the boy's
prompt reply. "But how can you believe that. If God is Love, why hasn't
he told someone to put better clothes on your body and shoes on your
feet." The boy was silent for a moment or two and then he made this
crushing reply, "I guess that God did tell someone, but that someone must
have forgot."

to develop its powers at the proper time. Cf. 2 Pet. 3: 18.

2. The injury inflicted upon others.

(1) If a man should see another person in danger of losing his life, and failed to do something about it when he had the opportunity, he would at least be held morally responsible for his death. But what of the man who remains silent while the character of another whom he knows to be innocent is being assailed?

(2) Acts 7: 57-8: 1; 22: 20.

But in order to be more specific, let us consider,

III. THE THINGS WE HAVEN'T SAID THIS YEAR

1. How many kind words did we leave unspoken? Eph. 4: 32; Matt. 26: 73.

2. Think of the times we should have stood for the truth. but kept silent for the sake of popularity. "Truth is not only violated by falsehood; it may be equally outraged by silence."—Amiel. Too many people are unwilling to be identified with an unpopular cause, although the cause itself may be proper and right.

3. The invitations we failed to extend.

(1) To those who should become Christians, Rev. 22: 17.

(2) To those who should attend the meetings of the church, Heb. 10: 24, 25.

IV. THE THINGS WE HAVEN'T DONE IN OUR HOMES

1. Family worship. Have we been faithful with it?

2. Family discipline. Have we properly appreciated and discharged it? Cf. Eph. 6: 4. The word "nurture," according to Thayer, involves *"the whole training and education of children* (which relates to the cultivation of mind and morals, and employs for this purpose now commands and admonitions, now reproof and punishment)."

3. Private Bible reading and prayer. How much of this have we really done?

V. THE THINGS WE HAVEN'T DONE FOR THE CHURCH

1. Grade yourself on the following, allowing 20 per cent for each question:

(1) Have you been faithful in your attendance at all the meetings of the church?

(2) Have you tried to do that which the Lord teaches with reference to giving? Cf. Heb. 8: 6; Luke 12: 48.**

**Lame Logic:* We say that tithing is not binding upon Christians; but in the next sentence, same paragraph, we say: "The gospel is founded upon better promises. We should give more than the Jews gave. The Jews gave a tenth. We should give at least that much. Where does that leave us? free or bound. Should we tithe? Oh, no, perish the thought! We should more than tithe!

Paul makes it clear that it must be voluntary, cheerful, of a willing heart; but if we should do more than the Jews, the cheerfulness and

(3) Have you been instrumental in leading any one to Christ? or have you endeavored to do so?

(4) Have you spoken well of the church among those about you? Remember that the church is the bride of Christ and your attitude toward her will affect him, accordingly.

(5) Have you done anything to make the church "more friendly?"

2. Having now had these things called to our attention, what will be our attitude toward them during the coming year? Cf. James 4: 17.

> He came to my desk with quivering lip—
> The lesson was done.
> "Dear Teacher, I want a new leaf," he said,
> "I have spoiled this one."
>
> I took the old leaf, stained and blotted,
> And gave him a new one, all unspotted,
> And into his sad eyes smiled,
> "Do better, now, my child."
>
> I went to the throne with a quivering soul—
> The old year was done.
> "Dear Father, hast thou a new leaf for me?
> I have spoiled this one.
>
> He took the old leaf, stained and blotted,
> And gave me a new one, all unspotted,
> And into my sad heart smiled,
> "Do better, now, my child."
>
> —*Kathleen Wheeler*

willingness cannot begin until the tenth is passed. All that is taught about the spirit and beauty of giving applies only after the tithe has been paid. We cannot begin to bud the grace of liberality until we have first matched percentages with the Jews. Paul had a lot of trouble with the Jews, and they are still a thorn in the flesh of spiritual Israel. We cannot get any credit for liberality until the Jews are disposed of; and some of our brethren find it necessary to revamp the whole Bible from cover to cover, and get the kingdoms, both human and divine, all scrambled, in order to provide a place in their philosophy for the Jews! Religiously speaking, we cannot eat our grapefruit without getting the Jews in our eyes!

When some of us say that tithing is not in force, we mean that it does not fall like gentle rain upon the roof; but of course it does come up like the dew in the night. It gets the same results—our logic is dampened. This is about on a par with our premillennial brethren who say that they would not be guilty of date setting (perish the thought!), still they insist with vehemence that Christ's coming is imminent. It may be momentarily expected. And the New Testament so taught nineteen hundred years ago!—W. E. Brightwell, *Gospel Advocate, Vol LXXX*, p. 1155.

"THE UNITY OF THE SPIRIT"
Eph. 4: 3

Introduction: 1. In spite of the organic political union of the Roman Empire of Paul's day, there were many divisions among the people, such as those which existed between Jew and Gentile, master and slave, rich and poor, and the learned and unlearned. The attitudes which grew out of these relationships produced barriers among the people which were almost insurmountable. The entire world was seamed and scarred by divisions which separated man from man. 2. It was into this kind of a situation that the gospel came with its appeal to men. This message was not limited to a favored few, but was for all men, regardless of their station or relationship in life. Cf. John 12: 32; Mark 16: 15, 16. 3. But the gospel did not call men to continue in their divisions; they were to be one in Christ. Cf. Col. 3: 9b-15. All of their former enmities and unholy attitudes toward one another were to be left behind when they came into Christ. Cf. Isa. 11: 6-9. 4. It was to people with this kind of a background that Paul addressed the exhortation of the text; and when we consider the fact that it is the unity which the Spirit himself brought about, the importance of the lesson will at once become apparent. But in studying this lesson, let us begin by considering,

I. THE GREAT SPIRITUAL MELTING-POT

1. Paul affirms in 1 Cor. 12: 13 that it was through the agency of the Spirit that we were "all baptized into one body." This baptism, of course, is water baptism, and is performed by the Lord's people as the Spirit directs. All classes, therefore, reach a spiritual equality before God in this body, which is the church. See Gal. 3: 26-28.

2. This unity is further confirmed and sealed by the fact that those baptized into Christ are "all made to drink of one Spirit." The word from which we have "drink" is *potizo,* meaning "to give to drink, to furnish drink." It came to mean "to water, irrigate," and that was the word which Paul used when he said, "I planted, Apollos *watered."* See 1 Cor. 3: 6-8. In its metaphorical sense, as used in the passage now before us, the word means, according to Thayer, "to imbue, saturate." Cf. Isa. 29: 10.

(1) A comparison of some of the translations may be helpful here. *Moffatt:* "we have all been imbued with one Spirit;" *Goodspeed:* "and we have all been saturated with one Spirit;" *The Expositor's Greek Testament:* "we were drenched" in one Spirit.

(2) The reference, of course, is to the reception of the Holy Spirit when one is baptized into Christ. "To drink of one Spirit" (1 Cor. 12: 13) and "ye shall receive the gift of the Holy Spirit" (Acts 2: 38) refer to one and the same thing—namely, the impartation of the Holy Spirit to obedient believers. Cf. John 7: 37-39; Acts 5: 32.

II. NEW CREATURES IN CHRIST JESUS

1. The change wrought in becoming a Christian is so radical that one is said to be "a new creature," or, as in the margin of the American Standard Version, "there is a new creation." See 2 Cor. 5: 17; cf. John 3: 3-5; Rom. 6: 3, 4; Gal. 6: 15. Paul says in Tit. 3: 5 that this "renewing" is done by the Holy Spirit, that is, that which is done to make one a new creature in Christ Jesus is accomplished by the Holy Spirit.

(1) The original word for "renewing" occurs only twice in the new Testament—Rom. 12: 2 and Tit. 3: 5, and it is defined by Thayer to mean "a renewal, renovation, complete change for the better; . . . effected by the Holy Spirit, Tit. 3: 5."

a. Is it possible to have a "new creature," or a "new creation," with anything less than a "renewal, renovation, complete change for the better?"

b. If there is a "new creature," or a "new creation," it must be accomplished by the power of God (cf. Psalm 51: 10, 11); and since Paul says that the "renewing" is accomplished by the Holy Spirit, we must accept it as a fact that the Holy Spirit is God's agent in bringing about the "new creation." "According to his mercy he saved us, through the washing of regeneration and renewing of the Holy Spirit." See Tit. 3: 5, 6.

c. The "washing of regeneration" is water baptism, while the "renewing of the Holy Spirit" is that which is done to make us new creatures in Christ. In the expression "renewing of the Holy Spirit" we have, according to Greek scholars, the *subjective genitive,* and the idea is that the "renewing" is wrought or accomplished by the Holy Spirit.

(2) There is no more mystery about God's making "new creatures" through the agency of the Holy Spirit, than there is about his saving the lost through the agency of Christ. They are both members of the Godhead and the divine side of redemption and sanctification is accomplished through them.

2. This unity, therefore, is preeminently the unity of the Spirit, since he is the author of it and it is accomplished through his agency. During the early age of the church miracles were employed in perfecting this unity, but since the completion of the New Testament the work is done according to the Spirit's revealed law. Read Eph. 4: 11-16. Cf. "the unity of the Spirit" (Eph. 4: 3) with "the unity of the faith" (Eph. 4: 13).

III. THE NATURE OF THE UNITY OF THE SPIRIT

1. It seems that some people have the idea that the unity of the Spirit consists primarily in a fraternal feeling toward each other, even though widely different viewpoints regarding teaching and practice may be held by them. In fact, there are those who contend that professed Christians can "keep the unity of the

Spirit in the bond of peace" while teaching conflicting doctrines and engaging in antagonistic practices.

(1) But the error of this viewpoint is easily seen when such passages as 1 Cor. 1: 10 and 2 Tim. 3: 16, 17 are considered. Do the Scriptures furnish the followers of Christ unto conflicting doctrines and antagonistic practices?

(2) Christians, of course, should be patient with each other and regard each other as brethren, while they are sincerely endeavoring to learn the way of the Lord more perfectly; but this does not imply that when some become confirmed in erroneous teaching and practice that they have the right to insist that those who "hold the pattern of sound words" endorse and fellowship them in their errors.

2. As has already been pointed out, the unity of the Spirit is the unity of which the Spirit is the author—the unity which results from following the teaching of the Spirit in becoming Christians and in living as Christians.

3. The cardinal points in this unity may be summed up as follows:

(1) Through the agency of the Spirit, or as directed by the Spirit, all those who are acceptable to God are "baptized into one body." Thus, through the simple ceremony of baptism they are all linked together in Christ. It matters not how widely different their former relationships may have been, when they were baptized into Christ they were all placed on a level of perfect equality.

(2) Not only are they one in Christ; they have all been created anew in him. "The old things have passed away; behold, they are become new." (2 Cor. 5: 17.) This, of course, is a "renewal, renovation, complete change for the better;" and it is also accomplished through the agency of the Holy Spirit. (Tit. 3: 5. 6.)

(3) Furthermore, those baptized into Christ and made new creatures in him were "all made to drink of one Spirit," that is, metaphorically speaking, they were all imbued, saturated, or drenched in one Spirit. As the human body (cf. 1 Cor. 12: 12) is animated by one spirit and all of its members controlled by one spirit, just so the body of Christ is animated by one Spirit and all its members controlled by one Spirit. It is hardly necessary to add that this controlling by one Spirit is now done through his revealed will. Cf. Rom. 8: 2, 14.

4. It is entirely erroneous, therefore, for any one to conclude that the unity of the Spirit is of such a nature as to permit wide differences in teaching and practice, so long as there is a fraternal feeling manifested toward all those who are professing to follow Christ. The teaching of the Spirit is a unit, and the unity of the Spirit requires that all of its adherents recognize the oneness of the Christian system. See Eph. 4: 4-6.

IV. HOW IS THIS UNITY TO BE KEPT?

1. There must be a diligent effort to keep it. "Giving diligence to keep the unity of the Spirit." To be diligent is to exert one's self, to interest himself most earnestly in the accomplishment of the task before him. This, of course, implies his interest in the soundness of the faith as it is in Christ Jesus (2 Cor. 13: 5) and his willingness to declare the whole counsel of God (Acts 20: 27.)

2. It is easy to have unity on certain phases of Bible teaching, or on misconceptions of New Testament doctrine, but *that* would not be the unity of the Spirit.

3. The unity of the Spirit must be kept *in the bond of peace*. This indicates the *sphere* in which unity is to be maintained. Such peace, however, is possible only when brethren are willing to remove from their hearts all selfishness and other sinful attitudes, and replace them with a gentle, long-suffering, and forbearing spirit, which seeks, not their own, but another's good.

◆ ◆ ◆

SUMMIT VIEWS
From the Five Peaks of John Fourteen

Introduction: 1. The portion of scripture from which this lesson is taken is a part of the discourse delivered by Jesus on the night of his betrayal. The heart and mind of the Saviour are in this matchless chapter. It is always new, as the latest sunrise; and the last word in its praise will never be spoken while the earth remains. Each verse, when considered alone, reminds one of a jewel of great price; and when they are all put together, one by one, the whole becomes, as it were, a rare necklace of great beauty. 2. When considered as a whole, the chapter appears as though we are moving along life's highway, with occasional heights from which we may look off on a boundless horizon and measure the life we are living as it begins in time and reaches out into eternity. 3. If one will pause on the five peaks of this chapter, he will be able to see the journey of life with the principal things which it involves; and as he leaves them he will be able to carry with him the vision which our Lord here gives of the pilgrimage to which he is calling us. But in studying this lesson, let us begin by considering,

I. LIFE'S DESTINATION

1. As we look upon life and see it verging toward the unknown, we naturally ask, "What is the goal of life?" The first summit view gives the answer. See verse 2.

2. Although there is a goal to be reached, we are too often conscious, almost wholly, of current events and experiences. Cf. Luke 8: 14; Col. 3: 1-4; 1 John 3: 1-3.

(1) If these events and experiences are pleasant, we are happy;

but if they are not, we are sad. Cf. Rom. 8: 28; 2 Cor. 4: 16-18; Luke 6: 22, 23.

(2) The common attitude of many may be compared to a boat on a river, the passengers of which are conscious only of that which they are passing on the banks, or that which they are doing on the boat.

3. People today, even Christians, do not talk much about the end of this earthly life, or of heaven; yet that is the goal toward which we are all traveling!

II. THE WAY

1. We may have a clear conception of the goal, but may not know the way. The second summit gives us a view of the way. See verse 6.

2. Jesus is our *Guide*. What he says we will believe, and where he leads us we will follow. *That which he asks us to believe and to do is our way home!* Cf. John 3: 36.

III. OUR OCCUPATION

1. The questions suggested in this study are all natural, and they come in their natural order. *We must have something to do.* Cf. Acts 22: 10.* The third summit reveals that which is expected of us. See verse 15.

2. Notice how this verse affects our daily manner of living. Cf. 1 John 5: 3; Matt. 25: 14-30.

3. Life in this world will never be that which it was meant to be, so long as men insist on regarding their talents as their own, and their strength and their time to be spent as they please. See Gal. 2: 20.

IV. STRENGTH FOR THE JOURNEY

1. There will be many obstacles in the way, and we may often become discouraged; but when we climb the fourth peak our spirits will be refreshed. See verses 16, 17.

2. Life is a strange partnership, the little member hardly knowing that he has any needs at all; proud, vain, and rather ignorant of all that which he has to face in life, while the great Partner knows all about the little member and all that which affects him.**

---

*Men go far astray in their conception of why these earthly years are given to us: therefore they do not spend them as they should. We should remember, however, that the things we do in this life are the things which will make heaven an agreeable and congenial place when we get there. Cf. Rev. 22: 3; Matt. 6: 10b. Heaven is a place where the inhabitants love to do God's will, where they are in perfect harmony with his will, and where they respond to the highest, the noblest, and the purest things. (John Edward Bushnell, Summit Views.)

**We are not unlike the child who starts forth in full strength by the side of the man, carrying his armful, refusing aid, and disdaining to be held even by the hand. The man and the child trudge along together and soon the little fellow unconsciously yields one little thing after another of his

3. There seems to be no effort made by the great Designer to make the path of life easy, but rather to furnish strength. Cf. Deut. 33: 25; 1 Cor. 10: 13; James 1: 5-8.

(1) The Comforter, as seen on this peak, is also called the Paraclete. See marginal note. This indicates one who stands by us to help us by pleading our cause, by admonishing and instructing us, and by imparting to us the consolation which we need.

(2) It is not courage, therefore, but fool's play to try to face the great mysteries of life in the confidence of one's own endurance.

V. THE MANNER OF OUR LIVING

1. We may have a clear vision from the other summits, but are we impressing the world as a company of pilgrims with happy hearts and gleaming faces, and with a consciousness that we are approaching a wonderful consummation? *We should recommend the way of life by the manner of our living.* The fifth summit will afford us this vision. See verse 27.

2. Do we show our faith in God when the clouds are about us. Cf. Acts 27: 25 and context.***

3. Let us take more frequent walks with the great Revealer of life amid these glorious summits!

◆ ◆ ◆

THE WISDOM OF THE WISE-MEN
Matt. 2: 1-12

Introduction: 1. One of the most interesting incidents in connection with the birth of Jesus is the visit of the Wise-men. The narrative which tells of this event has been read over and over

---

burden unto the other. And then, his load all gone, submits his hand to be held; and if one is near the journey's end he probably would see a strong man with child's things hung across one shoulder and on the other a little limp creature snuggling, no longer proud but quite content to be carried, upon the other.

So it often comes to us. Man is proud of his strength, his power of will; and, refusing partnership, he prefers to fight alone. But all the time Heaven is busy overhead, watching for the moment, which will surely come when the heart is prepared for it, to say, "Fear not. Be of good cheer;" and, according to one of the priceless, old sayings, he shall be privileged to "drink of the brook in the way." (Ibid.)

***The story is told of a father and his little daughter during their first experience of darkness after the wife and mother had been taken from them. They were in bed when the little girl called to her father and said, "Daddy, it is so dark. I do not think that I have ever seen it so dark before." Her father went to her side and assured her that he was near her, and that all would be well. Her fears were calmed, and she soon fell asleep.

Her father, more conscious of his loneliness, said, "It is so dark. I do not think that I have ever seen it so dark before." It was then that it seemed that God spoke to him and assuerd him that he was near him, and that all would be well. His fears were calmed, and he, too, soon fell asleep.

again; but it never grows old to those who delight to honor the Lord. The artist and the poet have portrayed these things in picture and song; and the result has been that multitudes of people have had their minds turned toward him whose coming was the greatest manifestation of God's love for man which the world has ever seen. 2. One of the proverbs (Prov. 13: 20) says, "Walk with wise men, and thou shalt be wise." It is our purpose in this study to apply this principle to ourselves, as we endeavor to walk with the Wise-men of the text. 3. While it is true that these men belonged to an order, known as "Wise-men" or "Magi," yet they displayed a wisdom worthy of imitation in their attitude toward Jesus; and it is to that wisdom that attention is now invited. Their wisdom is seen,

I. In the Object of Their Seeking

1. The record declares that they saw the star in the east, and then set out in search of the newly-born King of the Jews. These men were not Jews, but in some way they had learned of the coming King, and they went in search of him.

2. Their journey led them to Jerusalem, the capital city of the Jews, with its teeming life and temporal grandeurs, with its high priests and Herods, for they expected to find the "King of the Jews" in "David's royal city," but he was not there.

3. Thus do many of the quests of life turn out.

(1) Having seen some star of our desire, we begin our journey, and lo, in the place we hope to find the object of our search, we find only disappointment.

(2) But if we follow the wisdom of the Wise-men we shall not remain disappointed; for they were not baffled by disappointments nor discouraged by delays.

4. Refusing to be deceived by circumstances, they were willing to continue their search. God therefore again showed them the star, and it led them to the object of their seeking. They entered the house, worshipped the babe, and were satisfied. Cf. John 7: 17; Matt. 13: 12.

II. In Their Act of Worship

1. The record says, "And they came into the house and saw the young child with Mary his mother; and they fell down and worshipped him."

2. Wisdom always makes room for worship, for it recognizes that nothing is more vital, in its total effect, than worship; and nothing is more detrimental, in its ultimate issues, than its neglect.

3. The center of Christianity is worship, but unless it is the worship ordained of God, it will not prove a blessing to those who engage in it. See John 4: 24; Matt. 15: 9; Col. 2: 23; 2 John 9.

4. This great teacher (wisdom) therefore writes across all our folly the words of the psalmist, as found in Psalm 2: 10-12.

III. In Their Spirit of Giving

1. "And opening their treasures they offered unto him gifts, gold and frankincense and myrrh." Thus, by their gifts they proved the sincerity of their worship.

2. Giving has been described as the soul of Christianity, for apart from giving Christianity could not exist. Cf. John 3: 16; 2 Cor. 8: 9; Matt. 20: 28; Acts 20: 35.

3. Wisdom, indeed, has nothing in common with niggardliness, for it glorifies in generosity and knows that true giving is the secret of all real living.

Conclusion: Thus, we have seen that the Wise-men revealed their wisdom in their seeking, in their worship, and in their giving; and as a result they experienced great joy. Just so, may we, too, be "star-led" in our seeking, reverent and adoring in our worship, and kingly in our giving; that we also may know the unspeakable joy that comes through such wisdom.

◆ ◆ ◆

WALKING WITH GOD
Gen. 5: 21-24

Introduction: 1. The Hebrew people had a beautiful expression to describe those who were consistent in their every-day religion. They called it "walking with God." Such people felt the presence of God in every-day life, and not only in times of special events and emergencies. 2. The biography found in the Scriptures is highly interesting and instructive. It is designed for our spiritual advantage, in that it encourages us to imitate the good found in God's people and avoid their errors. 3. The language of the text seems to indicate that Enoch was distinguished from his contemporaries, as well as those who lived before and after him, because he walked with God; and the question naturally arises, What does it mean to walk with God—It means to have habitual fellowship with him. Enoch realized God's existence and he recognized his presence. Cf. Heb. 11: 5, 6. 4. Such an experience is possible for us today; and it may be likened to the companionship with a friend, with this difference: we can't spend many consecutive days with our dearest friends. But our fellowship with God need not be interrupted, for we can continue with him in all of our experiences as Christians. We can walk through life in his light, his assurance, his strength, and his confidence. But in studying this lesson, let us consider the expression,

I. And Enoch Walked with God

1. Human life is often represented as a course or way; and the activities of men are spoken of as walking in these ways. Cf. **Psalm 1: 1, 6.**

2. The phrase "walking with God" is frequently used throughout the Bible to represent a religious life. Cf. Gen. 6: 9; 17: 1; Isa. 2: 5. It is mentioned twice in the brief history of Enoch's life. See Gen. 5: 22, 24.

(1) It was evidently the most noticeable fact about him, and the information was passed down to others as his distinguishing mark.

(2) Some other instances in which the expression is used: 2 Kings 20: 3; Micah 6: 8; Rom. 8: 4; Eph. 4: 1; Col. 1: 10; 1 John 1: 6, 7.

3. What, then, are we to understand when we are told that Enoch walked with God, or that one walks with him now?

(1) *It implies that God is a person, as is the one who walks with him.* This two-fold conception is necessary to any adequate idea of religion, such as the one set forth in the Scriptures. Cf. Heb. 11: 5, 6.

(2) *It implies harmony.* But inasmuch as the carnal man is at enmity with God, there must first be a reconciliation with him, for "shall two walk together, except they have agreed?" See Amos 3: 3 and cf. Rom. 8: 6-8; 2 Cor. 5: 18-20.

(3) *To walk with God is to keep his commandments.* Obedience is the true test of a right heart, the only evidence of a living faith. Cf. 1 John 2: 3-6.

a. It is goodness, not greatness, that attracts the divine approbation. Enoch was not famed for worldly wealth, grandeur, or power, but for his personal purity.

b. Cf. Matt. 5: 8. "Only the pure in heart can see God, and only in the degree in which they are pure. The pure in heart behold him here. The impure could not see him ever there— the vision of God, the sight of the King in his beauty, and of the land that is very far off, is vouchsafed not to science but to sanctity, not to talent but to love."

(4) *To walk with God means progress.* Not only is progress being made, for in spiritual life, as in all other, there is no standing still. Maturity of religious consciousness is being attained. There is a sense of divine companionship and of harmony with a higher will. Cf. Matt. 7: 21.

(5) *To walk with God means rest.* Harmony comes through obedience, and obedience always brings rest.*

---

*There is harmony in music because in music there is no self-will. Music is built on law. Man did not make this law; he has simply discovered it. If he breaks it the music ceases. Each Hayden and Handel is as much bound by it as each amateur. The same is true of man's relation to his every act. Find out its principles, and all the genius of that art is yours. But disobey its principles; try to excel in any other way than by conformity to its nature, and all that art contends against you, and balks you at every step. We cannot change ocean current or tide, but we can build our ship and stretch our sail, and by adapting us to wind and wave we can gain any Liverpool or Queenstown. We cannot conquer

II. Enoch Was Not

1. Heb. 11: 5 says that "he was not found," suggesting that he was missed and sought for. Such a man, indeed, would be missed. This strongly implies that his life was not a solitary one.

2. He would be missed because his life was a good one. He lived in a busy but wicked world. Cf. Jude 14, 15.

3. The full significance ·of his noble life, doubtless, was not fully realized until he was gone. Such is usually the case. Cf. Matt. 13: 54-57; John 16: 7.

III. For God Took Him

1. The writer of Hebrews seems to imply that God took him because he was well pleased with him.**

2. What is signified by the expression "God took him?".

(1) It implies victory. Others had to die, but Enoch was spared that ordeal.

(2) Death for us, of course, is inevitable, unless we live till Jesus comes, but Christ has conquered the power of death by taking away its sting. See 1 Cor. 15: 55-57.

(3) However, let us remember our part in the conquest. God will give us the victory, only if we are faithful to him. Cf. 1 Cor. 15: 58. Enoch has taught us how to overcome, that is, by walking with God. He began his walk with God here on earth, and by faith was translated.

IV. How Do We Begin Our Walk with Him?

1. We have already seen the absolute necessity of walking with God, if we expect to please him, and the question now is, What must *we* do in order to walk with him?

2. The testimony of the Scriptures: John 6: 44, 45; Rom. 1: 16, 17; Mark 16: 15, 16; Acts 2: 1-42.

3. This principle of obedience, as has already been emphasized, must be extended to include all the activities of one's life as a Christian. Cf. Col. 3: 17; 2 Pet. 1: 5-11.

> Be with me, Lord—I cannot live without Thee,
> I dare not try to take one step alone,
> I cannot bear the loads of life, unaided,
> I need thy strength to lean myself upon.

---

lightning. Obedience pulls the sting out of lightning and makes it harmless. Fire is a bad master, but a good servant. So is it in the spiritual life. If we obey the law of God we have "rest and peace in the beloved."
—James Hastings.

**A little girl was once talking with another little girl about Enoch. The second little girl had never heard of him, and so the first, who was rich in Bible stories, told her by her mother, made up a version of the story of Enoch which had a very beautiful suggestion in it. Said the little girl to her friend, "God was accustomed to take walks with Enoch, and one day they went further than usual, and God said, 'Enoch, you are a long way from home; better come in and stay with me;' so he went, and has stayed ever since."—Ibid.

Be with me, Lord, and then if dangers threaten,
If storms of trial burst above my head,
If lashing seas leap ev'rywhere about me,
They cannot harm, or make my heart afraid.

Be with me, Lord! No other gift or blessing
Thou couldst bestow could with this one compare—
A constant sense of thy abiding presence,
Where'er I am, to feel that thou art near.

Be with me, Lord, when loneliness o'er takes me,
When I must weep amid the fires of pain,
And when shall come the hour of "my departure"
For "words unkonwn," O Lord, be with me then.

—*T. O. Chisholm*

✦ ✦ ✦

BY EVERY WORD
Matt. 4: 4

Introduction: 1. The baptism of Jesus marked the dividing
line between his private life and his public ministry here upon
earth. The inspired record informs us that following his baptism
he was "led up of the Spirit into the wilderness to be tempted
of the devil." See Matt. 3: 13-4: 11. 2. After he had completed
a fast of "forty days and forty nights," he hungered; and when
the tempter came to him, he said unto him, "If thou art the Son
of God, command that these stones become bread." But Jesus
answered and said, "It is written, Man shall not live by bread
alone, but by every word that proceedeth out of the mouth of
God." With the setting of the text thus before us, let us begin
the study of this lesson by considering,

I. GOD'S PRINCIPLE OF DEALING WITH MAN

1. The quotation given by Jesus in his answer to the devil
was taken from Deut. 8: 1-3, to which attention is now called.

2. By quoting Moses, Jesus shows that God employs the
same principle in dealing with man in both the Jewish and
Christian dispensations. Cf. Heb. 2: 1-3.

II. LIFE BY THE WORD OF GOD

1. When Jesus says that man shall *live* by God's word, he
assumes the fact of immortality; for he makes it plain that he
is not talking about mere physical life, supported by material
food. Cf. 1 Cor. 15: 32.

2. It is necessary, of course, that the body be properly cared
for, and the Lord has made ample provisions for that; but the
real emphasis must be placed upon that which sustains and develops the soul.

3. "Every word" of God contains a revelation and a commandment; for when God speaks to us it is to tell us something

which we do not know, and to bid us do something which we have not been doing. Cf. 2 Tim. 3: 16, 17.

4. *Truth and duty are always linked together.* There is no truth which has no corresponding duty; and there is no duty for which there is no corresponding truth.

(1) Too many people try to learn truths as if there were no duties belonging to them, and as if the knowing of them would make no difference in the way they live. Cf. John 7: 17; James 1: 23-25; 4: 17. *That is the reason their hold on the truth is so weak.*

(2) In like manner, there are those who are always trying to perform duties as if there were no truths behind them; that is, as if they were mere arbitrary things which rest on no principle and have no intelligible reasons. *That is the reason they do their duties so superficially and unreliably.*

(3) When every truth is rounded into its duty, and every duty is made to depend upon its truth, then we shall have a clearness, a consistency, and a permanence of moral and religious life of which we hardly dream now.

III. THREE LESSONS OF THE TEXT

1. *How to overcome temptation.* Cf. Heb. 4: 15; 1 Cor. 10: 13; Psalm 119: 11; James 1: 5ff. If we follow the example of Jesus, we must say, when tempted to do wrong, "It is written;" and then do as it is written. Of course, we could not speak and act in that way, unless we know that which is written.

2. *The two lives contrasted—the one by temporal food, and the other by every word of God.*

(1) Man is the most singular object of God's creation. The beasts and other forms of the lower creation can care for themselves to a large extent, but that is not true of man. He must be cared for in infancy and developed into manhood, if he is to reach his highest possibilities. And that which is true in the physical realm is also true in the spiritual. Man cannot please God without a guide. Cf. Jer. 10: 23. He is taught, therefore, by both precept and example.

(2) Examples of both types of life are clearly set forth in the Scriptures: Solomon sought to satisfy the lusts of the flesh, Ecclesiastes; while the attitude of Jesus is stated in John 4: 34.

3. *By every word.* This, of course, requires that the word be properly handled. See 2 Tim. 2: 15. This lesson may be illustrated by calling attention to some of the words of God by which we are to live:

(1) Grace, John 1: 17; Eph. 2: 8, 9.

(2) Faith, Heb. 11: 6; 2 Cor. 5: 7; Rom. 10: 17.

(3) Hope, Rom. 8: 24; 1 Pet. 1: 3; Heb. 6: 17-19.

(4) Love, Matt. 22: 37-40; 1 John 5: 3.

(5) Baptism, 1 Pet. 3: 21; Matt. 28: 18, 19; Mark 16: 15, 16.

IV. Our Responsibility Does Not End with Time

1. Regardless of how we may feel about the matter, we are developing one of these characters already referred to; for every responsible being is living on one or the other of these foods.

2. We may not obey the words of God in this life, but we may be sure that we shall meet them in the judgment. See John 12: 48-50.

◆ ◆ ◀

THE CHALLENGE OF THE NEW YEAR
Phil. 3: 13

Introduction: It is just as much a mark of progress to project ourselves mentally forward, as it is for us to swing ourselves backward in memory. Whether or not we can truthfully say that our best year is now closing, it is certain that we ought to be able to say with confidence that a better than the best will begin with the New Year. However, no man is prepared to predict the future unless he is able to estimate the past.* But as we pause, as it were, between the past and the future, let us consider some things that should help us during the coming months. There are three things which we want to think about in this study. They are,

I. The Ability to Forget

1. This is both the secret of true progress and the ground for enduring happiness; and its importance is at once seen when we consider that we must cultivate in the present the art of living in the future.

2. However, as we look toward the future we should ever remember that there must be a difference between what we dream and what we do. The story is told of an artist who was found standing before his masterpiece and looking at it with a saddened face. He had achieved magnificent success in his painting, and, knowing that, a friend asked him why he was so sad. "Because," he replied, "I am satisfied with my painting. I have enbodied

---

*The close of the career and life on one of Scotland's greatest writers, Sir Walter Scott, was both pathetic and sublime. His castle of red sandstone and granite, situated along the Tweed and built from the profits of his writings, was just completed in the very year which witnessed his financial failure. At fifty-five years of age he found himself $600,000 in debt, but with iron honesty and Scotch diligence he set himself to the task of paying every dollar of his indebtness.

He succeeded in six years, but it was at the cost of his life. He died at the age of sixty-one. Shortly before he passed away he uttered these words, "I am drawing near to the close of my career. I am fast shuffling off the stage. I have been perhaps the most voluminous author of the day, and it is a comfort to me to think that I have tried to unsettle no man's faith, to corrupt no man's principles, that I have written nothing that I should wish on my deathbed blotted."

all I can feel or think. I am sad because this marks the limit of my growth." It is a sad experience for any man when he reaches such a moment in his life. Cf. 2 Pet. 3: 18.

3. Memory is a precious heritage, for without it man would be a perpetual infant. But, as it is, he is the master of his memory and can train it to forget as well as to retain. Cf. Phil. 3: 12-16.

4. Therefore, if we go forward there are some things which we must forget, e. g., successes, failures, sins which have been forgiven, etc. Cf. 1 John 1: 7, 9.

II. THE ABILITY TO CONCENTRATE

1. It has been said that concentration is self-mastery. Those who succeed in life are the ones who hold themselves fast to one task. For example,

(1) Noah concentrated on the ark which he was building.

(2) Moses concentrated on the emancipation of Israel.

(3) Paul concentrated on turning men to God. Cf. his "one thing I do."**

2. The ability to concentrate is to have the power of discrimination. A man with only one idea is not necessarily a man with one talent. It may be that a dabbler at many things will gain quicker recognition in the world than the doer of one thing; but the dabbler will be forgotten when the doer of one thing goes right on being remembered for many years. Cf. Heb. 12: 1, 2; Acts 21: 7-14; 1 Cor. 15: 58.

III. THE ABILITY TO PERSIST

1. Persistency discovers and develops character. Cf. Matt. 24: 13.***

2. Persistency also releases the reserves of character. No

Happy it would be for each one of us if, looking back over the year which is just closing, we could truthfully say of all our words and deeds what the dying Sir Walter Scott said as he swept the whole past record of his career. Cf. Col. 3: 17.

**Atalanta of mythical fame offered to become the wife of any man who could outrun her in a race, but requiring that the penalty for defeat must be death. There were many suitors who risked their lives to win her hand, and many of them went to their death because of their failure to outrun her. At last Hippomenes came, bearing a gift from Aphrodite, consisting of three golden apples which he successively dropped along the race course. Atalanta, charmed by their beauty and confident of her fleetness, could not refrain from gathering them; but in doing so she was obliged to marry Hippomenes. The world drops its apples of wealth, pleasure, and ambition, along the course of life; and, stopping to gather them, we too may lose the race!

***Audubon spent three years in the forest among the haunts of birds and insects, and emerged with a complete set of drawings, the result of painstaking efforts. He entrusted them to a friend who carelessly allowed insects to get into them and destroy them. Audubon again plunged into the forest and began all over again; and after three more years of painstaking toil, he emerged with a new set of drawings, and reaped undying fame.

professed Christian should be satisfied to do less than his best
in the Lord's service. Cf. Luke 17: 10; James 2: 10; 4: 17.

   Conclusion: Therefore, as we enter the New Year, let us forget that which we should forget—that which will hinder our work;
and let us concentrate upon the right—that which will please God;
and let us continue stedfast unto the end of the way.

❦ ❦ ❦

A DIVINE CONTRAST
Psalm 1

   Introduction: 1. Whether intentional on the part of Jesus or
not, there seems to be a close relationship between this psalm and
the Lord's sermon on the mount. It is as if he preached an ex-
pository sermon on the main outline of this ancient poem. In
his sermon he pictured the ideal man of the kingdom and developed
four definite lines of thought—viz., his character, his influence, his
conduct, and his destiny. 2. To say the least of it, Jesus knew
the message of this great psalm, and he boldly addressed the principles which it sets forth to the people who heard him on that
day. He fully realized that the man who ignores God or shuts
him out of his life is on his way to eternal ruin. He taught that
the life that counts must have some strong refusals and some
equally great acceptances. 3. This psalm has been called "the
threshold psalm," for it forms an ideal portal to the whole
collections of psalms, as set forth in the Bible. It is a perfect
epitome of the whole book. The theme of this first psalm is the
blessedness of the righteous and the utter destruction of the wicked.
God alone can bless, and those who would enjoy his blessings
must enter into and continue in fellowship with him. This, of
course, implies that one's inner motives, desires, yearnings, and
thoughts be acceptable to God. 4. This psalm presents two por-
traits, one of which is the exact opposite of the other, involving
choice, character, influence, and conduct. The author knew that
there are three great perils which threaten human beings, and he,
accordingly, urges that care be taken in guarding the direction
of one's journey, his leisure, and his company. What a difference
it would make if every one would give heed to this admonition!
But in studying this lesson, let us consider,

I. Some Things Which Must Be Refused

   1. The great aim in every life should be that of character building—the kind of character that will be pleasing to God. See 2
Cor. 5: 9. But if this is done there are certain things which
must not be done.

   2. Some things which must be refused:

   (1) *The one who pleases God must not walk in the counsel of*

the wicked. The wicked are those who have no place in their thoughts and lives for God; and the righteous man therefore will avoid getting counsel or following the advice or example of such men.

(2) *He must not stand in the way of sinners.* Sinners are those who miss the mark, pass over the prohibited limits, transgress the law, or, in general, endeavor to block the progress of God's kingdom. The man who tries to please God will neither commit himself to their course nor spend his leisure hours with them. Such action would result in blunting one's moral sense and rendering his conscience flabby, weak, and ineffective. It is tragic to find a person who has allowed sin to rob him of his power of discernment. Cf. Heb. 5: 14.

(3) *He must not sit in the seat of scoffers.* Scoffers are those who scorn, mock, and deride truth and sacred things. Such people are coldly contemptuous of most things which others admire or believe in, especially things of moral or religious worth. Deliberate association with people of this sort must be carefully avoided by those who would please God.

3. Verse 1 of this psalm sets forth three successive steps in an evil career:

(1) The thoughtless might *walk* by a questionable place without any intention of going into sin. He merely wants to see what it is like.

(2) The next step is to *stand,* or loiter, around long enough to allow evil to get its grip on him. May be he does not realize it, but he is warming himself by the devil's fireside; or, which is the same thing, he is learning to like the things which he hears, sees, and experiences.

> Vice is a monster of so frightful mien,
> As to be hated needs but to be seen;
> Yet seen too oft, familiar with her face,
> We first endure, then pity, then embrace.

> *—Alexander Pope*

(3) The next step is to *sit,* that is, become confirmed, in the society of scorners. When one begins a life of sin, he easily goes from bad to worse; the road is down hill all the way.

This is the course of life which must be avoided by those who would have the Lord's blessings.

> Yield not to temptation, For yielding is sin;
> Each vict'ry will help you Some other to win;
> Fight manfully onward, Dark passions subdue,
> Look ever to Jesus: He'll carry you through.

II. Some Things Which Must Be Accepted

1. The man who endeavors to please the Lord is not the one who is ruled solely by negatives or who reacts to a succession of

"dont's." His heart and interests are somewhere else. He is in love with One who exerts a stronger influence over him: *his delight is in the law of Jehovah.*

(1) He delights to read and study the law of Jehovah and he is glad to do that which it commands. Cf. 1 John 5: 3; 2 Thess. 2: 10.

(2) He meditates on it day and night. To meditate on the law is to make a careful effort to learn its meaning, weighing it from all angles, so that he may follow its teaching. Cf. 1 Tim. 4: 15.

2. What are the results of such refusals and delights?

(1) *He shall be like a tree planted by the streams of water.* That is, he shall be rooted, anchored, and stedfast; and, fed and nourished from an unending fountain of rich treasures, he will be able to meet any situation and brave any storm.

(2) *He bringeth forth its fruit in its season.* He continues to be a vigorous, productive, fruit-bearing servant of the Lord all his days. See John 15: 8.

(3) *Whose leaf also doth not wither.* This indicates the perpetuity of this blessedness—an evergreen life. Cf. Psalm 23: 6.

(4) *And whatsoever he doeth shall prosper.* Cf. Joseph. whether in Potiphar's house or in prison; Rom. 8: 28.

III. The Wicked Are Not So

1. Having given a full-sized portrait of the righteous and the blessings which follow him, the psalmist next turns to the lot of the wicked. The wicked are those who choose to live by their own wills, rather than by the will of God. Cf. Matt. 7: 21-23.

2. They are the exact opposite of the righteous. Instead of being rooted and stedfast, continually nourished and fruitful, the wicked are like the dry, dead, and worthless chaff which the wind drives away. Cf. Jer. 2: 13.

3. The real character of the wicked is revealed in the hour of judgment—the testing time. The dry chaff has no root; it is helpless therefore before the storm. "Therefore the wicked shall not stand in the judgment, nor sinners in the congregation of the righteous." Cf. Matt. 7: 24-27.

IV. Jehovah Knows

1. See Gal. 6: 7, 8. The Lord carefully watches every life and rewards or punishes accordingly. See Eccl. 12: 14; 2 Cor. 5: 10.

2. The way of the righteous. Cf. Prov. 4: 18.

3. The way of the wicked. Cf. Prov. 4: 19.

FOUR ACTS OF RELIGION
Psalm 4: 4, 5

Introduction: 1. This is an evening psalm, and it was probably written during the same period in David's life as the morning prayer which precedes it. There is a gentler tone in this one, since the author seeks the conversion of his enemies, rather than their destruction. Then, too, there is less complaint here, and more joyous confidence. 2. The difference between the two psalms may be compared to the difference between a man rising in the morning to encounter by faith in the Lord a day of trial, and a man in the evening seeking rest in the conviction that all things work together for the good of the righteous; and that there is hope of repentance, even for the most hardened sinner. 3. The fourth and fifth verses of the psalm now under consideration contain a statement of the four acts which belong to the birth of a righteous life. These four acts are self-awakening, self-communion, self-confession, and self-abandonment. Cf. Matt. 16: 24. But in studying this lesson, let us consider the acts in the order named in the text.

I. SELF-AWAKENING—"STAND IN AWE, AND SIN NOT"

1. Our thoughts usually dwell more on the goodness, than on the severity of God. Instead of talking about awe, fear, trembling, and the like, we prefer to speak of joy, happiness, and peace. This, however, is not true of the man who has had a vision of the purity of God and the mid-night of alienation. Cf. Isa. 6: 1-5; 66: 2. Too many people spend their time in levity, as though God and duty were far removed from them, and were mere trifles. Cf. Matt. 7: 21; 2 Cor. 5: 9; John 12: 48-50.

2. If we do not stand in awe, we are likely to sin and think little about it. Different people have different ways of looking at sin.

(1) Some look at sin as being merely a moral mistake.

(2) Some view it as an irresponsible legacy from sinful parents.

(3) Others think of it as being nothing more than the legitimate outcropping from our animal nature. Being human, they say, we are not to be surprised at the lower vibrating strings of our humanity.

(4) Still others think of sin as a mere violation of the conventional ideas of the more respectable element of society. Not every one objects to the conduct of his fellows on the ground that it is a violation of the law of God. Cf. 1 John 5: 17. The term "unrighteousness," as used in this passage, means "a deed violating law and justice" (Thayer), and it includes every breach of duty and everything that comes short of the requirements of justice.

(5) Finally, there are those who regard sin as a transgression of the law of God; but since they lightly regard his law, no sensitive spot in their deeper nature is touched.*

II. Self-Communion—"Commune with Your Own Heart upon Your Bed, and Be Still."

1. Thus, after beholding the holiness of God, we are to conduct a soliloquy with ourselves. This is an appeal to the intellect and to the conscience. Cf. Isa. 2: 5; John 3: 19-21.

2. "Upon your bed" indicates the utmost secrecy. We are not to commune with others, lest we become satisfied with our own ways, while disobeying God's law. Cf. 2 Cor. 10: 12. Calvin is quoted as saying, Whoso goeth to his bed as to his grave, may go to his grave as to his bed.

3. "Know thyself" has for ages been considered desirable, but we must not overlook the real purpose of this exercise and knowledge.**

(1) *This communion, if we are to be benefited by it, must be characterized by uncompromising fidelity.* We must not turn away from painful inquiries when they awaken a slumbering conscience, or are found at war with some dearly loved indulgence. Cf. Mark 9: 43ff.

(2) *The Scriptures should be our guide in our self-communion, since the aim is to lead the one who communes with himself to seek communion with him by whom he can be transformed into the image of God.* See 2 Cor. 3: 18. This self-communion, then, should not be done as a mere duty, but rather to bring us

---

*John Lightfoot, in his *Works,* Vol. VI. p. III. tells a story about Origen which is filled with pathos. Origen had fallen into a foul and grievous apostasy, and, after some recovery from it, he came into a place where a group of people had gathered for worship. He was asked to preach. When he took the Bible into his hands, he accidently opened it at the Fiftieth Psalm. The first verses upon which his eyes fell were the sixteenth and seventeenth verses of that psalm, which read as follows:

> But unto the wicked God saith,
> What hast thou to do to declare my statutes,
> And that thou hast taken my covenant in thy mouth,
> Seeing that thou hatest instruction,
> And castest my words behind thee?

Upon reading these words he remembered his own fall; and, instead of preaching, he began to weep, and wept so bitterly that he caused the entire congregation to weep with him.

**What are our relations to God? What are our feelings toward him? In what spirit and manner do we fulfil the obligations which he has laid upon us? are questions which are to our highest interest to ask; and we can answer them only when we know our hearts and know them well.

We cannot take a purely abstract view of our own character. We must test ourselves by the things which affect us. When we comprehend the influence which our friends and loved ones, and business, pleasures, and the cares of this life have on us, we shall be better able to determine something of our standing before God. Cf. Matt. 10: 37-39; Luke 8: 14.

into the presence of our best Friend. The first effect will be to cast us down, and then to raise us up. It shows us our sins, so that we may go to the Great Physician.

4. This heart-communion should not be confused with reading, even though it be thoughtful, prayerful reading of the Scriptures. In reading we are seeking new truths, while in meditation we are applying them, that is, endeavoring to reduce that which we have learned to practice.

5. The self-communion here recommended is not the kind that appeals to the world, or that causes the self-righteous to trust further in themselves.

(1) It is the effort of the mind through the will of God to draw away its thoughts and affections from the earth to heaven. Cf. Col. 3: 1-3; Phil. 3: 17-19.

(2) It is for the trial of man's spiritual condition. See 2 Cor. 13: 5.***

(3) It is to convince us of sin, and to humble us into shame and repentance. *Many will confess their "sinfulness," while giving little or no heed to their "daily sins."*

(4) It should lead us on toward perfection. See 2 Tim. 3: 16, 17. It takes away our trust in self and shows us our need for Christ.

6. "Commune with your own heart upon your bed, *and be still.*" We are too much a part of a *busy* world. We need quiet hours, so that we may listen to the quiet tones of truth, as it speaks directly to our own hearts; but instead, we frequently look for the nod of our fellow men.

III. SELF-CONFESSION—"OFFER THE SACRIFICES OF RIGHTEOUSNESS"

1. What are the sacrifices of righteousness? The actions which are in accordance with God's will.

2. But whatever the words may have meant to the psalmist, they can have only one meaning to us who live in the light of the gospel age. When one has contemplated the holiness of God,

---

***The questions to be asked by one who sets about it are not merely concerning what he does, or what he feels, or what he fancies. The inquiry is not what he once was, or what he hopes to be, but what he is. What is the prevailing tone and bias of his mind? What does he take most pleasure in? From what motives does he act? What are his friendships, and his favorite haunts? What is he in the unrestrained intercourse of private life? For many are the self-deceits that men put upon themselves. Scarcely any danger indeed is more earnestly exposed in Scripture than the danger of fancying ourselves accepted sons of God whilst unmortified passions proclaim us children of the wicked one: the danger of speaking and thinking confidently of our religious hopes, whilst the entire or partial absence of the Spirit's fruits declare our hopes a lie. And when the psalmist calls us to self-communion, he would have us use it to test ourselves, by sound Scripture rules, whether the Spirit of Christ have real possession of us or not.—James Hastings.

and in self-communion has discovered his own need, he then turns to the Lord as his only hope and gladly does that which he is commanded to do. Cf. Psalm 119: 59, 60.

(1) The Israelites, when they brought their sacrifices, laid their hands upon the heads of the victims and confessed their sins. Cf. Psalm 51: 17. We, too, offer our sacrifices because of our sins; but unless we confess our sins, the sacrifices will avail us nothing. See 1 John 1: 8, 9; James 5: 16.

(2) The main thing that we must do first, however, is to bring to the Lord the offering which he has divinely appointed, that is, we must plead the blood of Jesus. See 1 John 1: 7; Heb. 9: 13, 14. Cf. Rom. 6: 3, 4.

IV. Self-Abandonment—"And Put Your Trust in Jehovah"

1. Observe the gracious manner in which the passage closes. The awe and the trembling converge in fruitful trust; and trust keeps the line of communication open between the soul and God. Cf. Phil. 4: 6, 7, 13.

2. But how are we to put our trust in Jehovah?

(1) We are to trust him as being willing to receive, forgive, and bless us. See Matt. 11: 28; John 6: 37.

(2) We are to trust in him as he reveals himself in Christ, that is, the promises made through Christ. Cf. John 14: 8, 9; Rom. 3: 24, 25; 2 Cor. 1: 20.

(3) We are to trust him by our willingness to do exactly as we are told to do. See Mark 16: 15, 16; Acts 2: 38-42.

(4) We are to trust him as being able by his Spirit to renew us. See Tit. 3: 5, 6; Rom. 12: 2; Eph. 4: 22-24.

◆ ◆ ◆

THE IDEAL GUEST IN GOD'S HOUSE
Psalm 15

Introduction: 1. Let us picture a beautiful estate with every conceivable comfort and luxury. The owner is a gracious host and wants to share his blessings with others, but he wants to make sure that there will be no one among those invited who will mar the fellowship or embarrass the host. He wants to be sure that each person invited will fit into the picture, enjoy the hospitality, and contribute to the higher atmosphere of the place. 2. Every thoughtful person will readily admit that such a host would have the right to lay down the rules and set up the standards of conduct for any who might want to partake of his hospitality. 3. The author of the psalm now before us used a figure similar to the one just presented in order to picture the ideal guest in God's house. Jesus, in his use of parables, often portrayed God as a host who invited men to share his bounty (cf. Matt. 22: 1-14;

Luke 14: 15-24), and Paul plainly spoke of the church as the house of God. See 1 Tim. 3: 14, 15. 4. God's presence is always holy, and we must remember that certain moral and spiritual requirements must be met before any one will be allowed to enter and remain there. We often make thorough preparation, with respect to our person, and carefully guard our words and deeds when we expect to be associated with the saintliest characters we know; and if we do that for them, how much more should we do for God! 5. The psalm which we are considering readily divides itself into three parts—viz: The question asked; the answer given; and the conclusion drawn. Let us now consider these parts in the order just given.

I. The Question Asked

1. The psalm had its setting in the Old Testament period of Bible history, and that accounts for the double-form of the question and the nature of God's dwelling place. The "tabernacle" was the tent erected by Moses, and was the temporary abode; while the "holy hill" referred to the temple as the permanent abiding place. Hence, they *sojourned* in the tabernacle, and *dwelt* in the holy hill. But we may, without doing violence to the Scriptures, ask, Lord, who shall be allowed to sojourn in the church here, and who shall dwell in heaven hereafter? Cf. Rom. 15: 4.

2. The question before us is not so much, How does one become a member of the church? as it is, What is the character of the person who is in the Lord's favor? What are the qualities of a righteous soul?

3. Of course one must *become* a member of the church before he can *live as* a church member. The teaching of the Lord on that subject is plainly set forth in such passages as Acts 2: 14-41.

II. The Answer Given

1. The ideal guest in God's house is a man of personal integrity, verse 2. This implies such moral perfection and rectitude as to render him incorruptible and blameless in character, incapable of being false to a trust, a responsibility, or his own standard of what is right. He must be thoroughly sincere and blameless. The positive virtues listed in verse 2 are three in number:

(1) *He walks uprightly.* He is characterized by utter honesty. There is no sham or hypocrisy about him. His entire life is governed by the word of the Lord.

(2) *He works righteousness.* He does that which is just and right toward both God and man, that is, he fulfils every obligation toward both, as set forth in the Scriptures. To work righteousness is to do that which God commands. Cf. Psalm 119: 172. The opposite of this characteristic is found in 1 John 5: 17 where, according to Thayer, the term "unrighteousness" means "a deed violating law and justice." It includes every breach of duty and everything that comes short of the requirements of justice.

(3) *He speaks truth in his heart.* The temptation to be untruthful, in one way or another, is one of the most common temptations among men. But the man who pleases God is one who is thoroughly sincere in his heart; and as long as that condition prevails he will not be untruthful anywhere else. Cf. Prov. 23: 7.

> This above all: to thine own self be true,
> And it must follow, as the night the day,
> Thou canst not then be false to any man.
> —*Hamlet,* Polonius to Laertes

2. It is not enough merely to claim that one possesses personal integrity; this claim must be translated into everyday living. This will involve negative tests, such as definite refusals, as well as positive conduct. Verse 3 lists three things which the ideal guest in God's house refuses to do. They are:

(1) *He slanders not with his tongue.* To slander a person is to give expression to a false and injurious report concerning him. The faithful Christian will not do this. In the first place he will not have anything like that in his heart to utter. If our hearts are pure, then the tongue will not be saying hurtful things. The tongue, after all, is only an instrument which gives expression to that which is in the heart. Cf. Prov. 4: 23; Matt. 5: 8.

Slander, in its very nature, is a diabolical practice. The words "Devil" and "slander," as used in the New Testament, come from the very same Greek word, *diabolos,* which, according to Thayer, means a calumniator or a false accuser. One has only to consider some of the facts concerning the practice in order to be convinced of its wickedness. For example,

a. "He that uttereth a slander is a fool." (Prov. 10: 18b.)

b. "Surely the serpent will bite where there is no enchantment; and the slanderer is no better." (Marginal reading, Eccl. 10: 11.)

c. A slanderer repeats (not necessarily originates) misleading and injurious reports regarding another without ascertaining whether or not they are true. He is simply not interested in finding out the truth regarding the reports which he circulates.

d. Slander is a cowardly practice, for he who engages in it will say in one's absence that which he does not have the moral courage to say in his presence.

e. It is a brutish practice, for he who engages in it is utterly insensible of the feelings of others.

f. It is contrary to the whole spirit and teaching of the New Testament. Cf. Matt. 7: 12; 2 Tim. 3: 3.

(2) *He does not do evil to his friend.* Many people place a very low estimate on the meaning and value of friendship, but the man of God will neither say nor do anything, knowingly, that will injure his friend.

> I like my friendships, as I like my fires,
>   Open, ruddy to the seasoned core;
> Sweet-fibered, hickory-hearted;
>   The sort to warm a life by, when, with storm,
> Winter smites hard on wall and pane and rooftree.
>   —*Hilton Ross Greer*

(3) *He will not take up a reproach against his neighbor.* The word "reproach" is here compared to a burden which, if the slanderer had not taken up and laid upon his neighbor, would have remained harmless. Cf. Ex. 23: 1. People whose sins thus affect others should remember this injunction. It is easy to ruin one's influence for life by a word or a deed which leaves the wrong impression. Shakespeare, in *Othello,* makes Iago say:

> Who steals my purse steals trash; 'tis something, nothing;
> 'Twas mine, 'tis his, and has been slave to thousands;
> But he that filches from me my good name
> Robs me of that which not enriches him
> And makes me poor indeed.

3. The ideal guest in God's house not only is characterized by personal integrity, which he translates into every-day living; he also has the ability to judge character and the moral courage to evaluate it just as it is. This trait is set forth in verse 4.

(1) *In whose eyes a reprobate is despised.* A reprobate is one who does not prove himself to be that which he ought to be. He is unable to meet the test of righteousness; and, being abandoned to sin, he is rejected. Cf. Jer. 6: 30, Authorized Version. The man who pleases God refuses to whitewash iniquity, it matters not what the sinner's standing may be before men; and it is for that reason that he despises, that is, rejects, the reprobate.

(2) *But he honors them that fear Jehovah.* To fear Jehovah is to reverence him. He respects and obeys that which he commands. The one who fears Jehovah is the exact opposite of the reprobate; and the Lord is pleased with the man who can and does discriminate between them.

(3) *He swears to his own hurt and changes not.* In evaluating the character of others the man of God is true to the principle of right and wrong; and now, as if to show that he does act from principle rather than from prejudice, he applies the same standard to himself. If he despises the reprobate, then he must meet the test of righteousness himself; for God is no respecter of persons. His whole life, therefore, is governed by principle, rather than by policy. When he makes a vow he keeps it; it matters not what the cost may be to him. Cf. Deut. 23: 21-23; Eccl. 5: 4, 5. The whole context shows that the psalmist is not talking about vows which involve disobedience to God if they are kept. That would be inconsistent with a life of righteousness.

4. Not only does the ideal guest in God's house have the proper attitude toward character, both his own and that of others,

he shows by his actual conduct that his whole aim in life is one of benevolence and equity.

(1) *He does not put out his money to interest.* Cf. Lev. 25: 35-37. The word for "interest," according to Brown, Driver, and Briggs, literally means "something bitten off," and its practical application is that he refuses to enrich himself at the expense of an unfortunate neighbor. Cf. Prov. 28: 8. There is no reference here, it seems, to the lending of money on interest which does not involve greed and oppression. Cf. Deut. 23: 19, 20. However, the man of God is more interested in laying up treasures in heaven than he is in augmenting his substance by interest and increase.

(2) *He does not take a reward against the innocent.* The term "reward" here is from a word which means a bribe for the purpose of perverting justice. The man whom God approves will not condemn the innocent in order to enrich himself or anybody else.

III. THE CONCLUSION DRAWN

1. *He that doeth these things shall never be moved, verse 5b.* This is the gracious promise of God to the man who meets his test of righteousness. It gives him a feeling of security and enables him to know that he has an anchor that will hold in any storm that may come upon him. *He shall never be moved.* Cf. 2 Pet. 1: 10.

2. This feeling of security brings a sense of perfect tranquillity to the guest in God's house which acts as an amazing tonic to the obedient believer. Cf. Isa. 26: 3.

> How firm a foundation, ye saints of the Lord,
> Is laid for your faith in his excellent word!
> What more can he say than to you he has said,
> You who unto Jesus for refuge have fled?
> "Fear not, I am with thee, O be not dismayed;
> I, I am thy God, and will still give thee aid;
> I'll strengthen thee, help thee, and cause thee to stand,
> Upheld by my gracious, omnipotent hand.
> "The soul that on Jesus hath leaned for repose,
> I will not, I will not desert to his foes;
> That soul, tho' all hell should endeavor to shake,
> I'll never, no never, no never forsake."

3. This place in God's house can be attained and kept only by complying with his law for the remission of alien sins (cf. Mark 16: 15, 16; Acts 2: 38, 39), and by continuing faithful in all his appointments until this life is over. Cf. 2 Tim. 4: 6-8.

◆ ◆ ◆

PEACE THROUGH FORGIVENESS
Psalm 32

Introduction: 1. It is generally agreed among Bible students that David, the royal psalmist, was the author of the psalm which serves as the text for this study. It appears to have been written to express his feeling of gratitude following the forgiveness of his sin with Bathsheba. The Fifty-first Psalm contains the confession of his sin and his cry for mercy, while the psalm now under consideration gives voice to the fact that the confession which was made won the forgiveness which was implored. It also states the blessedness of forgiveness and of trust in God. David knew what it meant to be forgiven and welcomed back into the favor of his Father. 2. The psalm now before us, as in the case of the fifty-first, can be properly understood only if it is studied in the light of the eleventh and twelfth chapters of Second Samuel. With the facts of those chapters in mind, let us begin our study by considering,

I. The Blessedness of Forgiveness, Verses 1, 2

1. These verses seem to indicate, not only the blessings which belonged to David following his forgiveness, but the blessed state of any man who has been forgiven. They have been called *the beatitude of forgiveness.*

2. In Psalm 51 David used three words to describe his wrongdoing, and in this psalm he repeats each of them and adds a fourth:

(1) *Pesha*—transgression: to rebel against God's authority; to set one's self against the will and law of God; to cross over a line, or do that which is expressly forbidden.

(2) *Chataah*—sin: to miss the mark which God has set for the man to aim at. Not only has God set bounds across which we must not go; he has also set a mark at which we must aim. To miss this mark, either by omission or commission, is to sin.

(3) *Avon*—iniquity: that which is turned out of its proper course or situation; anything that is morally distorted or perverted. This is the real source of our sin and transgression. Beginning with Adam, man was turned out of his proper course or condition by yielding to temptation, and as a result his nature became perverted from faithful obedience to God. Cf. Psalm 51: 5; Eph. 2: 1f.

(4) *Remiyah*—guile: deception, fraud, treachery. This term has the same basic meaning as the word "bait," which is used to allure fish—something put over the point of the hook, covering it up and thus deceiving the fish to its destruction. Cf. 2 Cor. 12: 16. David had used "guile" in his effort to deceive his victims and thereby cover up his sin, but the reproof of Nathan uncovered his soul before his own eyes, and exposed his secret and wicked intention.

3. With this fourfold description of sin before us, we are next made acquainted with the steps which are necessary to remove it:

(1) *Transgression is forgiven.* Forgiven *(nasa):* that which

is borne away, that is, by a vicarious sacrifice. Cf. Lev. 16: 6-10; 1 Pet. 2: 21-24. Thus, God sends away from his heart, and our own, our transgressions, and he has promised that he would remember them against us no more forever. See Heb. 10: 17.

(2) *Sin is covered.*. Covered *(kasah):* to cover or conceal; that which is hidden from sight. This is done for us by the blood of Christ. Cf. Rom. 3: 23-26; 1 John 1: 7.

(3) *Iniquity is not imputed.* Imputed *(chashab):* that, is reckoned or charged to one's account. Cf. 2 Cor. 5: 18-21.

(4) *The spirit is free from guile.* This means that the spirit is free from all deception, fraud, and treachery. Cf. John 1: 47. Sincerity and a willingness to confess one's sins is one of the very first conditions of forgiveness; and when this condition is met, moral purity is then possible. Cf. Tit. 3: 5, 6; 2 Cor. 5: 17.

4. Any man about whom these things can be said is indeed a happy man. It is in vain that any one looks for or expects happiness while the guilt and power of sin remain upon him.

II. A DARK AND PAINFUL MEMORY, VERSES 3, 4

1. The psalmist seems to indicate that there was an interval following his sins in connection with Bathsheba during which he failed to admit or say anything about them. This harmonizes fully with the record as set forth in 2 Sam., chapters 11 and 12.

2. But he tells us here something that is not recorded there— viz., the horror and suffering which he experienced during that period.

3. There was one thing, however, which David could be thankful for during his time of silence—his conscience was still alive and the hand of God was heavy upon him. Any man is to be pitied who does not feel the hand of God upon him while he remains impenitent. Cf. 1 Thess. 5: 19.

III. CONFESSION AND FORGIVENESS, VERSES 5-7

1. If there is anything clearly taught in the Scriptures it is that confession of sin must precede forgiveness. Cf. Prov. 28: 13; 1 John 1: 9.

2. In making his confession David used the very words to describe his wrong-doings which he had earlier used in the Fifty-first Psalm to set forth the three aspects of sin—viz., sin, iniquity, and transgression.

3. To confess one's wrongs is to admit or acknowledge that he has sinned.

(1) The Greek word for "confess" is *homologeó* and its literal meaning, according to Thayer, is to say the same thing as another, that is, to agree with him. Thus, when God says that we have sinned we agree with him and say the same thing when we confess our sins.

(2) The Hebrew word for "confess" is *yadah* and it means that when one confesses his sins he ceases to try to cover them, that is, he admits or acknowledges them. Cf. Prov. 28: 13.

4. There are some definite things implied in a sincere confession of sin. For example,

(1) *Confession of sin reveals a consciousness of guilt.* If this were not true we would have no confession to make. But just because a man does not feel that he is guilty of sin, that, in and of itself, does not necessarily prove that he is not a sinner. It may be that his power of spiritual perception is at a low ebb, or that he is not sufficiently acquainted with that which God says about sin. Cf. John 16: 7ff; 3: 19-21.

(2) *Confession of sin reveals a need for pardon.* When a man's sins are ever before him he must get relief from them, if he is to survive. But we should remember, however, that it is not always an easy thing for one to confess his sins. Cf. an unfaithful husband confessing his sin of adultery to his wife.

(3) *Confession of sins shows a humble desire to be pure in heart and life, or, which is the same thing, to be different from other sinners.* There can be no progress in spiritual life without this desire. But a confession which is not followed by repentance and obedience to God's law is simply a useless recitation, unheard in heaven.

5. Because God is merciful and always ready to forgive when the sinner turns to him, the psalmist urges every godly person to pray for forgiveness while the Lord may be found. Cf. Isa. 55: 6, 7.

(1) The "godly" man is one whose heart is softened and whose conscience disturbs him. Cf. Heb. 4: 7.

(2) The psalmist knew something of the blessings that come from God to his restored child; and in keeping with his vow to "teach transgressors thy ways" (Psalm 51: 13), he sings of some of those benefits, verses 6b, 7.

> O safe to the Rock that is higher than I,
> My soul in its conflicts and sorrows would fly;
> So sinful, so weary, thine, thine would I be;
> Thou blest Rock of Ages, I'm hiding in thee.
>
> How oft in the conflict, when pressed by the foe,
> I've fled to my Refuge and breathed out my woe;
> How often, when trials like sea-billows roll,
> I've hidden in thee, O thou Rock of my soul.
> —*William O. Cushing*

IV. GOD'S GRACIOUS PROMISE, VERSES 8, 9

1. It is possible and very probable that verses 8 and 9 are the words of the Lord to the forgiven penitent. They were, it seems, spoken in response to David's expression of confidence in him. At least we know that that is what God does for every

one who will listen to him.

2. After making known something of his benevolent attitude and helpful guidance, the Lord cautions against any obstinacy on the part of man.

3. If man is to be benefited by God's goodness, he must react to it understandingly; for God follows certain definite principles in his dealing with men. For example,

(1) *He appeals to their reason.* Cf. Isa. 1: 18. He wants us to recognize the facts in the case. We must endeavor to see ourselves as God sees us—to realize something of what it means to be a sinner, to understand what it means to be forgiven and to have God's gracious promises.

(2) *He appeals to them by experience.* Cf. 2 Tim. 1: 12. It is not God's will to force obedience on the part of his people. The service which he requires is reasonable, and no one who follows him has ever been led astray. However, there is always an element of venture in faith; for the Lord never tells one where he will lead him. Cf. Heb. 11: 8.

> When we walk with the Lord in the light of his word,
> What a glory he sheds on our way!
> While we do his good will, he abides with us still,
> And with all who will trust and obey,

(3) *He draws them by their affection.* Cf. Rom. 2: 4. God's providence is one of his greatest gifts to men.

V. THE LOTS OF THE WICKED AND RIGHTEOUS CONTRASTED, VERSES 10, 11

1. "Many sorrows shall be to the wicked." It is always true that the way of the transgressor is hard, Prov. 13: 15. Cf. Eccl. 8: 11-13.

2. "But he that trusteth in Jehovah, loving kindness shall compass him about." Cf. Isa. 26: 3; Rom. 8: 28.

3. A final exhortation, verse 11. As Adam Clarke observes, man was made for happiness, but his happiness must be founded on holiness; and holiness, the kind that pleases God, comes only from him and must be maintained by continual union with him.

◆ ◆ ◆

A CRY FOR MERCY
Psalm 51

Introduction: 1. There is no poem or prayer which surpasses the Fifty-first Psalm in depth of feeling or ardor of expression. It is a classic in the literature of penitence. During the long years of its life it has proved itself to be both a challenge and a solace to countless thousands of men and women who, having realized something of the enormity of their sins, have been filled with self-loathing and a longing for reconciliation with God. Even after thirty centuries this psalm is frequently found in the hands or upon the lips of those who fear God. The One Hundred and Thirtieth Psalm is comparable to it, but it is less personal and quickly soars to hope. 2. The psalm now before us presents one of the most pathetic scenes in human experience. It deals with a problem which is beyond human solution. Even though its subject is a king with armies and mighty men to do his bidding, and with multitudes of animals for sacrifice at his disposal, he is, nevertheless, a helpless sinner, naked and defenseless, and without any possible means of escape or deliverance. But with all that he is not without hope, for he can turn to God and that is exactly what he does. In deep penitence he confesses his sin and implores God for mercy. But in order to appreciate the full significance of the scene now before us we must consider it in the light of the facts as set forth in 2 Sam., chapters 11 and 12. With this background in mind, let us begin our study of this psalm with

I. David's Cry for Mercy Based on His Contrite Confession, Verses 1-6

1. Man's greatest need is for forgiveness, but he must realize that it can be obtained only through the loving kindness and tender mercy of God.

2. But even though God delights to forgive the sins of his people, the sinner has no right to expect that blessing until he confesses his wrong-doing, turns away from it, and then does that which God requires of him.

3. David, therefore, promptly turned his attention to his sin, and he emphasized the magnitude of it by using three words to picture the different aspects of sin.

(1) *Pesha*—transgression: to rebel against God; to set one's self against the will and law of God. David had done that very thing and he knew it. He made no effort to conceal his transgression—"Thou art the man"—"I am the man." His act was one of high treason against the Sovereign Ruler of the universe, and he freely confessed it. Cf. 2 Sam. 12: 9.

(2) *Avon*—iniquity: a perversion or distortion; that which is bent or twisted; in its moral application, depravity of conduct. See 1 John 3: 4, where the meaning is to have a contempt for and live in violation of law; a manifest disregard for law. Cf. Matt. 7: 21. (The words "lawlessness"—John 3: 4, and "iniquity"— Matt. 7: 23, are from the same Greek original.)

(3) *Chattath*—sin. The literal meaning of this term is *missing the mark*, that is, God's mark for man. When man sins he fails to reach and remain on God's plane for his life.

4. Viewing his sin from these three angles, the psalmist makes a threefold request for God's help in his deplorable condition:

(1) *Machah*—blot out: erase, cancel, obliterate. David real-

ized that God alone could erase the sorry record which he had made.

(2) *Kabas*—wash. The psalmist pleads that his whole being, inside and out, be cleansed, so that the holy eyes of God may be pleased with what they see when they look upon him.

(3) *Taher*—*cleanse:* make free from guilt and therefore pure in God's sight. Cf. Hab. 1 : 13 ; Psalm 11 : 4, 5 ; 34 : 15, 16.

5. In his confession of wrong-doing David not only bewailed his act of sin, but likewise the disposition which led to the act. See verses 5, 6. As a consequence of the fall of Adam man inherited a fallen nature, a proneness to sin ; and since this was true in the case of the psalmist, he realized that he was the *very opposite* of what he ought to be.

II. A PRAYER FOR FULL CLEANSING AND A NEW HEART, VERSES 7-12

1. David not only prayed that he might be received into God's presence again, but that he might be fit for his presence, verses 7-9. Cf. Isa. 1 : 18.

2. God's cleansing from sin is spoken of as a "creation." Cf. 2 Cor. 5 : 17 ; Tit. 3 : 5, 6. This fact should call to our attention something of the destructive nature and power of sin. *Creation,* not merely repair, was the psalmist's desperate need. Cf. John 3 : 1-5. His *whole* heart had to be changed. See the author's *One Hundred Sermons, p. 140ff.*

3. In a pathetic tone he begged God not to cast him away from his presence. Cf. Gen. 4 : 9-16. In the case of David, to be cast away from God's presence was equivalent to being denied the privilege of worship and service according to the law.

4. "Take not thy holy Spirit from me." Cf. Eph. 4 : 30 ; Acts 7 : 51 ; 1 Thess. 5 : 19. David knew that he had grieved the Holy One and that he deserved to be deprived of the indwelling Spirit. His prayer shows that the Spirit does not dwell in God's children merely through the word. He dwells in them personally. Cf. 1 Cor. 6 : 19, 20.

III. A SOLEMN VOW, VERSES 13-17

1. One of the first impulses of a man who realizes what it means to be saved from the terrors of sin is to tell others about that salvation. He knows the certainty of God's grace, and he himself is the most effective witness of what that grace can do for the penitent sinner.

2. "My tongue shall sing aloud of thy righteousness, . . . and my mouth shall show forth thy praise." Every really converted sinner will be an active evangelist in the cause of redeeming lost souls. Cf. Acts 8 : 4.

3. Along with stating his vow, the psalmist gives again his conception of the way to please God, verses 16, 17. Cf. Isa.

66: 2; Micah 6: 6-8. No man can please God who ignores God's law for *him*. Cf. Prov. 28: 9.

4. Inasmuch as verses 18, 19 treat a wholly dissimilar subject, it is very probable that they do not belong to the psalm which includes verses 1-17. It is possible that they originally formed a psalm of themselves.

Conclusion: Some one has said that certain notes dominate this psalm: 1. sin; 2. personal responsibility; 3. confession, repentance, and prayer; 4. forgiveness; and 5. a resolution to tell others the story of salvation. It is certain that it is a psalm that should be known alike by every saint and sinner.

◆ ◆ ◆

THE CROWNING OF THE YEAR
Psalm 65: 11

Introduction: 1. It has been said that the harvest is the plainest display of the divine bounty, and the crown of the year. The Lord himself conducts the coronation, and sets the golden crown upon the brow of the year. God always works in an ascending scale, and the idea here is one of culmination. 2. The harvest, rather than the seedtime is the crown of the year; for there is certainly no likeness of such a crown in the seed which the farmer sows in the field. Who would ever imagine that there are poems or beautiful essays in an alphabet, or that a helpless infant may some day become a philosopher, a scientist, a missionary, or a leader of men? But in studying this lesson, let us begin by considering the words of the text.

I. "Thou Crownest the Year with Thy Goodness"

1. God is here represented as placing the crown of completeness and perfection upon a long process. The preceding verses of the psalm, verses 9 and 10, contain a graphic picture of the preparation for the harvest.

2. Jehovah crowns the world of men, just as he does the world of nature. Human life, character, and experience, have their supreme culminating moments. For example, love comes to crown the solitary life; success, legitimate ambition—not forgetting that there may be true success in honorable failure; influence, character; friendship, the longings of the heart; and trust and admiration, the life lived in honest toil.

3. But culmination is a process, and the crown is sometimes long deferred. It is deferred in nature, but experience has taught us to expect it. It frequently looks as if nothing is being done during the dreary months of winter; but if our hearing were keen enough, we might place our ear to the ground in December and hear the pulse still beating in the earth's mighty bosom. From this we should learn not to become discouraged when there is

a winter season in our mental growth, our spiritual experience, and our church life. The crown in these higher fields is often long withheld; but if one is all the time reading, observing, studying, and thinking, the rapturous emancipation will come in due season.*

II. THE HARVEST CROWN COMES AS A REWARD OF HUMAN LABOR

1. Man is called upon to be a co-worker with God. Cf. 2 Cor. 6: 1. Nature may do her best; but without the toil of man the harvest would be but a heap of wild and tangled weeds. God never gives a rich and bountiful harvest unless man gives his work, care, and supervision over it.

2. The world and the church are great harvest fields, and each man therein should do his part. There is no room for idlers. Fruits are produced in some tropical countries, but the strongest of men are not there!

III. THE HARVEST IS THE GIFT OF GOD AND SHOULD LINK MAN TO HIM

1. At best man does but little. He must work and wait—for God. For aught we know, God could give the harvest immediately after the sowing, but he has chosen to wait on man's co-operation. He keeps his hold on man by the mysterious element in things. If we could explain the harvest, we could go a long way in explaining God! That, however, can never be.

2. In the harvest time the Greeks saw the good goddess Ceres bearing the golden sheaves; but the modern farmer too often sees only the result of his own knowledge, labor, and the best fertilizer. But we pity the poor heathen Greeks!

IV. THE CROWN OF HARVEST IS WOVEN IN THE LOOM OF WINTER

1. June always comes after December, and the crown follows the cross. Cf. Rom. 8: 16, 17; 2 Tim. 2: 11-13.

2. The people tried to give Christ a crown of gold, but he waited for the crown of thorns. Few men are brave enough to forego the crown of gain, in order that they may wear with Christ the crown of sacrifice.

3. It has been said that the greenest grass grows where the forest fires have burned; and it is certain that some of the most beautiful graces spring from tribulation.

---

*Tennyson had passed his eightieth milestone when he wrote "Crossing the Bar." When he showed the poem to his son, the latter exclaimed, *"That is the crown of your life's work!"* ."But," replied the aged poet,* "it came in a moment." Yes, but however instantaneous the inspiration for it may have been, the poem had behind it a lifetime of careful, painstaking, and even fastidious work.

V. The Crown of Harvest Is Not for Ornament and
Beauty Only; It Is for Utility and Beneficence
As Well

1. The ripe grain is not only used for food, but the best of it
becomes the seed for future harvests. Just so must men do in
other realms. They must sacrifice the best they have in self,
time, rest, ease, comfort, pleasure, etc., if they would reap a rich
harvest in the end. Cf. Matt. 16: 24-26; Heb. 12: 1, 2.

2. One does not always see at the time of sowing what the
result will be. Cf. 1 Pet. 3: 1, 2; 2: 11, 12.*

◆ ◆ ◆

GETTING THE BEST OUT OF THE WORST
Psalm 84: 6

Introduction: 1. For one to be able to get the best out of a
troublous situation is one of the most important victories of life.
This should be evident to every one, for trouble is sure to come
to every normal individual. Cf. Job 5: 7. Some one has said,

> If every man's internal care
> Were written on his brow,
> How many who our envy share
> Would have our pity now.

The kind of person described in the psalm from which the text is
taken is what all of us need to be today. When a person who
trusts in God, and is conscious of the help he receives from him,
finds himself in a disagreeable and omnious place, he can do more
than merely go through it; he can creatively make something
worthwhile out of it. 2. That this ability is our need should be
obvious to every one. Many people are cracking up both morally
and emotionally, and are coming out of the experience in a worse
condition than when they entered it. On the other hand, many
are learning lessons they never learned before, are having strength

---

*There is a story told of a night of seemingly fruitless toil which
resulted in great blessing. A woman missionary in India, utterly tired
out, was one evening about to return home, when the son of the head-man
of an important village, who had been poisoned, was hurriedly brought
into the compound.

The missionary soon saw that it was impossible to save him, yet she
kept careful watch over him and rendered him the most menial service—
service hardly fit for the village scavenger.

The father and brothers watched all the time; and although the missionary returned home utterly exhausted the next morning, feeling as if
nothing had been accomplished; yet all the time the chief and his family
had watched, and as they did so, they were judging between Hinduism
and the religion of Christ; and within six months the whole of the large
family of the village chief was baptized. It was not long before a school,
along with the church, was founded in the village, and from that one
chief's family, so the report goes, there were developed no fewer than
ten evangelists and Bible women.

called out of them which was never called out before, and are so handling the experience as to make them wiser and better because of it. *To which group are we going to belong?* 3. Every right-thinking person should count on this much to start with, viz., a desire not to be among the number who merely drag through a crisis or who go to pieces under its stress, but rather among those who creatively make something out of it and out of themselves in it, and who come out of the experience wiser and stronger because of it. 4. The real list of war casualties is much longer than that which is published in the papers; for it includes many men and women on the home front who are shot to pieces, whose faith is wrecked, whose morale is broken, and whose emotional life is flooded by discouragement, cynicism, vindictiveness, and hate, resulting in their progressive personal deterioration. But in studying this lesson let us ask, What are the qualities of mind and character which enable a man passing through this valley of Weeping to make it a place of spring? We should be able to get a fairly clear answer to this question by considering some of the common attitudes of life. Let us notice,

I. The Attitude of Merely Enduring

1. There are some people in a disastrous time like this who take the attitude of merely enduring, or managing in some way or other to stand it, while others are aroused by it, intellectually and spiritually stimulated, so that they learn things which they had never known before.

2. This negative attitude of mere endurance is natural and should not be lightly thought of; but that attitude alone is not enough; for if that is all that one has it will eventually turn into a dull, weary, and self-pitying attitude. People generally think more of a person who has been aroused intellectually and spiritually, and who has seen things which he never saw before, has learned things he never knew before, and who has become something he never was before.

3. Many of the troubles which come upon the Lord's people are providentially used by him for their good and his glory. Cf. Phil. 1: 12; 1 Cor. 10: 13. We should not, therefore, allow them to get the best of us, or assume the attitude of mere endurance. Paul has assured us that all things will work out for the good; and if we cannot see their purpose now, we can know "that the messages of God are not to be read through the envelope in which they are inclosed." Cf. Gen. 41: 51, 52; 45: 5, 8; 50: 20.

4. It is true that the difference between people which is now being considered is temperamental and is not altogether within our control, but not entirely so; for any ordinary person can have something to say as to whether or not he will be among those who merely manage to get by, or in the company of those

who are intellectually and spiritually aroused to think and to do and to be that which was never within their scope before.

II. THE EMOTIONAL ATTITUDE WHICH WE ARE DEVELOPING

1. There are some who are emotionally infected by the passions which accompany a crisis, such as the present global catastrophe through which we are passing. They are flooded by its bitterness, its prejudices, its hatred, and its vengefulness; while others are enlarged in their vision to take the whole world in, and to see and feel the impossibility of welfare for any without the welfare of all. *Thus, the question before each of us is, Are we coming out of this experience with a bitter spirit, filled with prejudice and vindictiveness, or shall we be more humane, possessing a wholesome world vision, and magnanimous?*

2. People continually reveal their own quality by that which they see in and get out of the ordinary things of life. Even the Bible is not the same to all men. The good man sees in it the message of divine love, while to others it is "that splendid mine of invective." One sees in the Sermon on the Mount the highest type of moral, ethical, and spiritual teaching, while to another that sermon is "the Sarcasm on the Mount." If the Bible can produce such widely differing reactions, what can a wartime era like this do?

3. The vision we need is illustrated by Isaiah's experience and message in connection with the deliverance of Israel from Babylonian captivity. See Isa. 49: 6. While in the valley of Weeping, he caught a vision of world-wide significance. Cf. Acts 13: 47.

III. THE ATTITUDE TOWARD SPIRITUAL RESOURCES

1. Some face exhausted spiritual resources and see their strength and courage fail, while others realizing their need for greater strength to carry on are able to tap the proper source, with the result that the greater strain brings the greater strength. Cf. Deut. 33: 25; Psalm 50: 15; 2 Kings 19: 14-19 and context. Many people have grown from stature to stature, as burdens became heavier and tragedy deeper, revealing qualities which no one knew were in them.

2. If a man's religious faith does not bring him greater strength, then there is something seriously wrong with it. See Psalm 27: 13; James 1: 5-8; Phil. 4: 6, 7, 19; Rom. 8: 28; 2 Cor. 4: 16-18; Matt. 28: 20.

3. It is not so much what the situations are which come to us, but rather what we do with those situations. Cf. 2 Cor. 5: 10; Matt. 25: 14-30.

THE USE OF THE WORD "REVEREND" AS A TITLE FOR PREACHERS
Psalm 111: 9

Introduction: 1. The word "reverend" is used by denominational and other worldly people as a title of esteem for preachers. The custom has grown until it is considered by many a lack of respect not to use the term when addressing preachers, or when referring to them. 2. In considering this practice, the question naturally arises, How and when did the custom originate? The answer to this inquiry is found in connection with that which took place in the early days of the apostasy. It will, therefore, be necessary for us to examine some of the facts as they relate to the early departure from the Lord's plan, if we are to have anything like a clear idea of the use of the term now before us. In studying this lesson, then, let us begin with a consideration of,

I. The Distinction between the So-Called "Clergy" and "Laity"

1. One of the first departures from the original pattern was a change in the form of church government; and a direct result of this change was a distinction between that which came to be known as the "clergy" and the "laity."

2. The New Testament order provided for a universal priesthood of all Christians; but under the perverted system "the clergy claimed for themselves the prerogatives, relations, and authority of the Jewish priesthood," thus constituting themselves a mediating office between God and man.

3. This arrangement sought to invest the propitiating priest with *awful* sanctity, and raised him above the people; and while the priests were being resolved into a sacerdotal caste, the people were being reduced to a distinct and inferior order.

4. Both groups began to feel the force of conflicting interests and claims; and the result has been that never again have the two groups occupied together the original New Testament ground of common priesthood of all believers.

II. The Misuse of the Term Clergy

1. It is thought by some authorities that the practice of calling the "ministers of the sacraments" the clergy goes back to the Greek *Klēros* (lot), as if they were, in some special sense, consecrated to God, "either because they are the lot of the Lord, or else because the Lord himself is their lot and portion."

2. However, as has already been indicated, both the doctrine and practice of setting apart a class known as the *clergy,* as distinguished from the "laity," belong to the apostate church,* and

---

*In the apostolic Church no abstract distinction of clergy and laity, as to privilege or sanctity, was known; all believers were called to the prophetic, priestly, and kingly offices in Christ (1 Pet. v. 3). The Jewish

are specifically condemned in the Scriptures. See Matt. 23: 8-10; 1 Pet. 2: 5, 9; Rev. 1: 5, 6.

3. The term "clergy" may be traced through the Latin *clericus,* a priest; the Greek *klērikos,* belonging to the clergy; to the Greek *klēros,* the clergy as opposed to the laity. Cf. the Septuagint rendering of Num. 18: 20; Deut. 18: 2.

4. The word *klēros* occurs in the New Testament in the following places: Matt. 27: 35 (lots); Mark 15: 24 (lots); Luke 23: 34 (lots); John 19: 24 (lots); Acts 1: 17 (portion, margin, lot); 1: 26 (twice: lots, lot); 8: 21 (lot); 26: 18 (inheritance); Col. 1: 12 (inheritance); 1 Pet. 5: 3 (charge allotted.)

(1) There is nothing in any of these passages, nor in any other part of the New Testament, which indicates that those to whom *men* have applied the term "clergy" are in any special sense the Lord's *lot,* or that the Lord is their *lot,* any more than is true of any other Christian.

(2) The word, however, is used to designate, not the clergy, but those whom the denominational world calls the "laity!" See 1 Pet. 5: 3.

III. THE ORIGIN AND MEANING OF THE TERM "REVEREND"

1. The English word *reverend* is from the Latin *reverendus,* the latter being the gerundive of *revereri.*

(1) The meaning is, according to Webster, "worthy of reverence; entitled to respect or honor, as on account of age or position; inspiring reverence; revered."

(2) Tennyson speaks of "the *reverend* walls;" and Milton makes reference to "a *reverend* sire." "As you are old and reverend, you should be wise." (Shakespeare.) "Judges ought to be more learned than witty, more reverend than plausible, and more advised than confident. Above all things, integrity is their portion and proper virtue." (Bacon.)

2. The Hebrew word from which we have the term *reverend* is *yare;* and when the relation between the English and Latin (already pointed out) is considered, it becomes quite probable that the translation of the Hebrew *yare* by the English *reverend* in the King James Version was due largely, if not altogether, to the influence of the Vulgate (the Latin Version of the Scriptures).

---

antithesis of clergy and laity was at first unknown among Christians; and it was "only as men fell back from the evangelical to the Jewish point of view" that the idea of the general Christian priesthood of all believers gave place, more or less completely, to that of the special priesthood or clergy . . . Indeed, from the third century onward, the term *clerus (klēros, ordo)* was almost exclusively applied to the ministry to distinguish it from the laity. As the Roman hierarchy was developed, the clergy came to be not merely a distinct order (which might consist with all the apostolical regulations and doctrines), but also to be recognized as the only priesthood and the essential means of communication between man and God.—M'Clintock and Strong.

(1) The Septuagint (Greek Version of the Hebrew Old Testament) renders the expression, "Holy and fearful is his name;" while Dr. John R. Sampey (in a letter to the author) suggests, "Holy and terrible is he."

(2) *The Complete Bible—An American Translation*, by Smith and Goodspeed, has this rendering, "Holy and terrible is his name."

IV. The Scriptural Use of the Term Reverend

1. Many people, in giving their reason for not using the term "reverend" when referring to preachers, say that the word occurs only one time in all the Bible, and is there applied to God; and since men are not worthy to have the same language applied to them, it is not proper to use the term "reverend" when referring to preachers.

(1) These same people, however, seemingly overlook the fact that the term "holy" is used in exactly the same relation to God in the text now before us. According to the argument just referred to, would it be proper to apply the term "holy" to men? Cf. 1 Pet. 1: 15, 16; Lev. 11: 44, 45; 19: 2; 20: 7.

(2) Then, too, many of the same people who object to the use of "reverend" as a title for preachers, do not hesitate to speak of them as "Elder" So and So!

(3) But if we will only stop and think, it will not be hard to see that even in the passage now under consideration, Psalm 111: 9, the term "reverend" is NOT used as a title for God. It is merely a term used to denote something of the character of his name. In addition to being *holy,* his name is *reverend,* that is, worthy of reverence, entitled to respect or honor.

2. The word *yare* (from which we have the term "reverend" in Psalm 111: 9) occurs 376 times in the Old Testament—327 times in the Qal-form; 44 times in the Niphal-form; and 5 times in the Piel-form. The form in Psalm 111: 9 is the Niphal.**

(1) The Septuagint translates this Hebrew *yare* by *phobeomai.* Leaving the Septuagint and coming into the New Testament, we find this same Greek word, in its various forms, used in the New Testament 143 times. See Acts 9: 26, *"afraid* of him;" Gal. 4: 11, *"afraid* of you;" Eph. 5: 33, *"fear* her husband;" Heb.

**In explanation of the NIPHAL term, it may be said that Hebrew has seven verb terms: QAL, NIPHAL, PIEL, PUAL, HIPHIL, HOPHAL, HITHPAEL. In a sense these are called voices; again, they may be called a kind of conjugation, or, maybe, moods. Speaking in an elemental way, QAL is the simple active meaning, NIPHAL is its passive; PIEL is the intensive active meaning, PUAL is the intensive passive; HIPHIL is the causative active meaning, HOPHAL is the causative passive; HITHPAEL carries the reflexive and reciprocal idea. So the NIPHAL of YARE is the passive participle, translated here in Psalms 111: 9 by the Latin passive participle (gerundive) "reverendus," English "reverend" or "to-be-feared."—J. O. Garrett.

10: 27, *"fearful* expectation of judgment;" Heb. 10: 31, "a *fearful* thing to fall;" Heb. 12: 21, "so *fearful* was the appearance." Cf. all of these references in the King James Version.

(2) The Hebrew *yare* ("reverend" of Psalm 111: 9) is translated, in the King James Version, by "be afraid," 76 times; "dread," 1 time; "fear," 242 times; "reverence," 2 times; "afraid," 3 times; "fearful," 2 times; "be feared," 4 times; "be had in reverence," 1 time; "dreadful," 5 times; "fearful," 2 times; "fearfully," 1 time; "reverend," 1 time; "terrible," 24 times; "terrible acts," 1 time; "terribleness," 1 time; "terrible things;" 4 times; "affright," 1 time; "make afraid," 2 times; and "put in fear," 2 times.

(3) As already stated, the Niphal-form of the verb *yare* is found 44 times in the Old Testament. These occurences may be listed as follows: masculine participle, 34 times; feminine, 1 time; feminine plural, 9 times.

a. This form of *yare* (the same as in Psalm 111: 9) occurs in the following passages: Ex. 15: 11, *fearful* in praises;" Deut. 1: 19 *"terrible* wilderness;" Deut. 7: 21, "a great God and a *terrible;"* Deut. 8: 15, "great and *terrible* wilderness;" Deut. 10: 17, "the great God, the mighty, and the *terrible;"* Deut. 28: 58, "fear this glorious and *fearful* name, JEHOVAH THY GOD;" Judg. 13: 6, "the countenance of the angel of God, very *terrible;"* 1 Chron. 16: 25, "to be *feared* above all gods;" Neh. 1: 5, "the great and *terrible* God;" Neh. 4: 14, "remember the Lord, who is great and *terrible;"* Neh. 9: 32, "the great, the mighty, and the *terrible* God;" Job. 37: 22, "God hath upon him *terrible* majesty;" Psalm 47: 2, "For Jehovah Most High is *terrible;"* Psalm 66: 3, "How *terrible* are thy works!" Psalm 66: 5, "He is *terrible* in his doing toward the children of men;" Psalm 68: 35, "O God, thou art *terrible* out of thy holy places;" Psalm 76: 7, "Thou even thou, art to be *feared;"* Psalm 76: 12, "He is *terrible* to the kings of the earth;" Psalm 89: 7, "A God very *terrible* in the council of the holy ones;" Psalm 96: 4, "He is to be *feared* above all gods;" Psalm 99: 3, "Let them praise thy great and *terrible* name;" Psalm 139: 14, "for I am *fearfully and* wonderfully made;" Isa. 18: 2, 7, "a people *terrible* from their beginning onward;" Isa. 21: 1, "from a *terrible* land;" Isa. 64: 3, "When thou didst *terrible* things;" Ezek. 1: 22, "like the *terrible* crystal to look upon;" Dan. 9: 4, "the great and *dreadful* God;" Joel 2: 11, "for the day of Jehovah is great and very *terrible;"* Hab. 1: 7, "they (the Chaldeans) are terrible and dreadful;" Zeph. 2: 11, "Jehovah will be *terrible* unto them;" Mal. 1: 14, "My name is *terrible* among the Gentiles;" Mal. 4: 5, "before the great and *terrible* day of Jehovah come."

b. Thus, it can be seen that the Niphal of the verb *yare,* that is, the passive participle of the verb, the same construction that is found in Psalm 111: 9 and there translated "reverend," is used, not only with reference to Jehovah, but also with reference to people (the Chaldeans, Hab. 1: 7, and, apparently, the Ethiopians, Isa. 18: 1ff), an angel, works, a wilderness, a crystal, a day, etc. Cf. Josh. 4: 14, 24.

3. It is not correct, therefore, to say that the word occurs only one time in the Bible, and that it refers only to Jehovah; for, as we have seen, the word actually occurs 376 times in the Hebrew Scriptures; and if we add to that number the 143 times the corresponding Greek term is found in the New Testament, we have the root idea appearing 519 times in our English Bible; for in each instance the original word is translated by an English equivalent.

(1) Thus, it can be seen that the conventional argument, that is, the argument based on the idea of the single occurrence of the word *reverend* in the Bible, is not a valid argument against the practice of applying the term "reverend" as a religious title to preachers.

(2) Error cannot be convincingly refuted by erroneous reasoning. Any one should be commended who tries to combat error; but no one is justified in passing Jerusalem in his flight from Rome. The Bible contains the truth on every such question, and a correct application of its teaching will expose any erroneous position.

4. It is proper to apply the descriptive term "reverend" to any person, if his character warrants it; but it is not proper to use the term as a religious title, as in the case of preachers, for the following reasons:

(1) There is no scriptural basis for the distinction between the so-called "clergy" and "laity." The system which calls for such is a direct result of the departure from the Lord's plan for his people. Cf. 2 Tim. 3: 16, 17; 1 Pet. 4: 11; Gal. 1: 6-10.

(2) Jesus specifically condemned the use of such religious titles for his people. See Matt. 23: 8-10.

◆ ◆ ◆

A GOOD AND PLEASANT RELATIONSHIP
Psalm 133: 1-3

Introduction: 1. Unity among the Lord's people is a relationship which is pleasing to the Lord, and pleasant and beneficial to those who maintain it. In fact, no one can please the Lord or grow into the kind of person he wants him to be, without giving this question his most earnest consideration and attention. 2. However, it should be kept in mind that the unity which pleases the Lord and benefits his people is that unity which is based entirely upon his word. Unity is oneness—oneness of faith and purpose. It does not consist in a number of incongruous or antagonistic elements brought together into a combination or union. There must be a common spirit of unity animating and premeating those who are thus bound together. 3. Not only does such a relationship please the Lord and benefit those involved, it also has a profound effect upon those who are not directly concerned with it. And, too, if the Lord's people cannot maintain such a state of unity, how can any one expect those who are not giving this matter the attention they should to come to the unity of the faith? But in studying this lesson, let us observe that

I. UNITY IS AN INDIVIDUAL OBLIGATION

1. The testimony of the Scriptures: Eph. 4: 3; 1 Cor. 1: 10; cf. John 17: 20, 21.

2. Let it be remembered, however, that unity is not to be sought by sacrificing the truth or compromising with error and sin. Cf. Matt. 10: 34-39.

II. THE IMPORTANCE OF UNITY IS SEEN IN THAT WHICH DEPENDS UPON IT

1. An unobstructive plea for unity cannot be made to the denominational world as long as division exists within the church. The consistency and force of our plea for unity, then, depends upon our maintaining unity among ourselves.

2. The strength and influence of the church against all erroneous teaching and sin is destroyed by a lack of peace and harmony in the church itself. This fact should have a powerful effect upon the church for good.

3. The successful accomplishment of the mission of the church (self-edification, evangelization, and benevolence) depends upon the right measure of cooperation. Division makes cooperation impossible and robs the church of the strength necessary in fulfilling its mission.

4. Furthermore, the acceptance of Christian worship depends upon the members of the church holding the right attitude toward each other. Consider, for example,

(1) The power of unity in prayer, Matt. 18: 19, 20.

(2) The hope for forgiveness, Matt. 6: 12, 14, 15.

(3) The acceptance of our worship in general depends upon our effort to be at peace with our brethren, Matt. 5: 23-26; cf. Rom. 12: 18.

III. SOME THINGS WHICH DESTROY THE UNITY OF THE CHURCH

1. *Selfishness.* Cf. Matt. 16: 24; Phil. 2: 1-5; This attitude involves,

(1) A lack of love for Christ and his cause.

(2) A headstrong desire to have one's own way.

(3) A failure to regard properly the rights of others.

2. *An undue regard for teachers.* See 1 Cor. 1: 11-15; 3: 1-4; Acts 17: 11. Cf. 1 Cor. 4: 14-17; 2 Cor. 12: 15. There is a difference in loving or having a high regard for a teacher, and in blindly accepting any and everything he says.

3. *Speculative and hobbyistic teaching.* Cf. Tit. 2: 7; 3: 9-11; 2 Tim. 2: 14, 23-26; 2 Pet. 1: 16-2: 2.

4. *Uncontrolled tongues.* See James 1: 26, Prov. 16: 28 (margin); Col. 4: 6.

5. *Peevishness, impatience, or being easily provoked.* Such an attitude is intolerant of opposition or anything which does not suit its possessor. In its chronic state it usually finds in any petty matter an occasion for its exercise. Cf. 1 Cor. 13: 5. *Love will not permit such a disposition.*

IV. SOME MEANS OF PROMOTING UNITY

1. *Generosity, self-sacrifice, a willingness to give over to others in matters of judgment.* See Phil. 2: 3-5; Rom. 12: 3-5; 16-19.

2. *Unity in faith, teaching, and practice.* Cf. Acts 2: 42; 4: 32, 33.

3. *Insofar as it is possible within ourselves, be at peace with all men.* See Rom. 12: 18-21. Refuse to become a party to differences among people, especially brethren.

4. *Cultivate the characteristics of love.* Cf. 1 Cor. 13: 4-7.

5. *Genuine love for the Lord and his cause, and stedfastly refusing to allow the body of Christ to be divided.* Cf. 1 Cor. 1: 10; Gal. 5: 12. Jesus and his disciples prayed for those who persecuted and killed them; but neither he nor they ever prayed for any one who divided the church of the Lord.

INDEX